BRIAN WOOD   KRISTIAN DONALDSON

SUPERMARKET

Written by
Brian Wood

Art by
Kristian Donaldson

Lettered by
Robbie Robbins

Original Series Edited by
Chris Ryall

Designed by
Neil Uyetake and Robbie Robbins

Collection Edited by
Justin Eisinger

Operation
Moshe Berger, Chairm
Ted Adams, Chief Executive Offic
Greg Goldstein, Chief Operating Offic
Matthew Ruzicka, CPA, Chief Financial Offic
Alan Payne, VP of Sale
Lorelei Bunjes, Dir. of Digital Servic
Marci Hubbard, Executive Assista
Alonzo Simon, Shipping Manag

Editori
Chris Ryall, Publisher/Editor-in-Chi
Scott Dunbier, Editor, Special Projec
Andy Schmidt, Senior Edit
Justin Eisinger, Edit
Kris Oprisko, Editor/Foreign Li
Denton J. Tipton, Edit
Tom Waltz, Edit
Mariah Huehner, Assistant Edit

Desig
Robbie Robbins, EVP/Sr. Graphic Art
Ben Templesmith, Artist/Design
Neil Uyetake, Art Direct
Chris Mowry, Graphic Art
Amauri Osorio, Graphic Art

ISBN: 978-1-60010-353-7
11 10 09 08   1 2 3 4
www.idwpublishing.com

SUPER
market™

SUPERMARKET

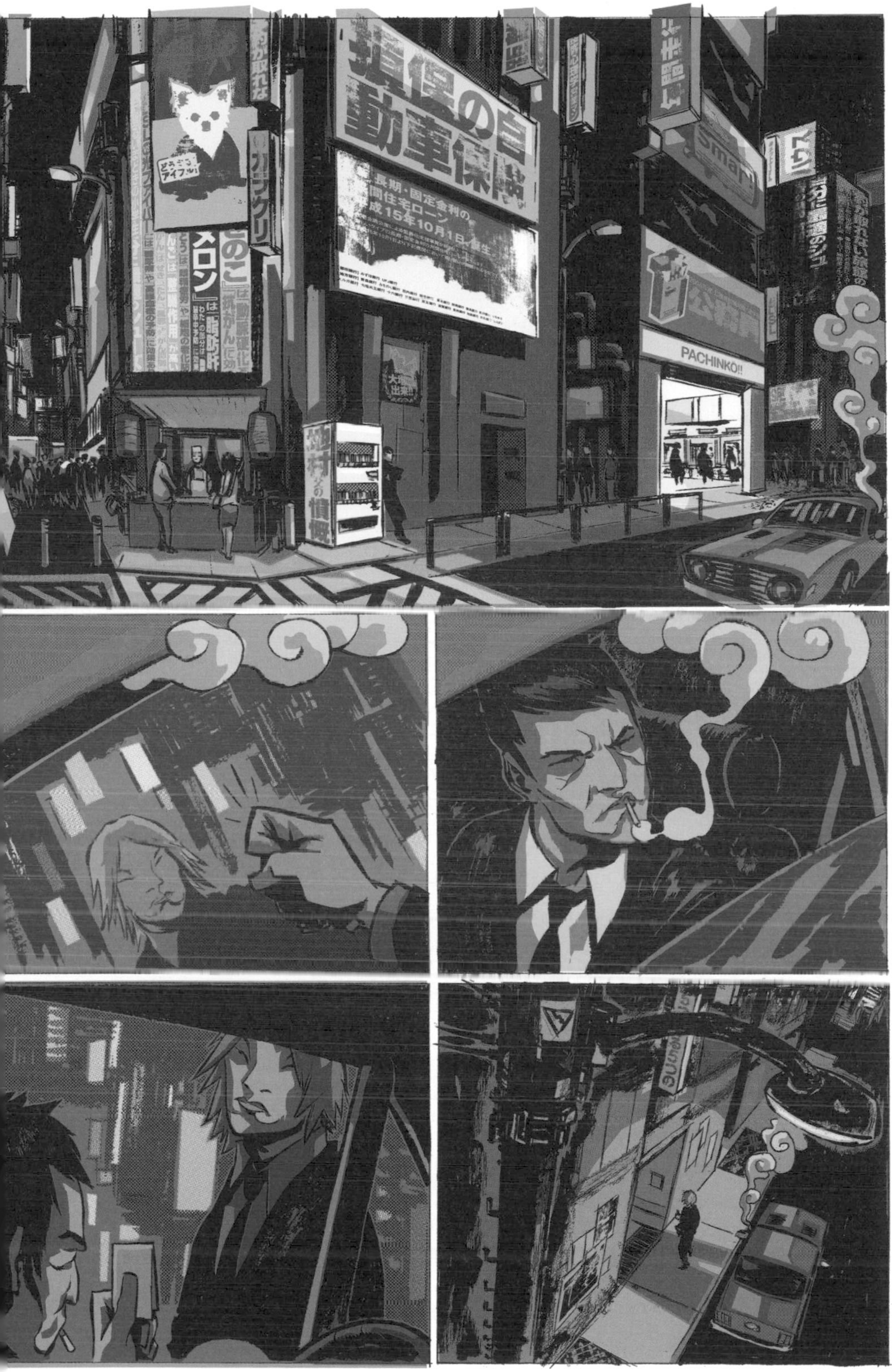
PACHINKO!!

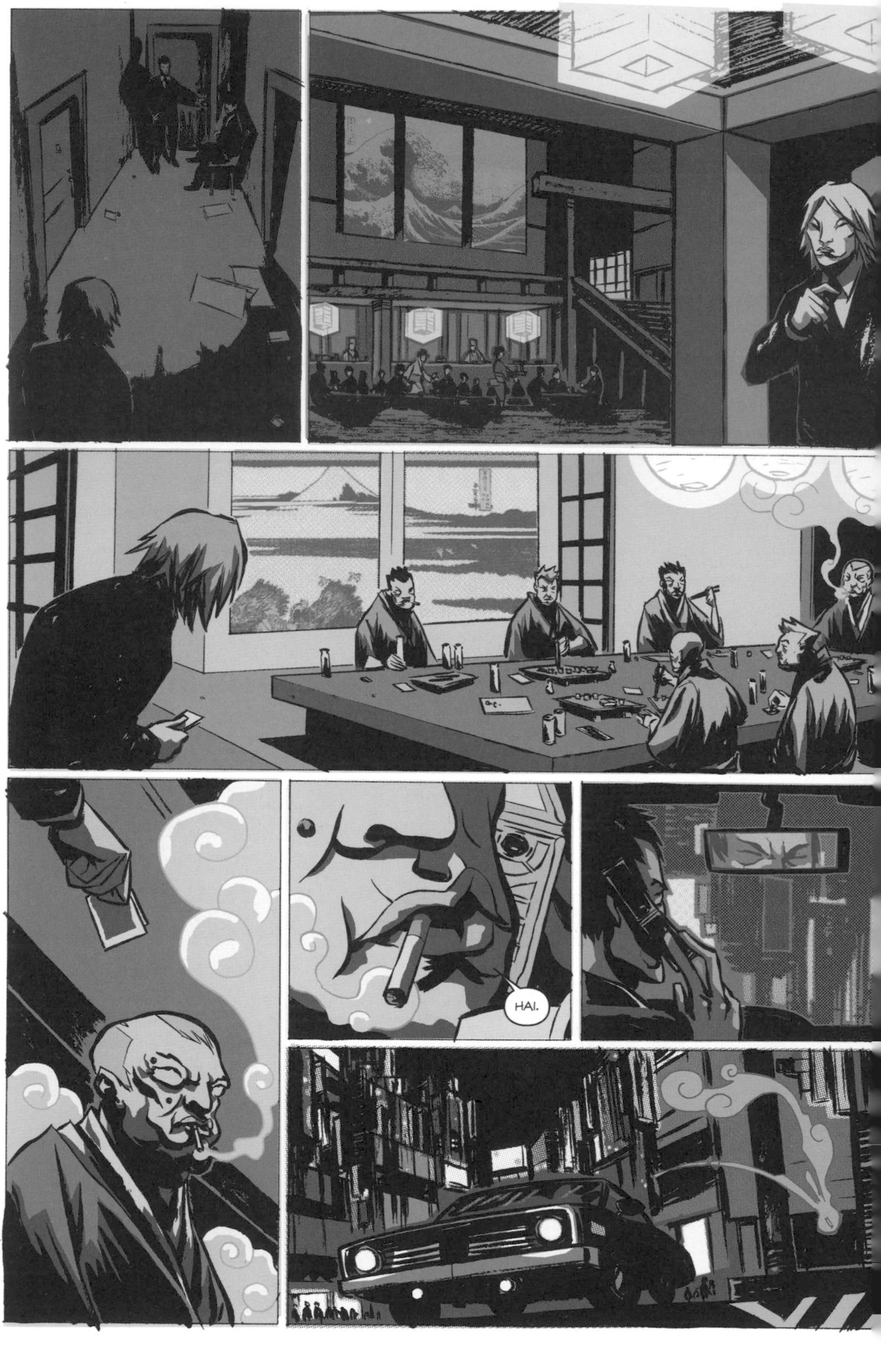
HAI.

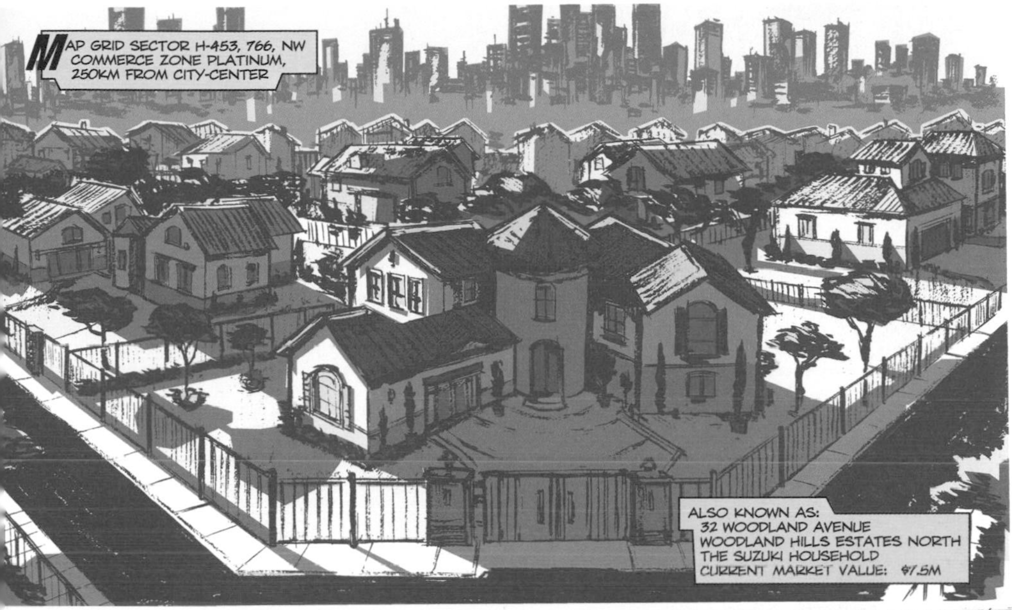
MAP GRID SECTOR H-453, 766, NW
COMMERCE ZONE PLATINUM,
250KM FROM CITY-CENTER
ALSO KNOWN AS:
32 WOODLAND AVENUE
WOODLAND HILLS ESTATES NORTH
THE SUZUKI HOUSEHOLD
CURRENT MARKET VALUE: $7.5M

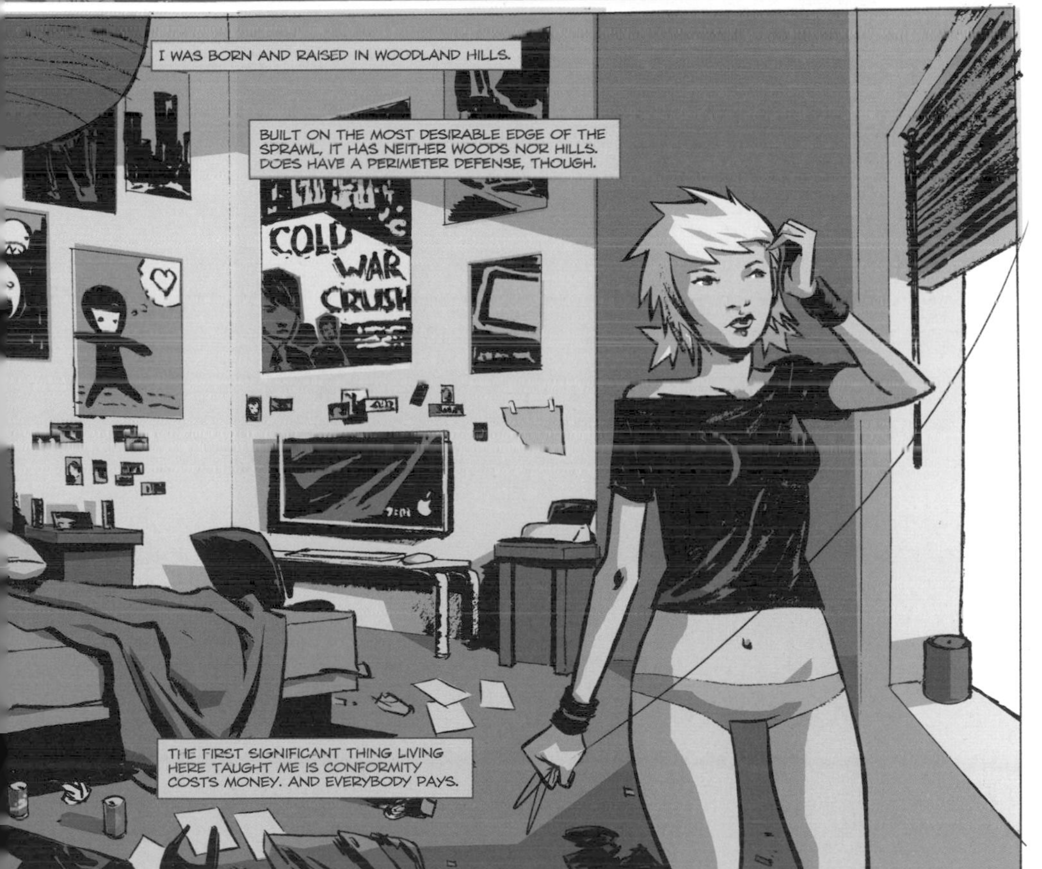
I WAS BORN AND RAISED IN WOODLAND HILLS.
BUILT ON THE MOST DESIRABLE EDGE OF THE SPRAWL, IT HAS NEITHER WOODS NOR HILLS. DOES HAVE A PERIMETER DEFENSE, THOUGH.
COLD WAR CRUSH
THE FIRST SIGNIFICANT THING LIVING HERE TAUGHT ME IS CONFORMITY COSTS MONEY. AND EVERYBODY PAYS.

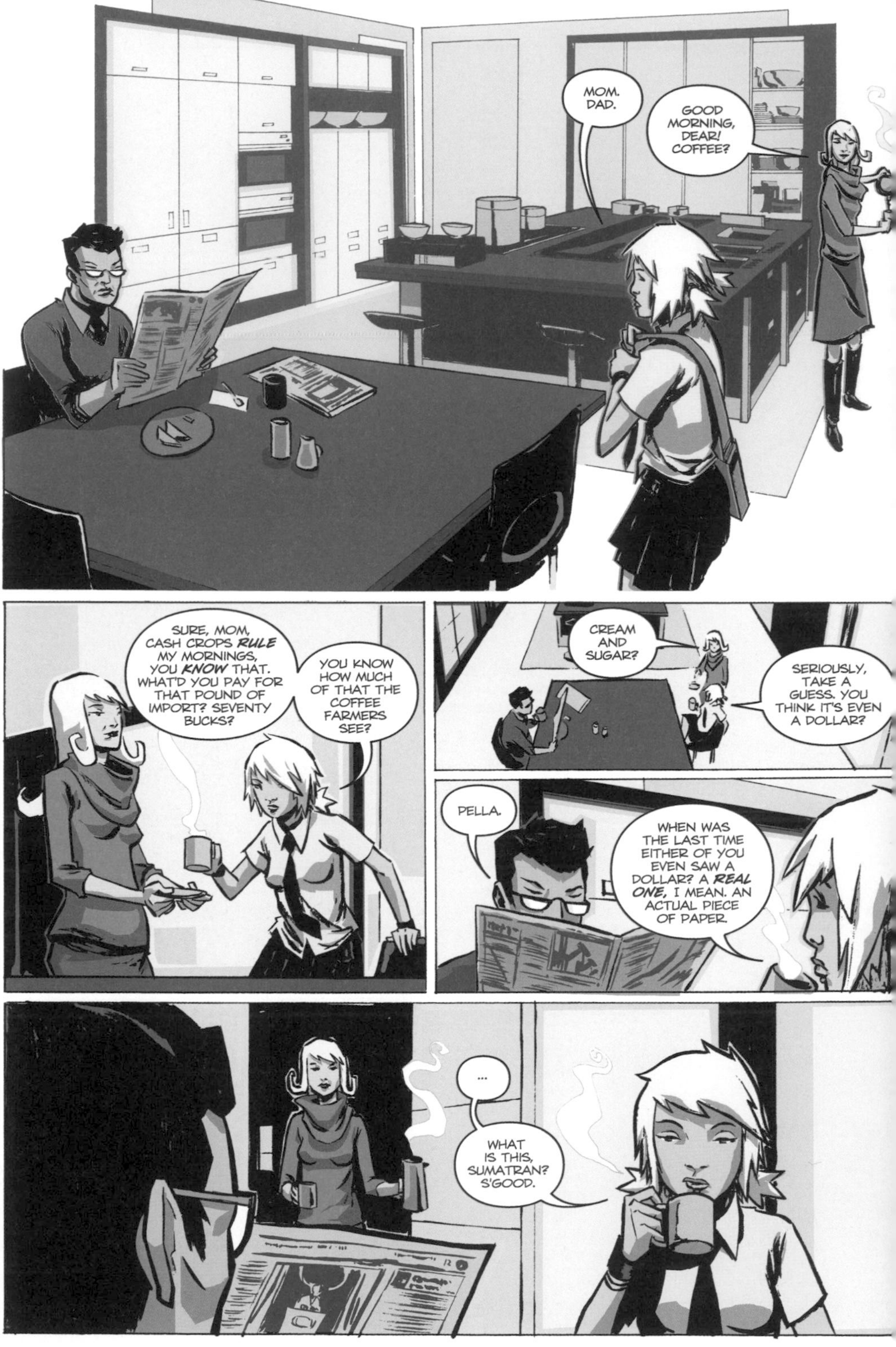
MOM. DAD.
GOOD MORNING, DEAR! COFFEE?
SURE, MOM, CASH CROPS RULE MY MORNINGS, YOU KNOW THAT. WHAT'D YOU PAY FOR THAT POUND OF IMPORT? SEVENTY BUCKS?
YOU KNOW HOW MUCH OF THAT THE COFFEE FARMERS SEE?
CREAM AND SUGAR?
SERIOUSLY, TAKE A GUESS. YOU THINK IT'S EVEN A DOLLAR?
PELLA.
WHEN WAS THE LAST TIME EITHER OF YOU EVEN SAW A DOLLAR? A REAL ONE, I MEAN. AN ACTUAL PIECE OF PAPER.
...
WHAT IS THIS, SUMATRAN? S'GOOD.

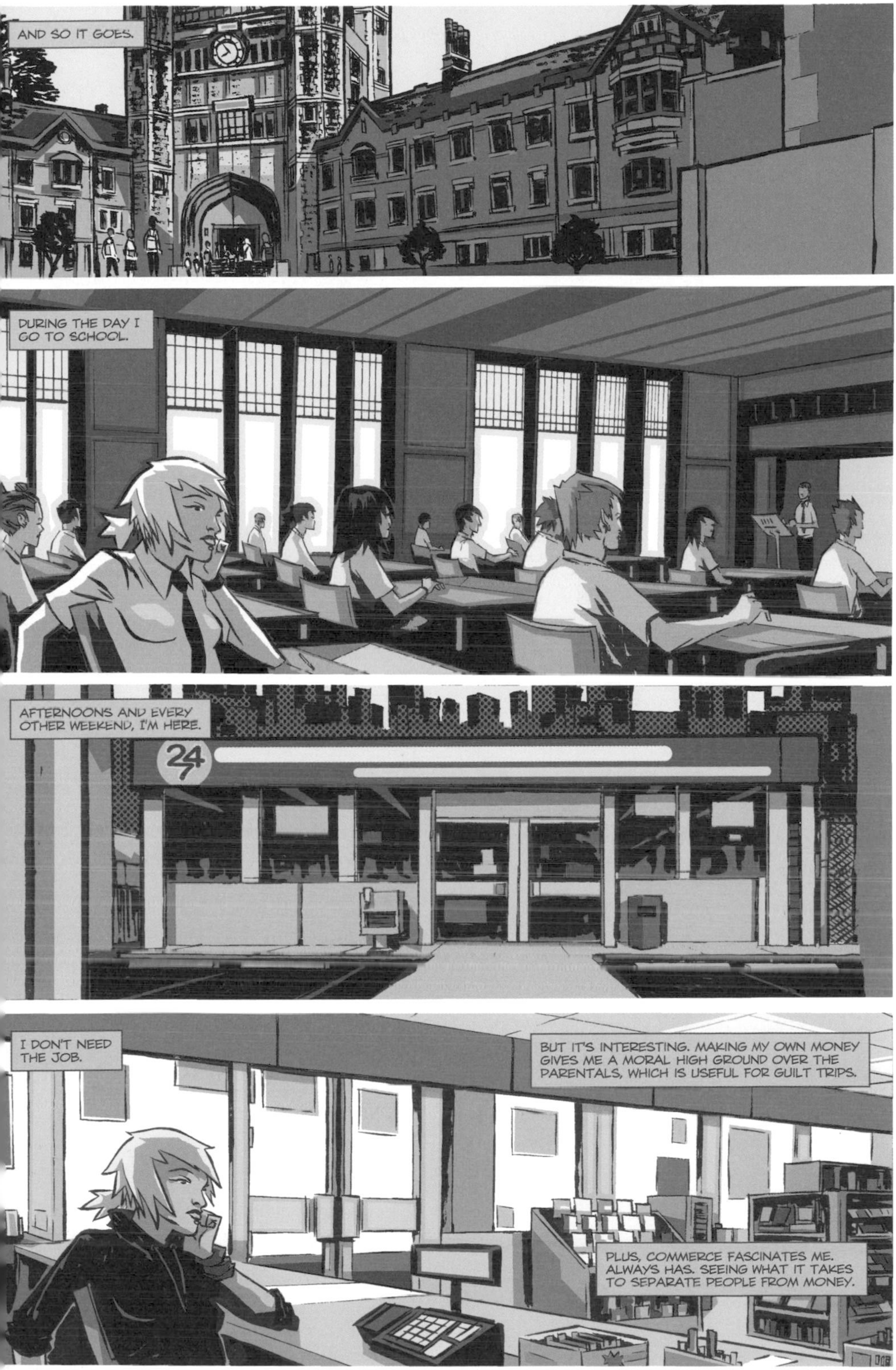
AND SO IT GOES.
DURING THE DAY I GO TO SCHOOL.
AFTERNOONS AND EVERY OTHER WEEKEND, I'M HERE.
24/7
I DON'T NEED THE JOB.
BUT IT'S INTERESTING. MAKING MY OWN MONEY GIVES ME A MORAL HIGH GROUND OVER THE PARENTALS, WHICH IS USEFUL FOR GUILT TRIPS.
PLUS, COMMERCE FASCINATES ME. ALWAYS HAS. SEEING WHAT IT TAKES TO SEPARATE PEOPLE FROM MONEY.

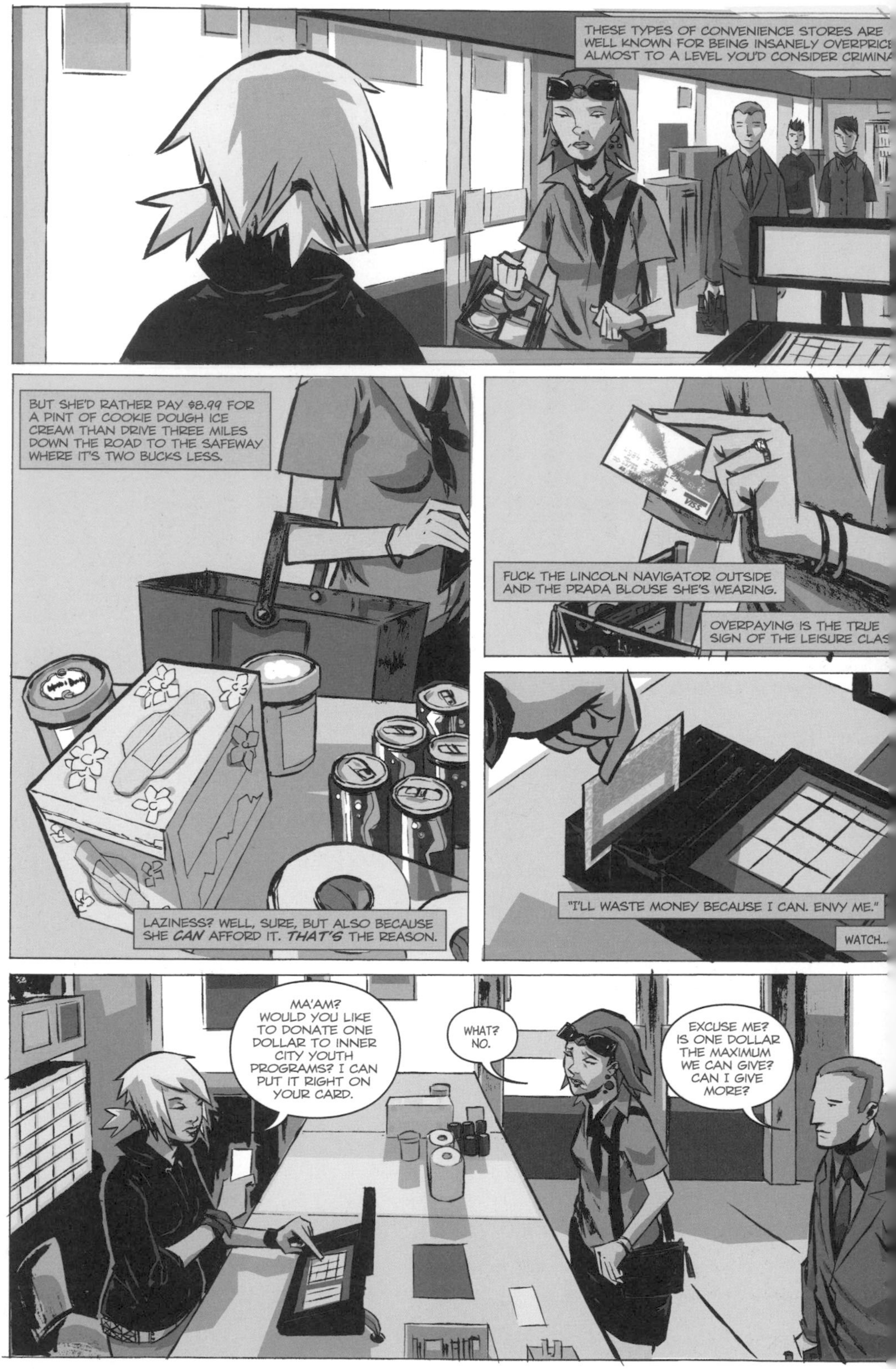
THESE TYPES OF CONVENIENCE STORES ARE WELL KNOWN FOR BEING INSANELY OVERPRICE ALMOST TO A LEVEL YOU'D CONSIDER CRIMINA
BUT SHE'D RATHER PAY $8.99 FOR A PINT OF COOKIE DOUGH ICE CREAM THAN DRIVE THREE MILES DOWN THE ROAD TO THE SAFEWAY WHERE IT'S TWO BUCKS LESS.
LAZINESS? WELL, SURE, BUT ALSO BECAUSE SHE CAN AFFORD IT. THAT'S THE REASON.
FUCK THE LINCOLN NAVIGATOR OUTSIDE AND THE PRADA BLOUSE SHE'S WEARING.
OVERPAYING IS THE TRUE SIGN OF THE LEISURE CLAS
"I'LL WASTE MONEY BECAUSE I CAN. ENVY ME."
WATCH...
MA'AM? WOULD YOU LIKE TO DONATE ONE DOLLAR TO INNER CITY YOUTH PROGRAMS? I CAN PUT IT RIGHT ON YOUR CARD.
WHAT? NO.
EXCUSE ME? IS ONE DOLLAR THE MAXIMUM WE CAN GIVE? CAN I GIVE MORE?

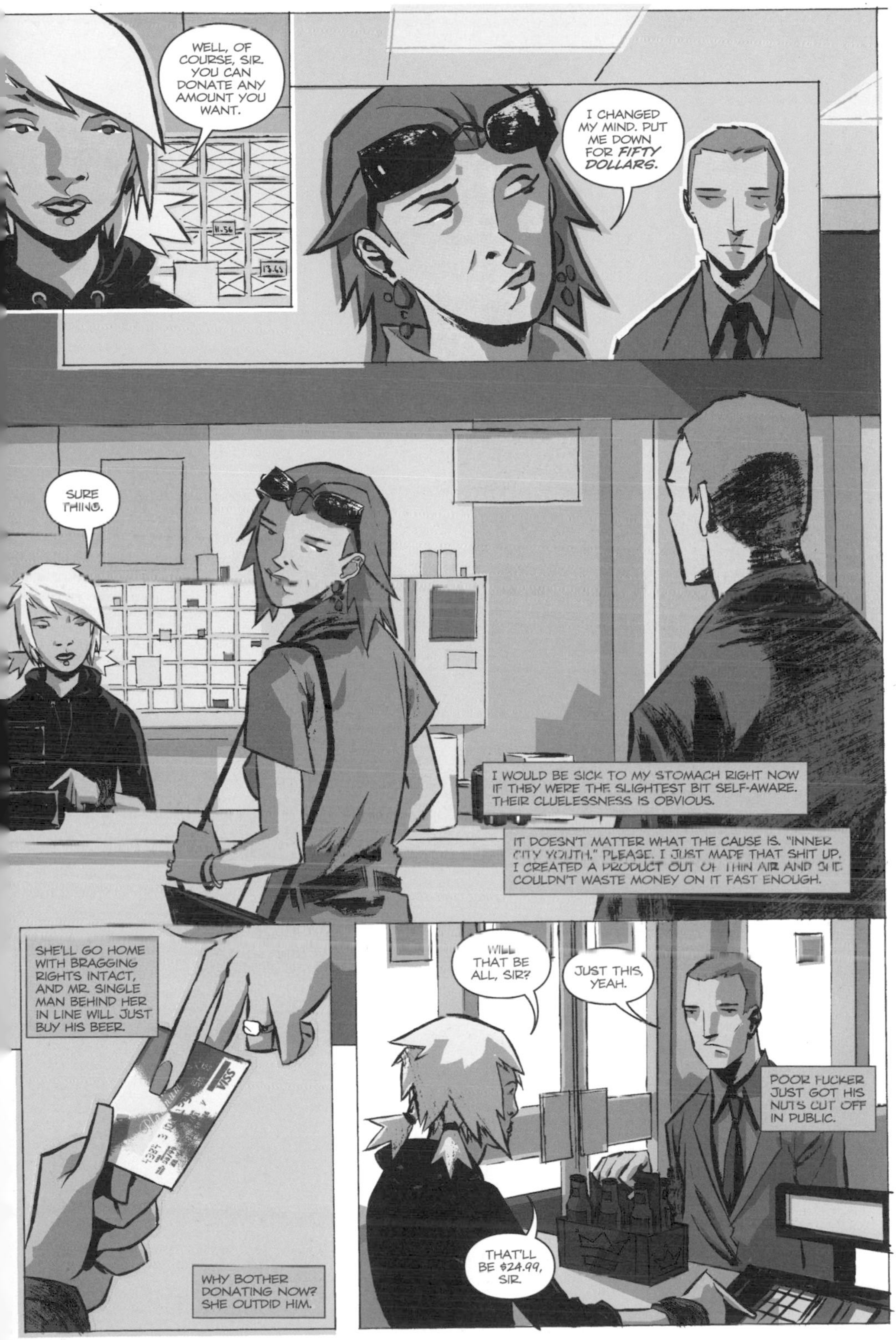
WELL, OF COURSE, SIR. YOU CAN DONATE ANY AMOUNT YOU WANT.
I CHANGED MY MIND. PUT ME DOWN FOR FIFTY DOLLARS.
SURE THING.
I WOULD BE SICK TO MY STOMACH RIGHT NOW IF THEY WERE THE SLIGHTEST BIT SELF-AWARE. THEIR CLUELESSNESS IS OBVIOUS.
IT DOESN'T MATTER WHAT THE CAUSE IS. "INNER CITY YOUTH," PLEASE. I JUST MADE THAT SHIT UP. I CREATED A PRODUCT OUT OF THIN AIR AND SHE COULDN'T WASTE MONEY ON IT FAST ENOUGH.
SHE'LL GO HOME WITH BRAGGING RIGHTS INTACT, AND MR. SINGLE MAN BEHIND HER IN LINE WILL JUST BUY HIS BEER.
WHY BOTHER DONATING NOW? SHE OUTDID HIM.
WILL THAT BE ALL, SIR?
JUST THIS, YEAH.
POOR FUCKER JUST GOT HIS NUTS CUT OFF IN PUBLIC.
THAT'LL BE $24.99, SIR.

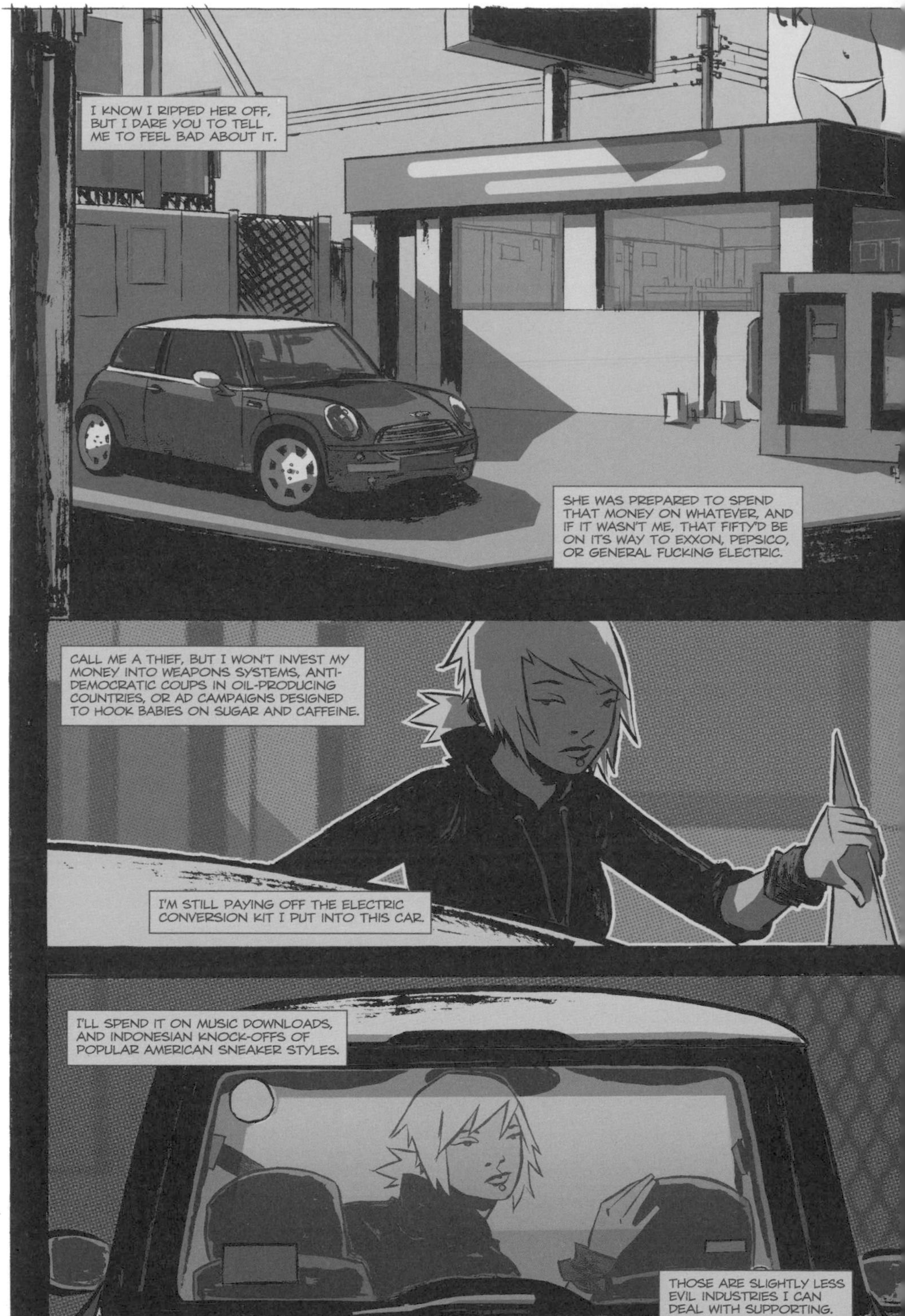
I KNOW I RIPPED HER OFF, BUT I DARE YOU TO TELL ME TO FEEL BAD ABOUT IT.
SHE WAS PREPARED TO SPEND THAT MONEY ON WHATEVER, AND IF IT WASN'T ME, THAT FIFTY'D BE ON ITS WAY TO EXXON, PEPSICO, OR GENERAL FUCKING ELECTRIC.
CALL ME A THIEF, BUT I WON'T INVEST MY MONEY INTO WEAPONS SYSTEMS, ANTI-DEMOCRATIC COUPS IN OIL-PRODUCING COUNTRIES, OR AD CAMPAIGNS DESIGNED TO HOOK BABIES ON SUGAR AND CAFFEINE.
I'M STILL PAYING OFF THE ELECTRIC CONVERSION KIT I PUT INTO THIS CAR.
I'LL SPEND IT ON MUSIC DOWNLOADS, AND INDONESIAN KNOCK-OFFS OF POPULAR AMERICAN SNEAKER STYLES.
THOSE ARE SLIGHTLY LESS EVIL INDUSTRIES I CAN DEAL WITH SUPPORTING.

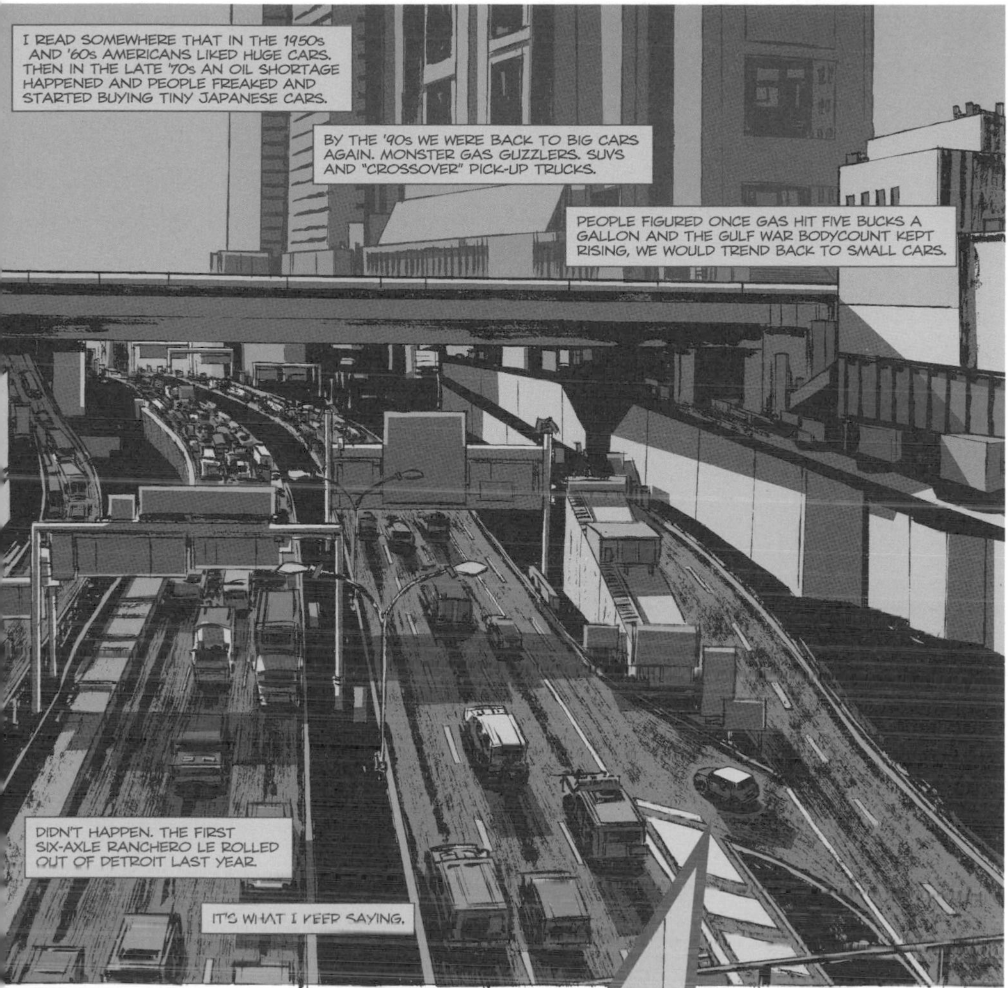
I READ SOMEWHERE THAT IN THE 1950s AND '60s AMERICANS LIKED HUGE CARS. THEN IN THE LATE '70s AN OIL SHORTAGE HAPPENED AND PEOPLE FREAKED AND STARTED BUYING TINY JAPANESE CARS.
BY THE '90s WE WERE BACK TO BIG CARS AGAIN. MONSTER GAS GUZZLERS. SUVS AND "CROSSOVER" PICK-UP TRUCKS.
PEOPLE FIGURED ONCE GAS HIT FIVE BUCKS A GALLON AND THE GULF WAR BODYCOUNT KEPT RISING, WE WOULD TREND BACK TO SMALL CARS.
DIDN'T HAPPEN. THE FIRST SIX-AXLE RANCHERO LE ROLLED OUT OF DETROIT LAST YEAR.
IT'S WHAT I KEEP SAYING.

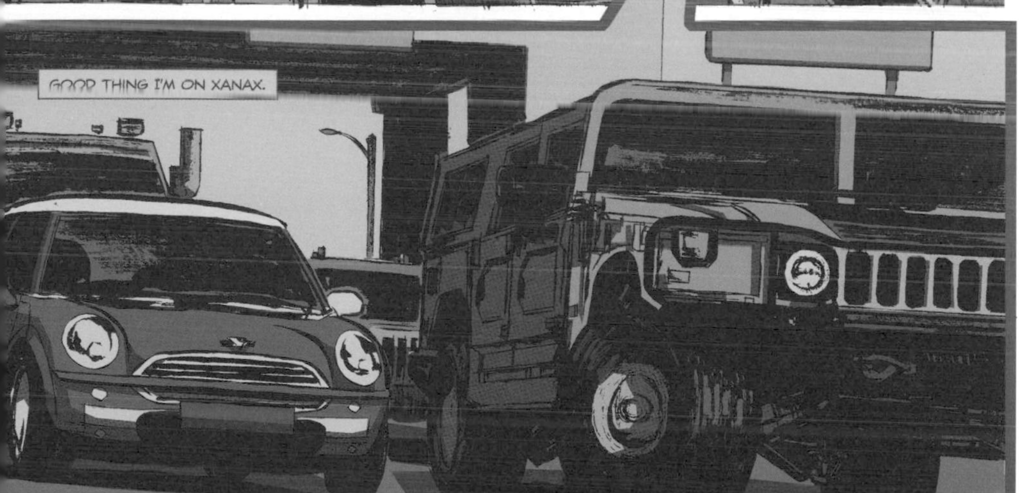
GOOD THING I'M ON XANAX.
I'D NEVER SURVIVE THIS COMMUTE OTHERWISE.

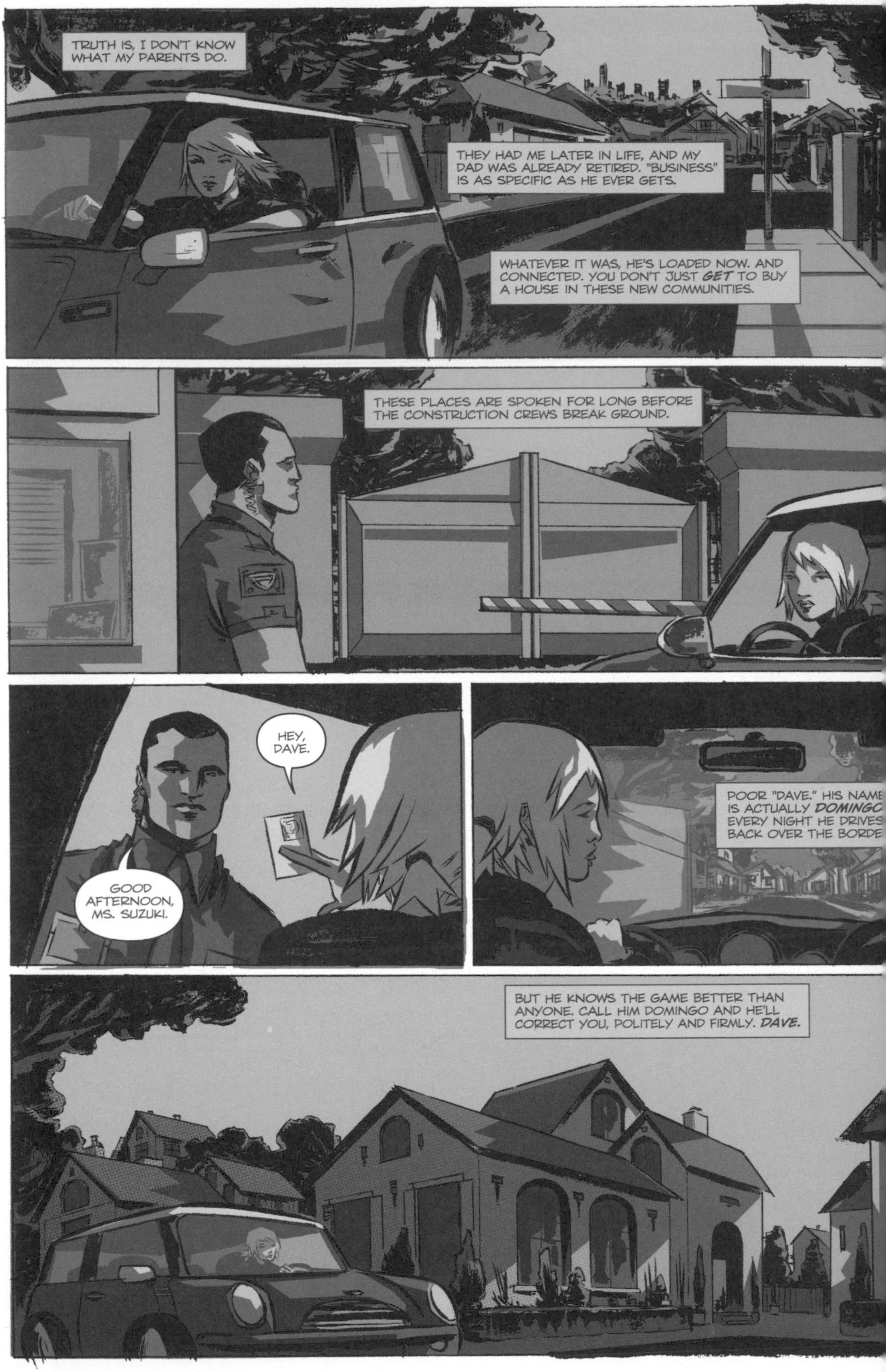

TRUTH IS, I DON'T KNOW WHAT MY PARENTS DO.
THEY HAD ME LATER IN LIFE, AND MY DAD WAS ALREADY RETIRED. "BUSINESS" IS AS SPECIFIC AS HE EVER GETS.
WHATEVER IT WAS, HE'S LOADED NOW. AND CONNECTED. YOU DON'T JUST *GET* TO BUY A HOUSE IN THESE NEW COMMUNITIES.
THESE PLACES ARE SPOKEN FOR LONG BEFORE THE CONSTRUCTION CREWS BREAK GROUND.
HEY, DAVE.
GOOD AFTERNOON, MS. SUZUKI.
POOR "DAVE." HIS NAME IS ACTUALLY *DOMINGO* EVERY NIGHT HE DRIVES BACK OVER THE BORDE
BUT HE KNOWS THE GAME BETTER THAN ANYONE. CALL HIM DOMINGO AND HE'LL CORRECT YOU, POLITELY AND FIRMLY. *DAVE.*

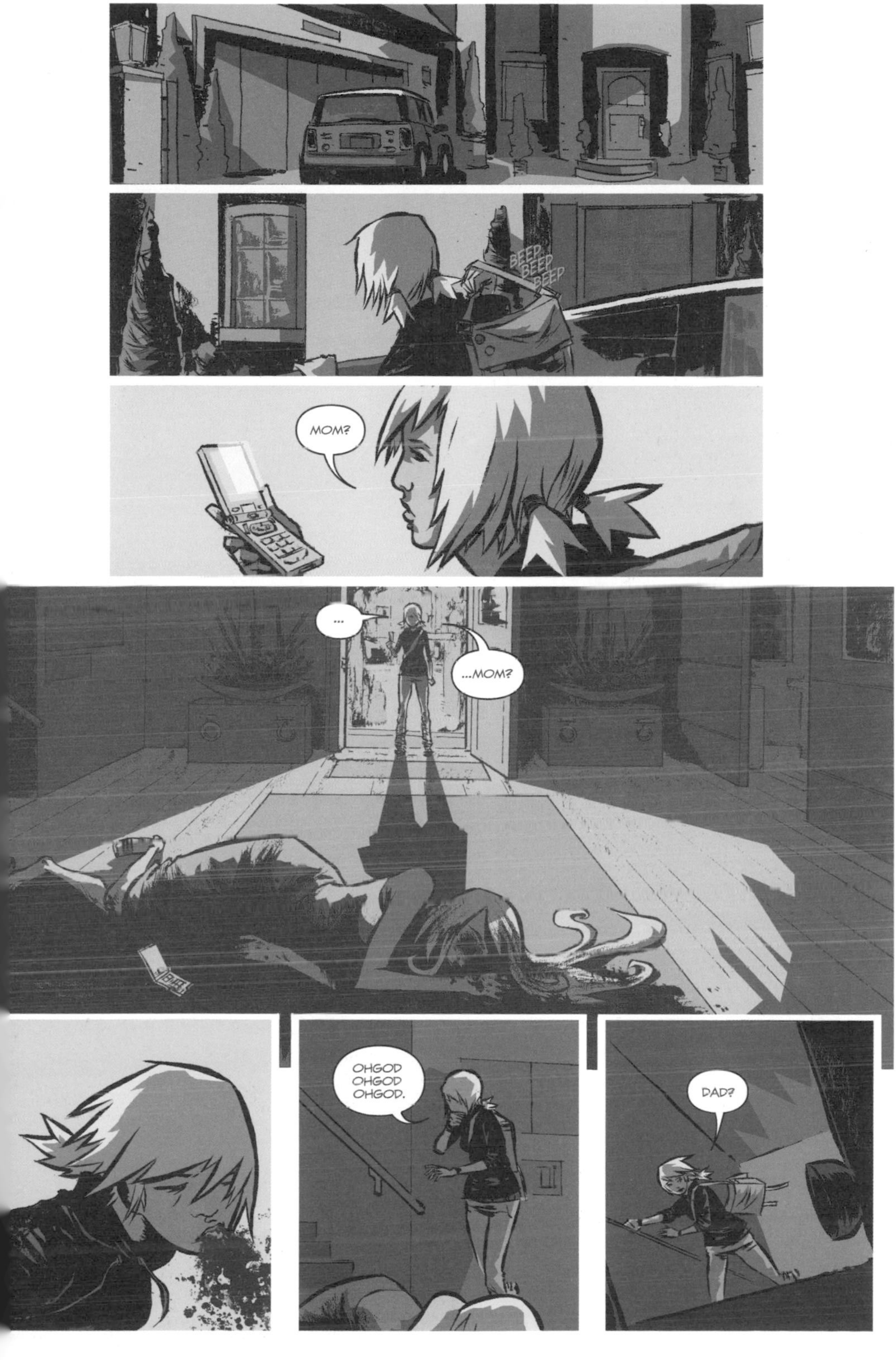
BEEP
BEEP
BEEP
MOM?
...
...MOM?
OHGOD
OHGOD
OHGOD.
DAD?

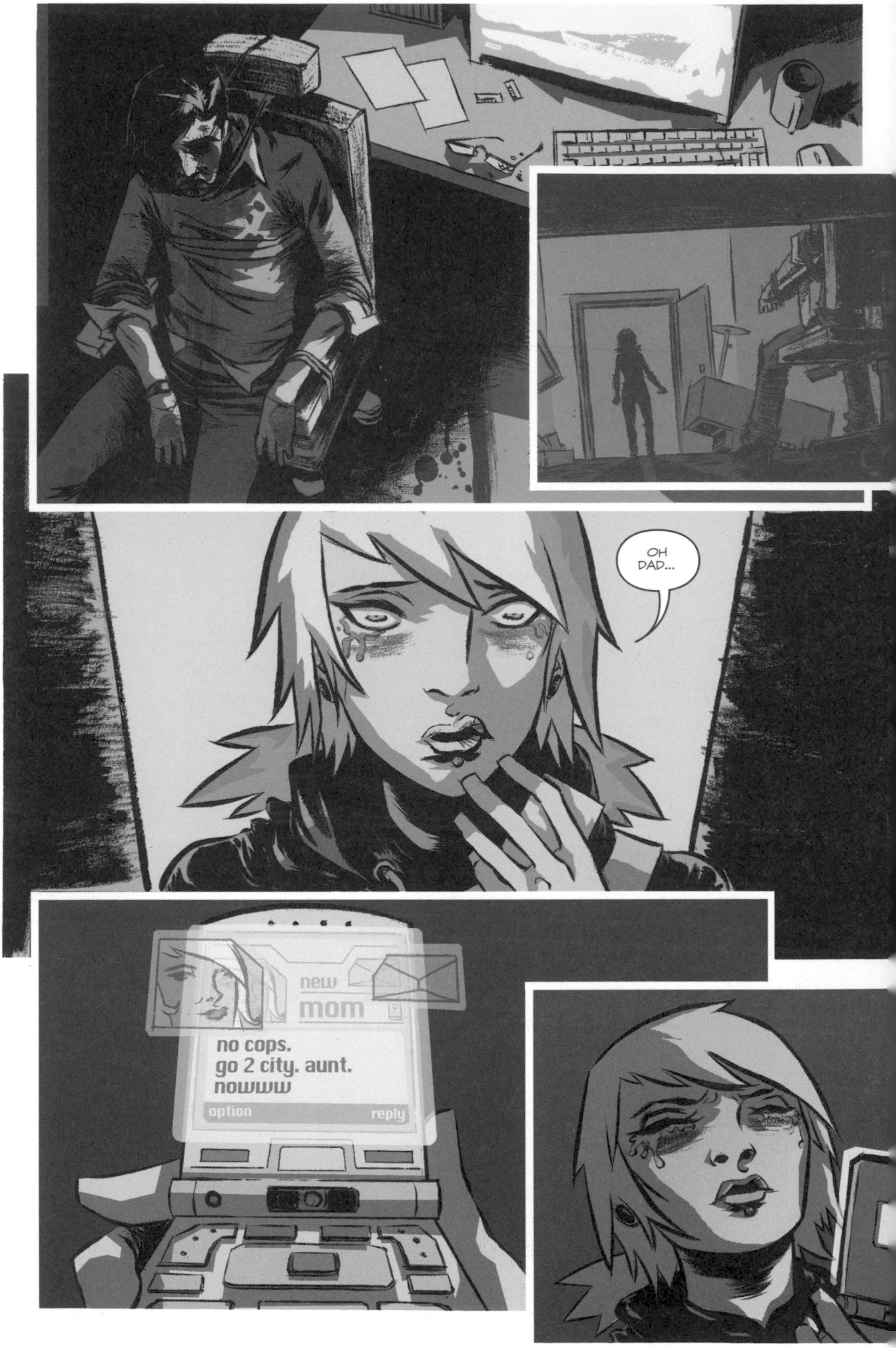
OH DAD...
new
mom
no cops.
go 2 city. aunt.
nowww
option
reply

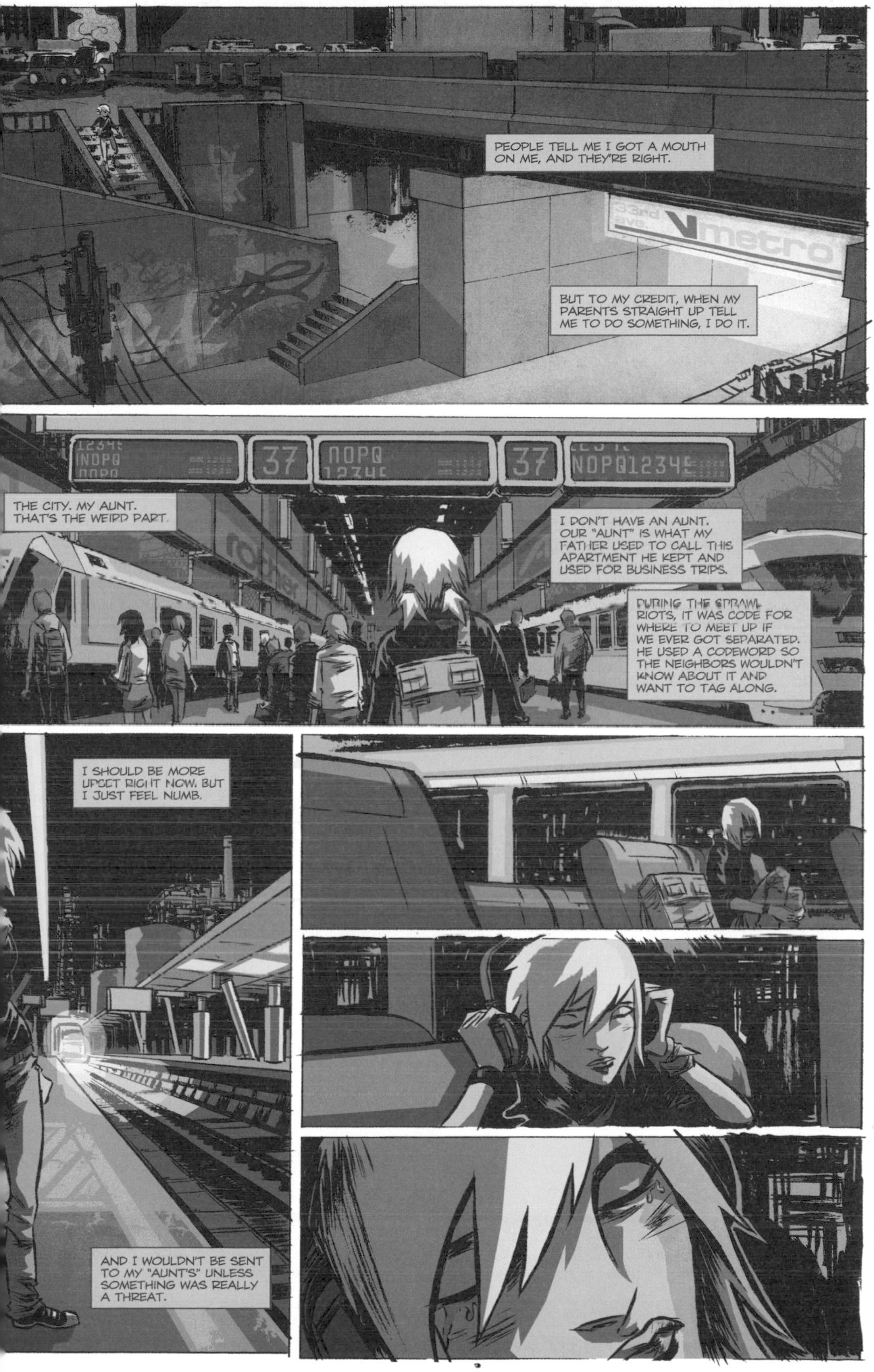
PEOPLE TELL ME I GOT A MOUTH ON ME, AND THEY'RE RIGHT.
33rd ave.
metro
BUT TO MY CREDIT, WHEN MY PARENTS STRAIGHT UP TELL ME TO DO SOMETHING, I DO IT.
37
37
THE CITY. MY AUNT. THAT'S THE WEIRD PART.
I DON'T HAVE AN AUNT. OUR "AUNT" IS WHAT MY FATHER USED TO CALL THIS APARTMENT HE KEPT AND USED FOR BUSINESS TRIPS.
DURING THE SPRAWL RIOTS, IT WAS CODE FOR WHERE TO MEET UP IF WE EVER GOT SEPARATED. HE USED A CODEWORD SO THE NEIGHBORS WOULDN'T KNOW ABOUT IT AND WANT TO TAG ALONG.
I SHOULD BE MORE UPSET RIGHT NOW. BUT I JUST FEEL NUMB.
AND I WOULDN'T BE SENT TO MY "AUNT'S" UNLESS SOMETHING WAS REALLY A THREAT.

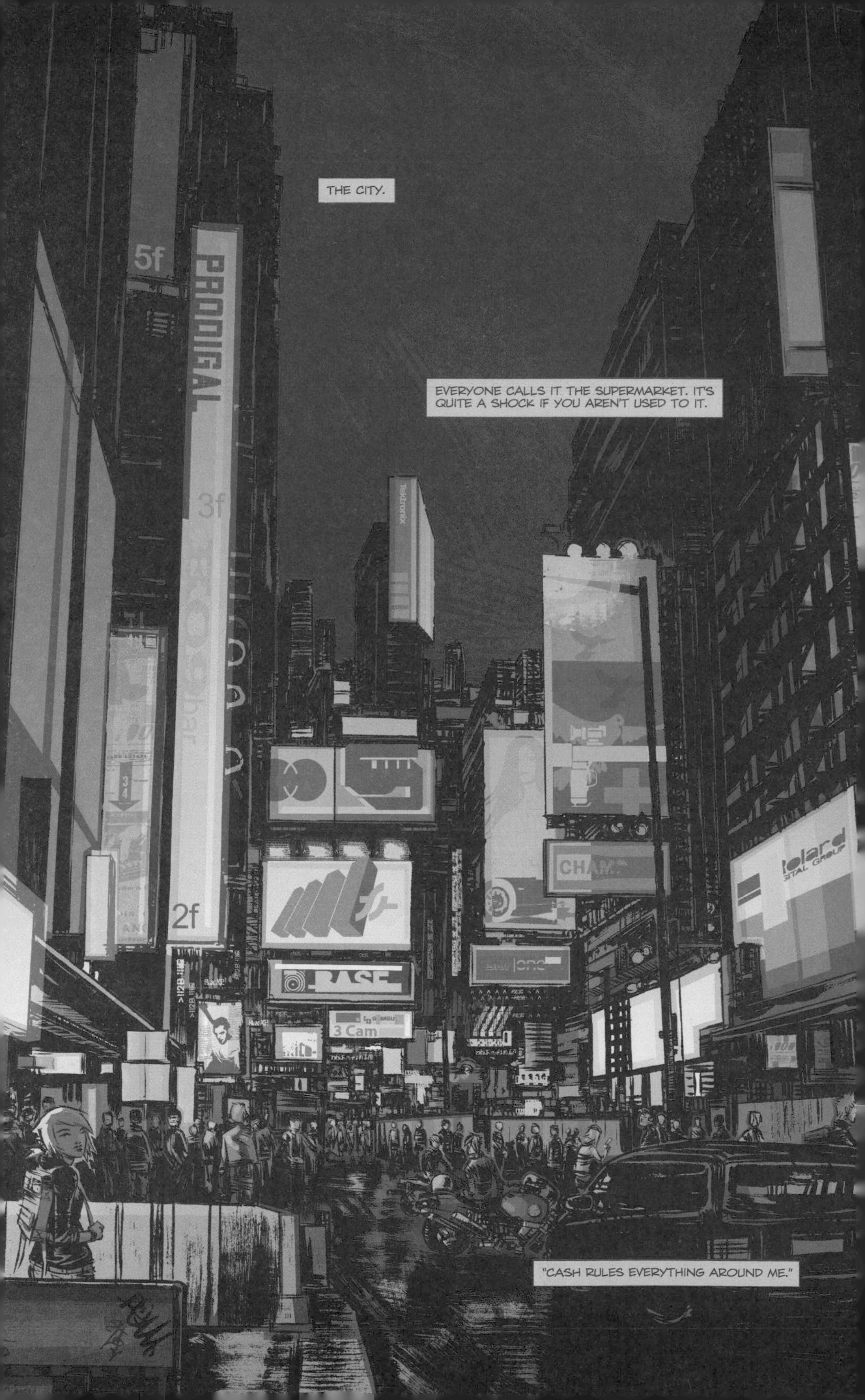
THE CITY.
EVERYONE CALLS IT THE SUPERMARKET. IT'S QUITE A SHOCK IF YOU AREN'T USED TO IT.
"CASH RULES EVERYTHING AROUND ME."
PRODIGAL
3 Cam
CHAMP

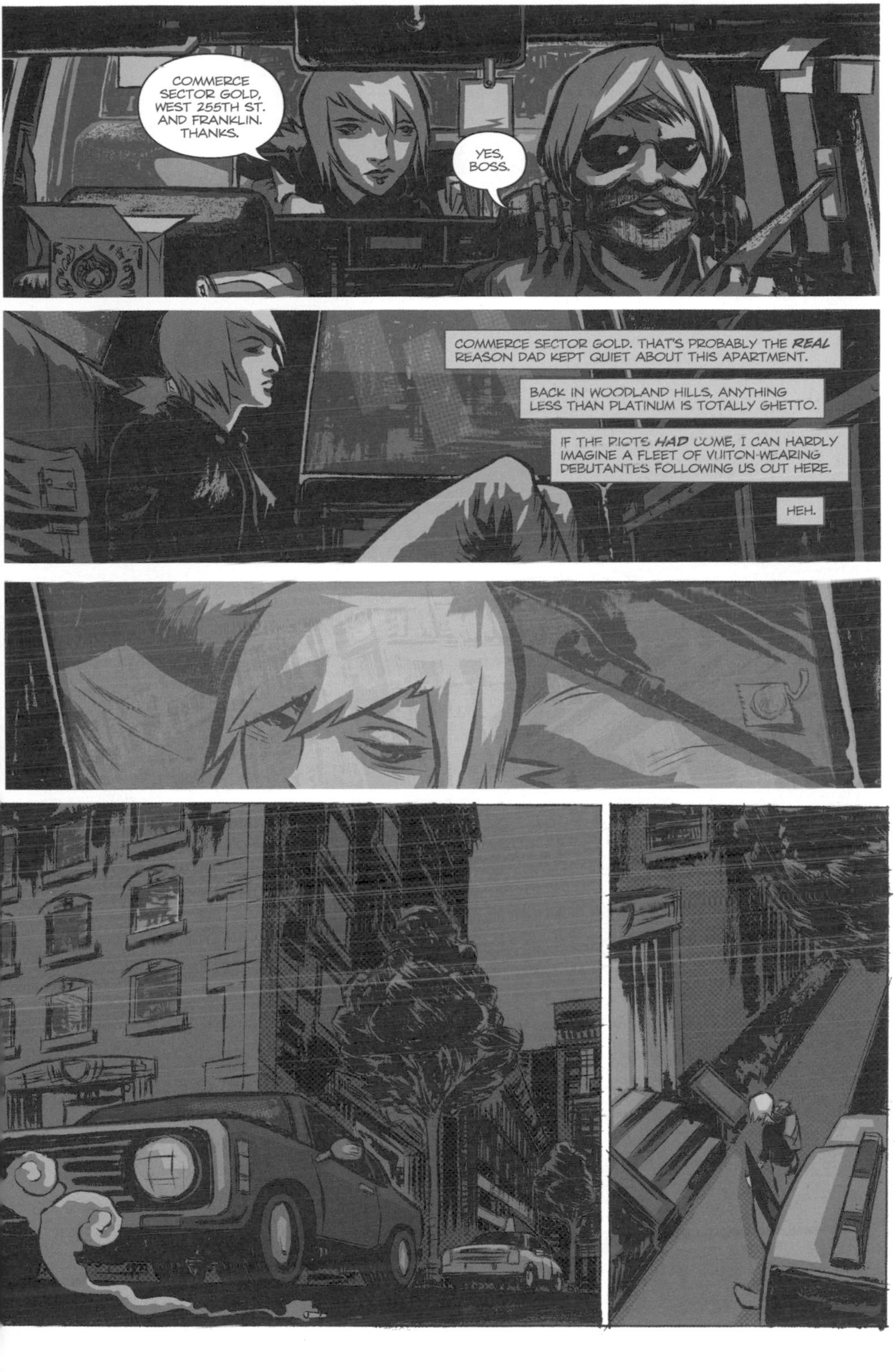
COMMERCE SECTOR GOLD, WEST 255TH ST. AND FRANKLIN. THANKS.
YES, BOSS.
COMMERCE SECTOR GOLD. THAT'S PROBABLY THE REAL REASON DAD KEPT QUIET ABOUT THIS APARTMENT.
BACK IN WOODLAND HILLS, ANYTHING LESS THAN PLATINUM IS TOTALLY GHETTO.
IF THE RIOTS HAD COME, I CAN HARDLY IMAGINE A FLEET OF VUITON-WEARING DEBUTANTES FOLLOWING US OUT HERE.
HEH.

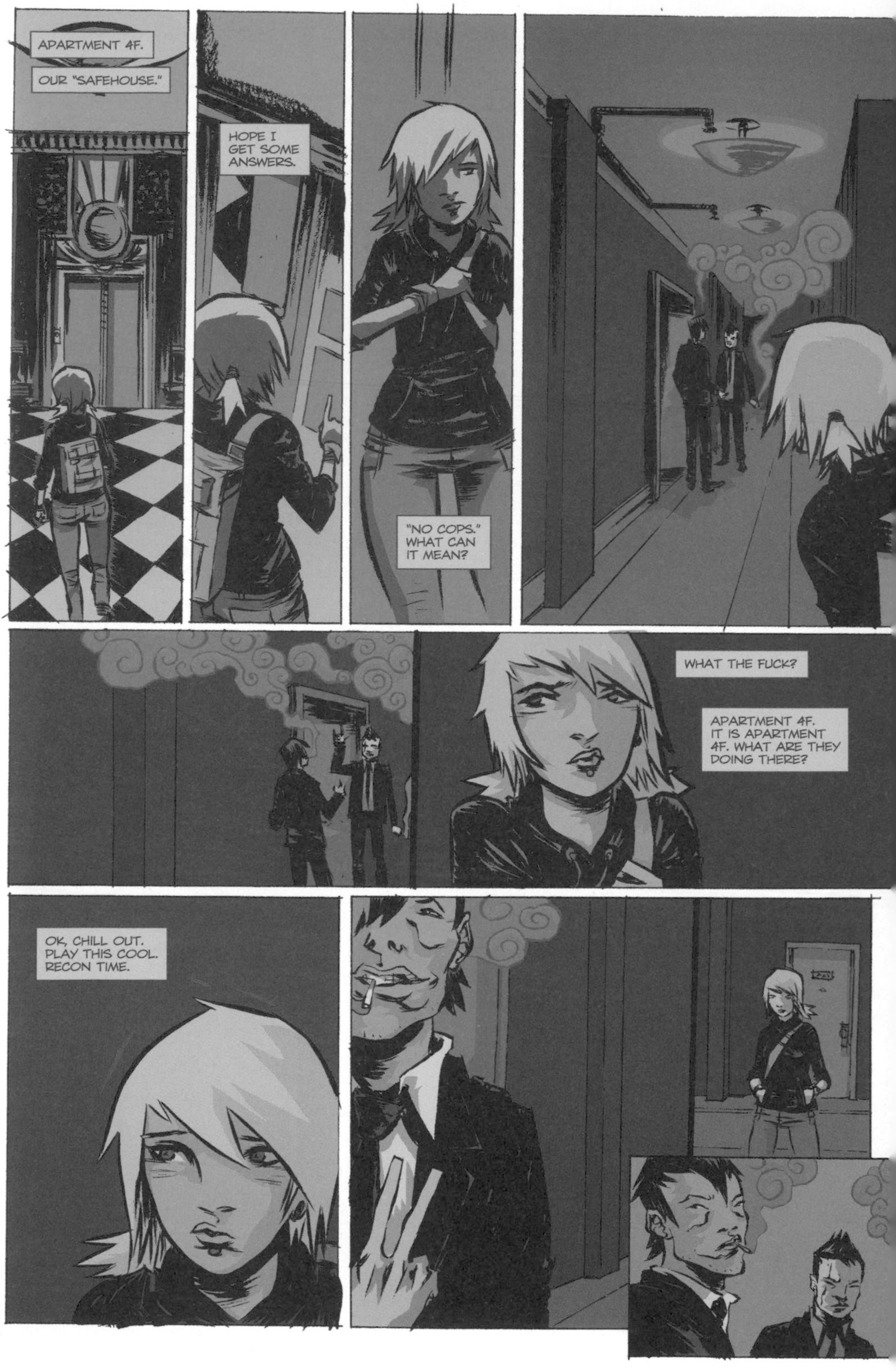
APARTMENT 4F.
OUR "SAFEHOUSE."
HOPE I GET SOME ANSWERS.
"NO COPS." WHAT CAN IT MEAN?
WHAT THE FUCK?
APARTMENT 4F. IT IS APARTMENT 4F. WHAT ARE THEY DOING THERE?
OK, CHILL OUT. PLAY THIS COOL. RECON TIME.

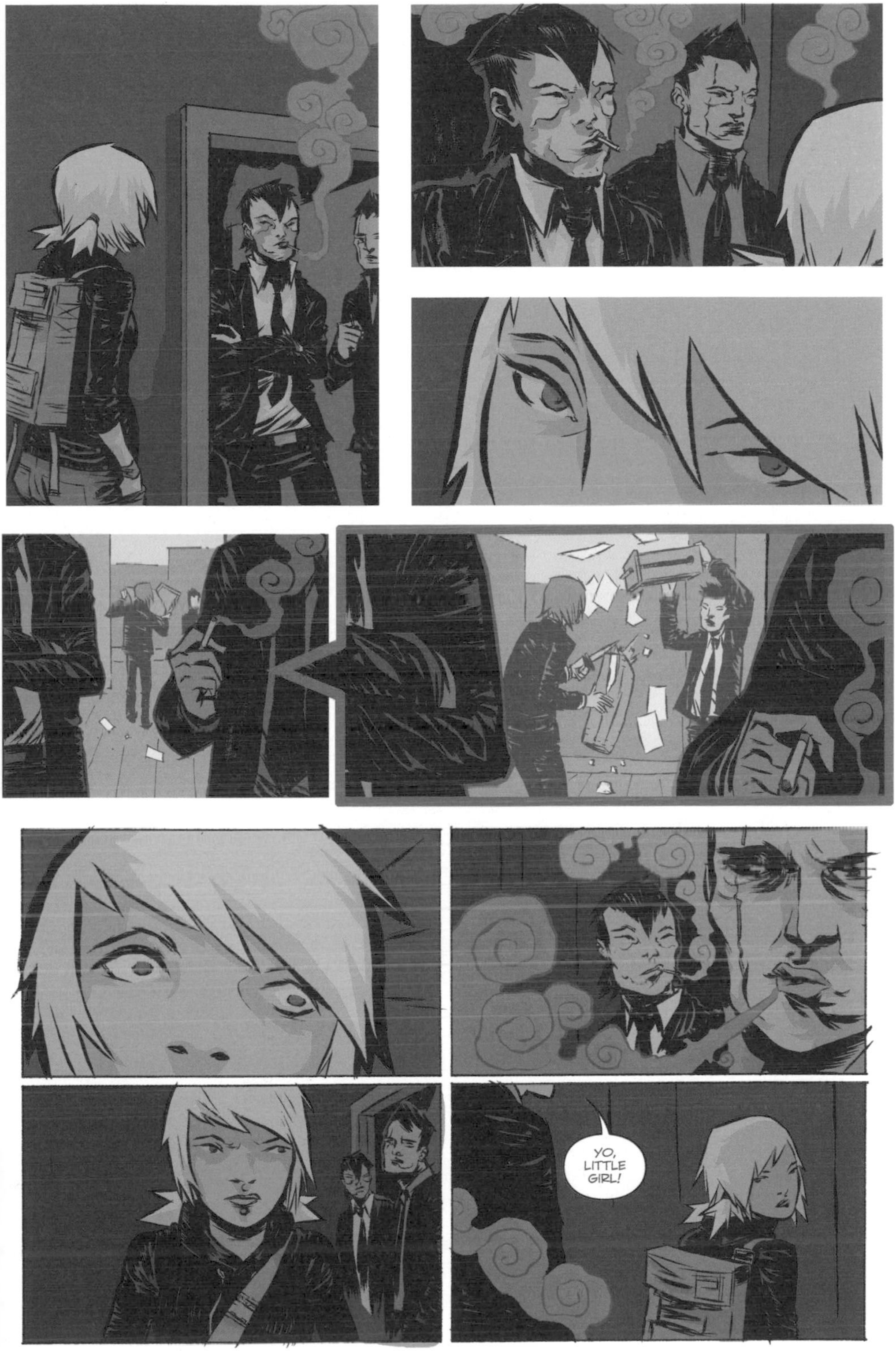
YO, LITTLE GIRL!

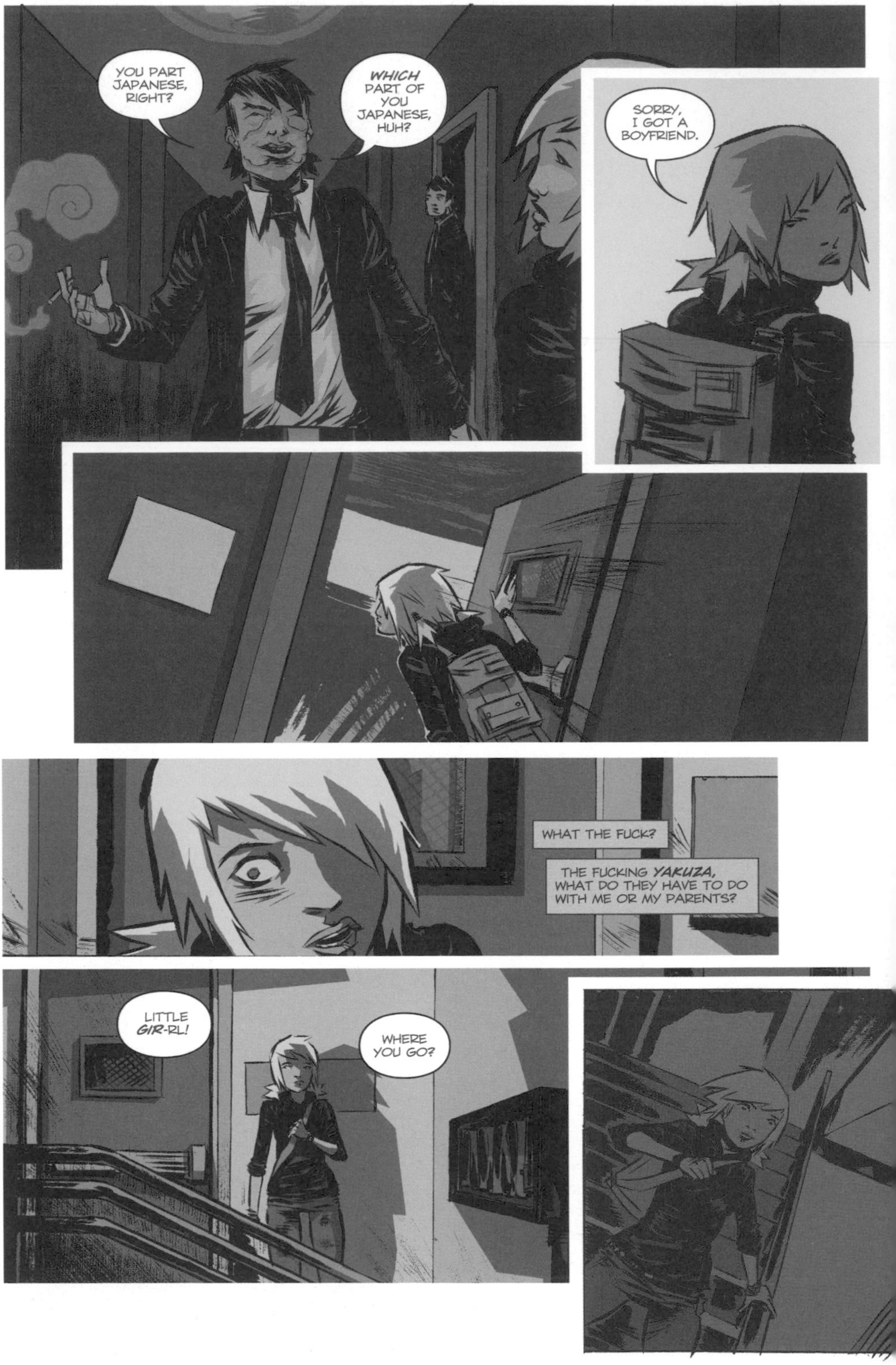

YOU PART JAPANESE, RIGHT?
WHICH PART OF YOU JAPANESE, HUH?
SORRY, I GOT A BOYFRIEND.
WHAT THE FUCK?
THE FUCKING YAKUZA, WHAT DO THEY HAVE TO DO WITH ME OR MY PARENTS?
LITTLE GIR-RL!
WHERE YOU GO?

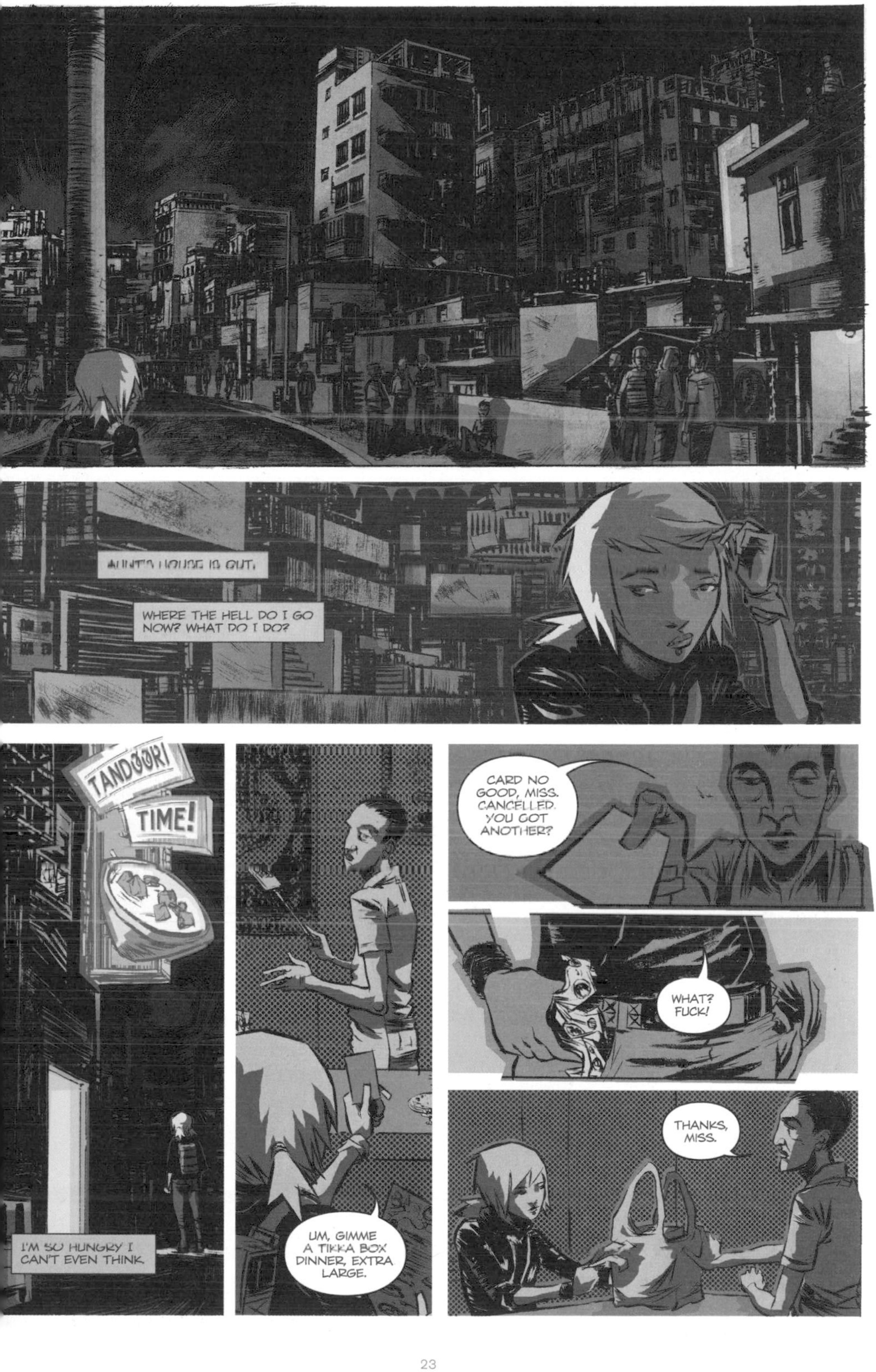

AUNT'S HOUSE IS OUT.
WHERE THE HELL DO I GO NOW? WHAT DO I DO?
TANDOORI TIME!
I'M SO HUNGRY I CAN'T EVEN THINK.
UM, GIMME A TIKKA BOX DINNER, EXTRA LARGE.
CARD NO GOOD, MISS. CANCELLED. YOU GOT ANOTHER?
WHAT? FUCK!
THANKS, MISS.

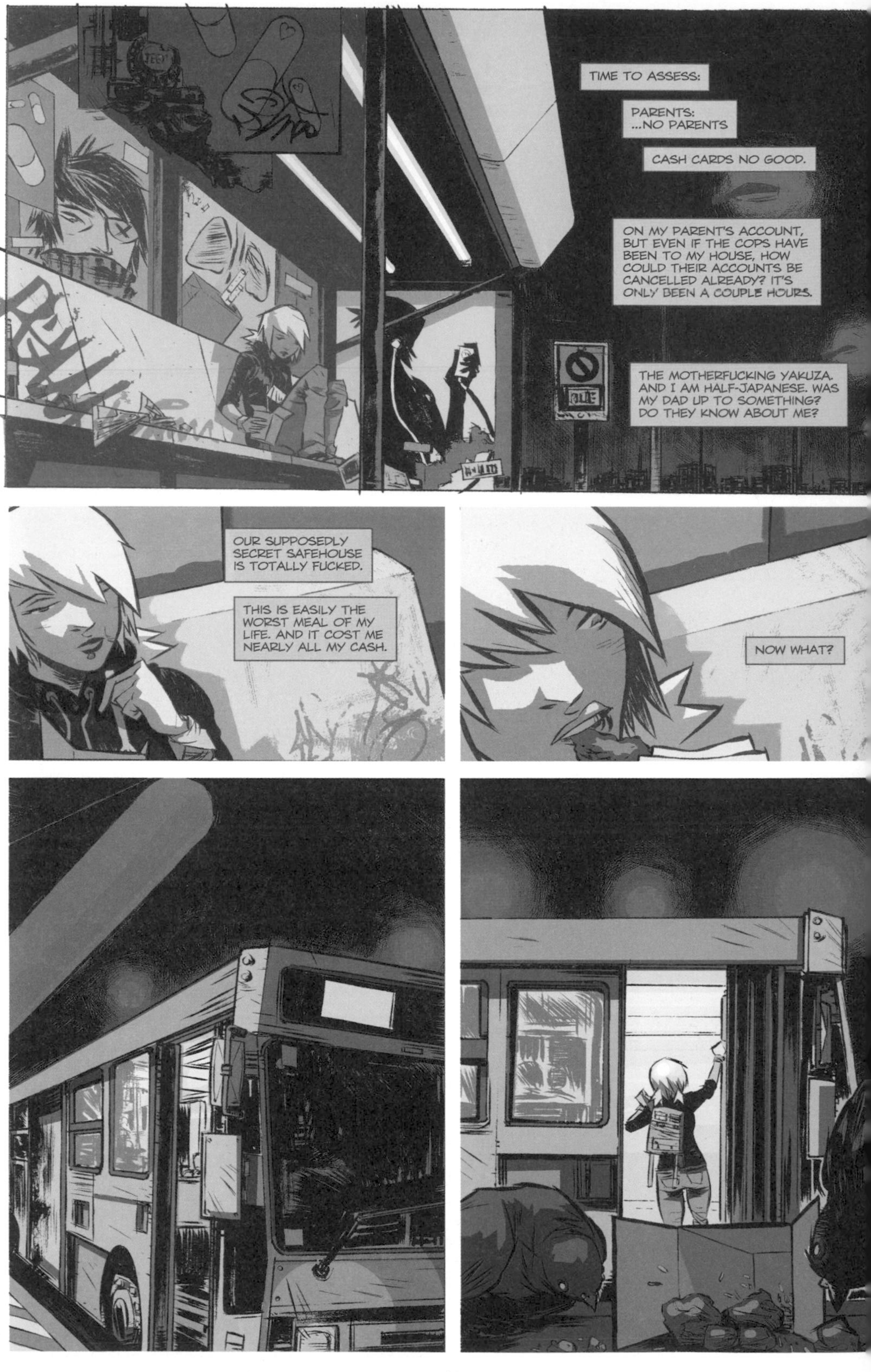
TIME TO ASSESS:
PARENTS:
...NO PARENTS
CASH CARDS NO GOOD.
ON MY PARENT'S ACCOUNT, BUT EVEN IF THE COPS HAVE BEEN TO MY HOUSE, HOW COULD THEIR ACCOUNTS BE CANCELLED ALREADY? IT'S ONLY BEEN A COUPLE HOURS.
THE MOTHERFUCKING YAKUZA. AND I AM HALF-JAPANESE. WAS MY DAD UP TO SOMETHING? DO THEY KNOW ABOUT ME?
OUR SUPPOSEDLY SECRET SAFEHOUSE IS TOTALLY FUCKED.
THIS IS EASILY THE WORST MEAL OF MY LIFE. AND IT COST ME NEARLY ALL MY CASH.
NOW WHAT?

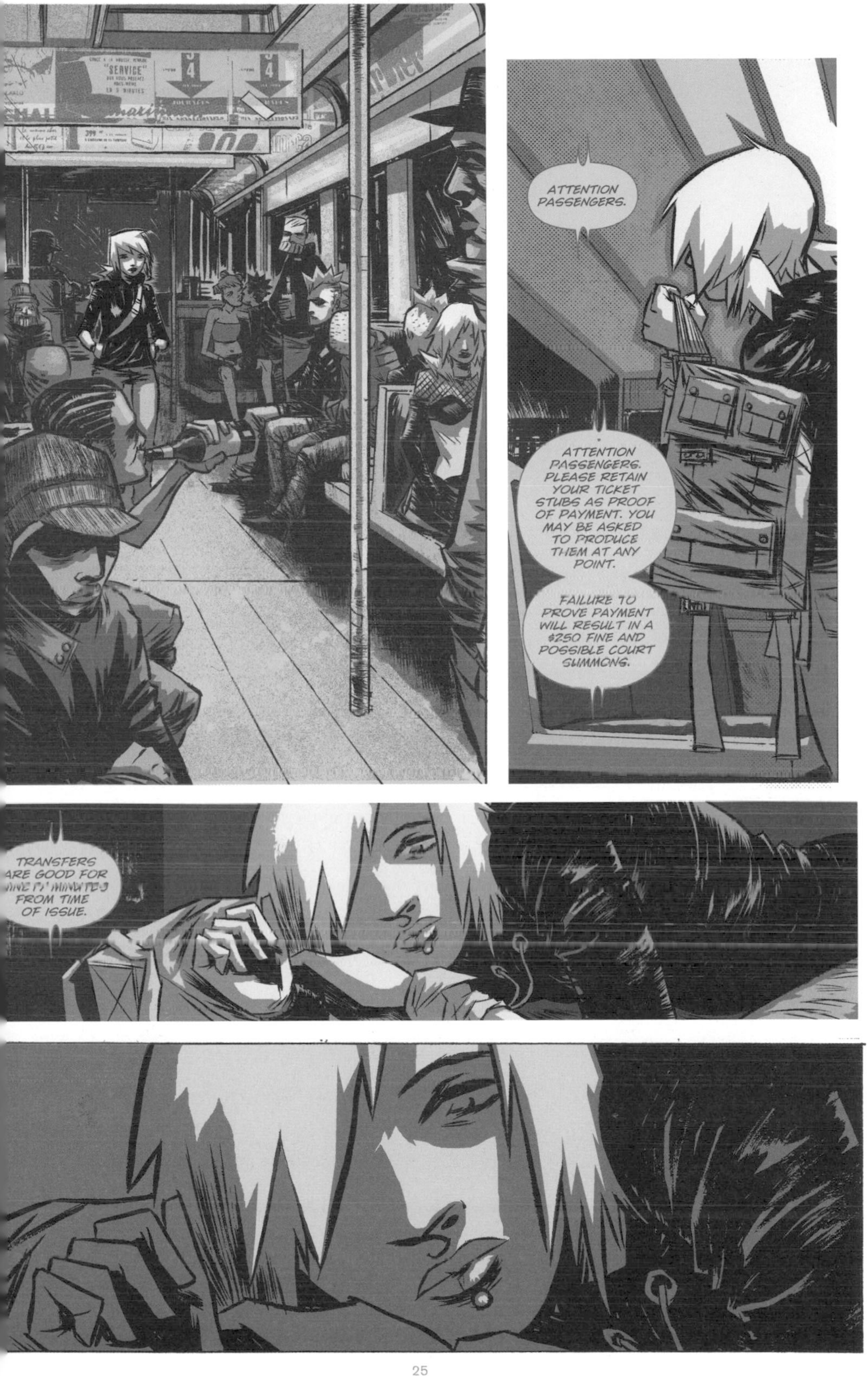
ATTENTION PASSENGERS.
ATTENTION PASSENGERS. PLEASE RETAIN YOUR TICKET STUBS AS PROOF OF PAYMENT. YOU MAY BE ASKED TO PRODUCE THEM AT ANY POINT.
FAILURE TO PROVE PAYMENT WILL RESULT IN A $250 FINE AND POSSIBLE COURT SUMMONS.
TRANSFERS ARE GOOD FOR
FROM TIME OF ISSUE.

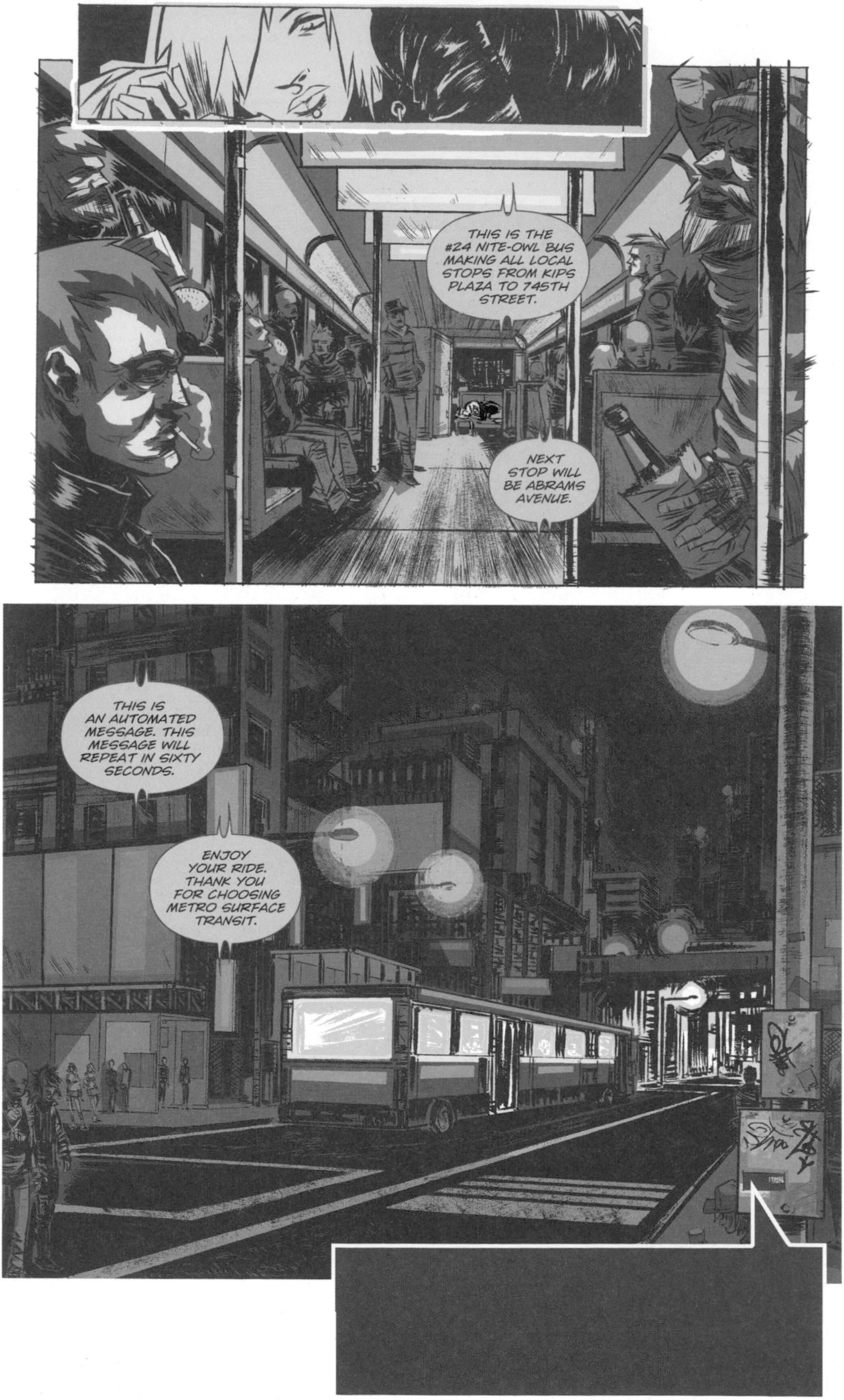
THIS IS THE #24 NITE-OWL BUS MAKING ALL LOCAL STOPS FROM KIPS PLAZA TO 745TH STREET.
NEXT STOP WILL BE ABRAMS AVENUE.
THIS IS AN AUTOMATED MESSAGE. THIS MESSAGE WILL REPEAT IN SIXTY SECONDS.
ENJOY YOUR RIDE. THANK YOU FOR CHOOSING METRO SURFACE TRANSIT.

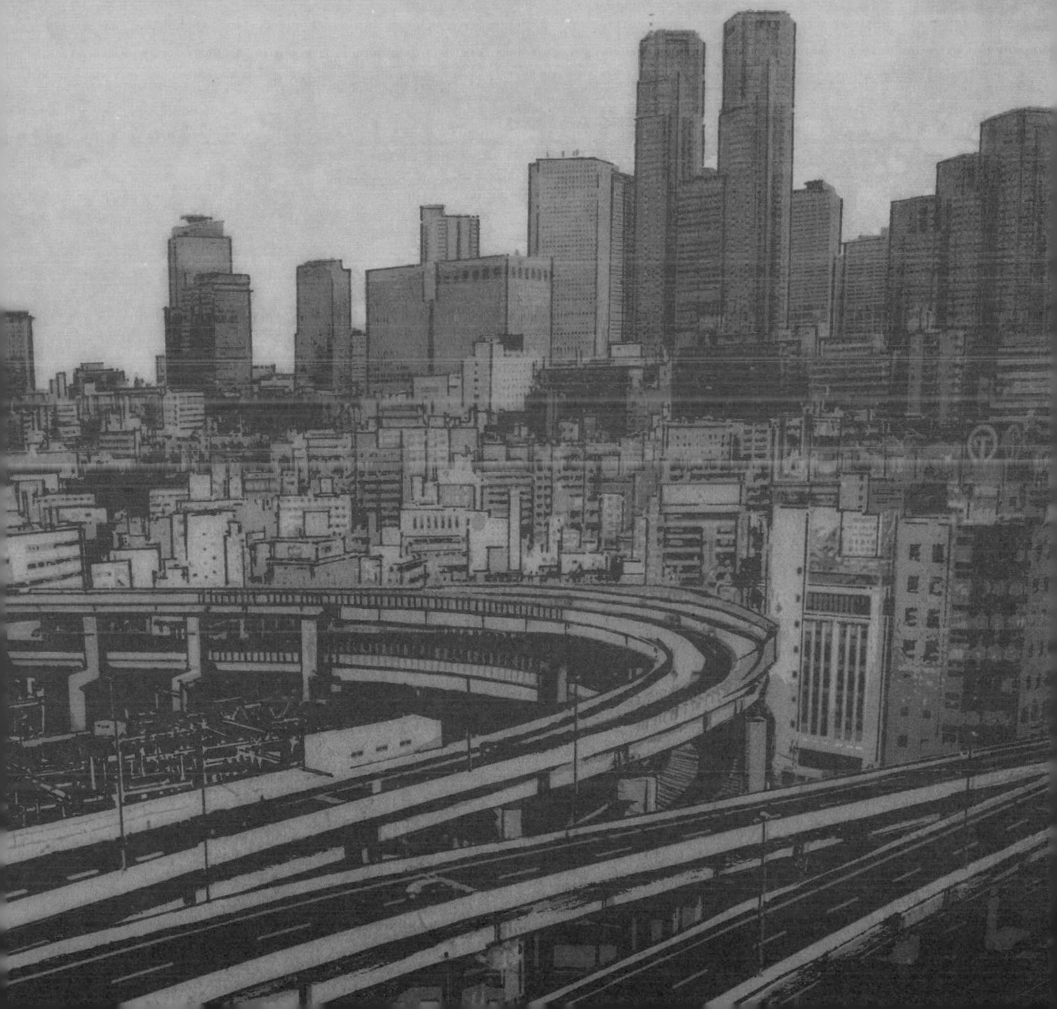

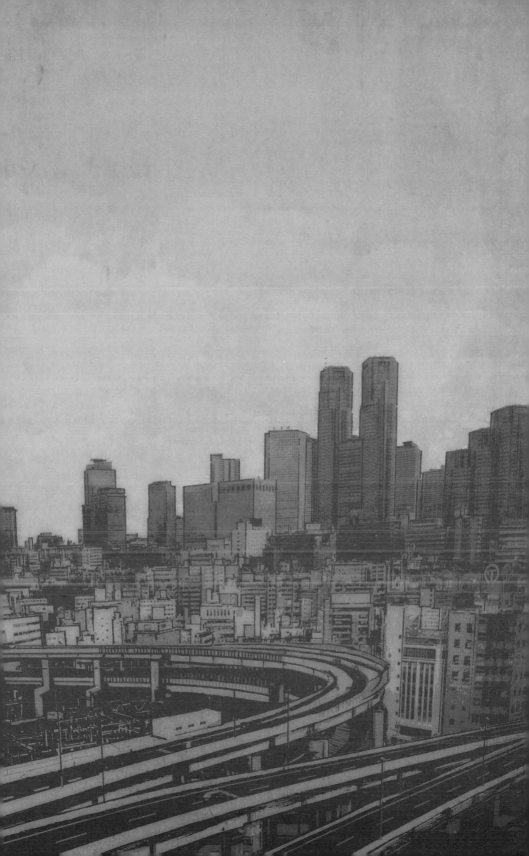

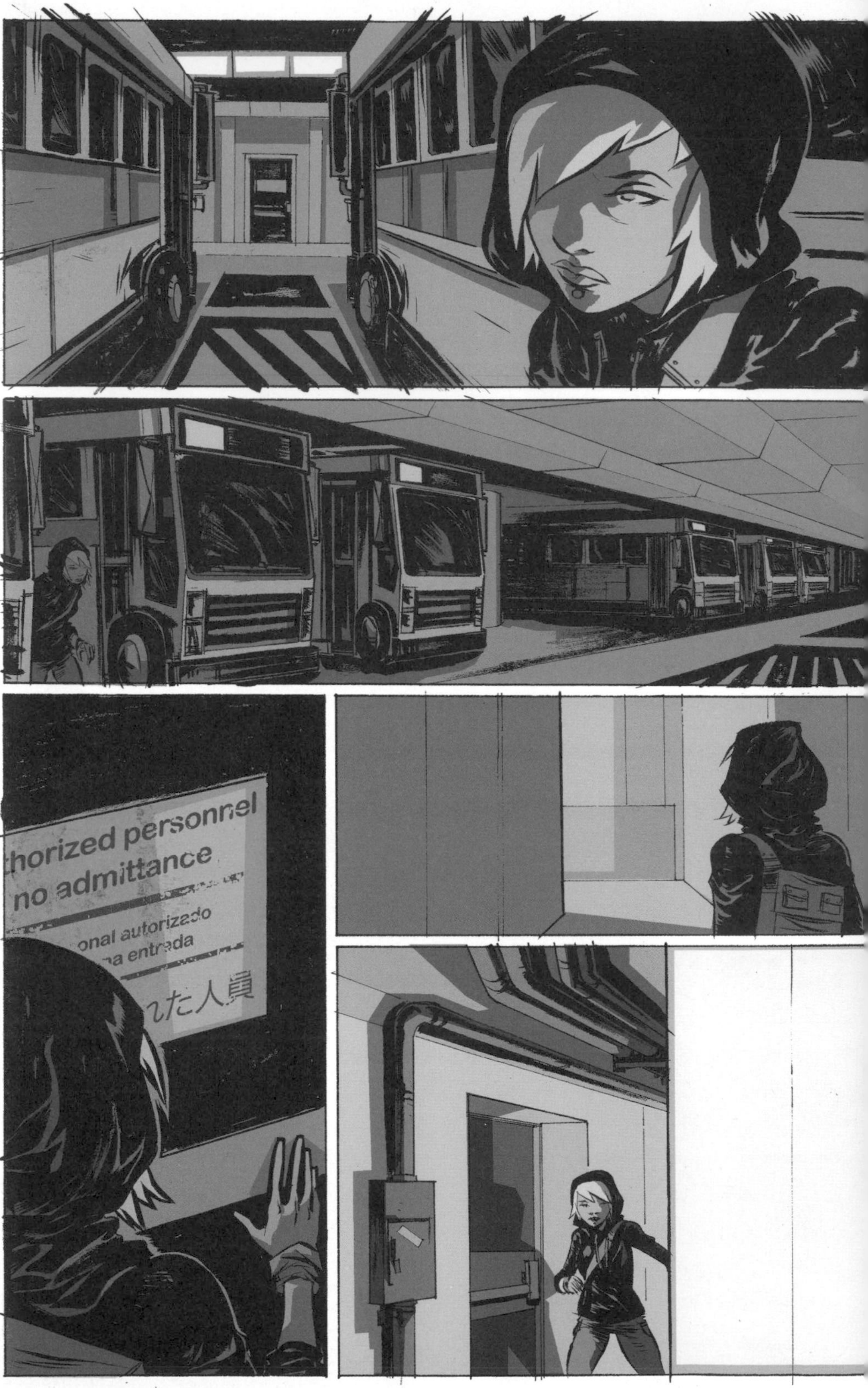
thorized personnel
no admittance
onal autorizado
na entrada
た人員

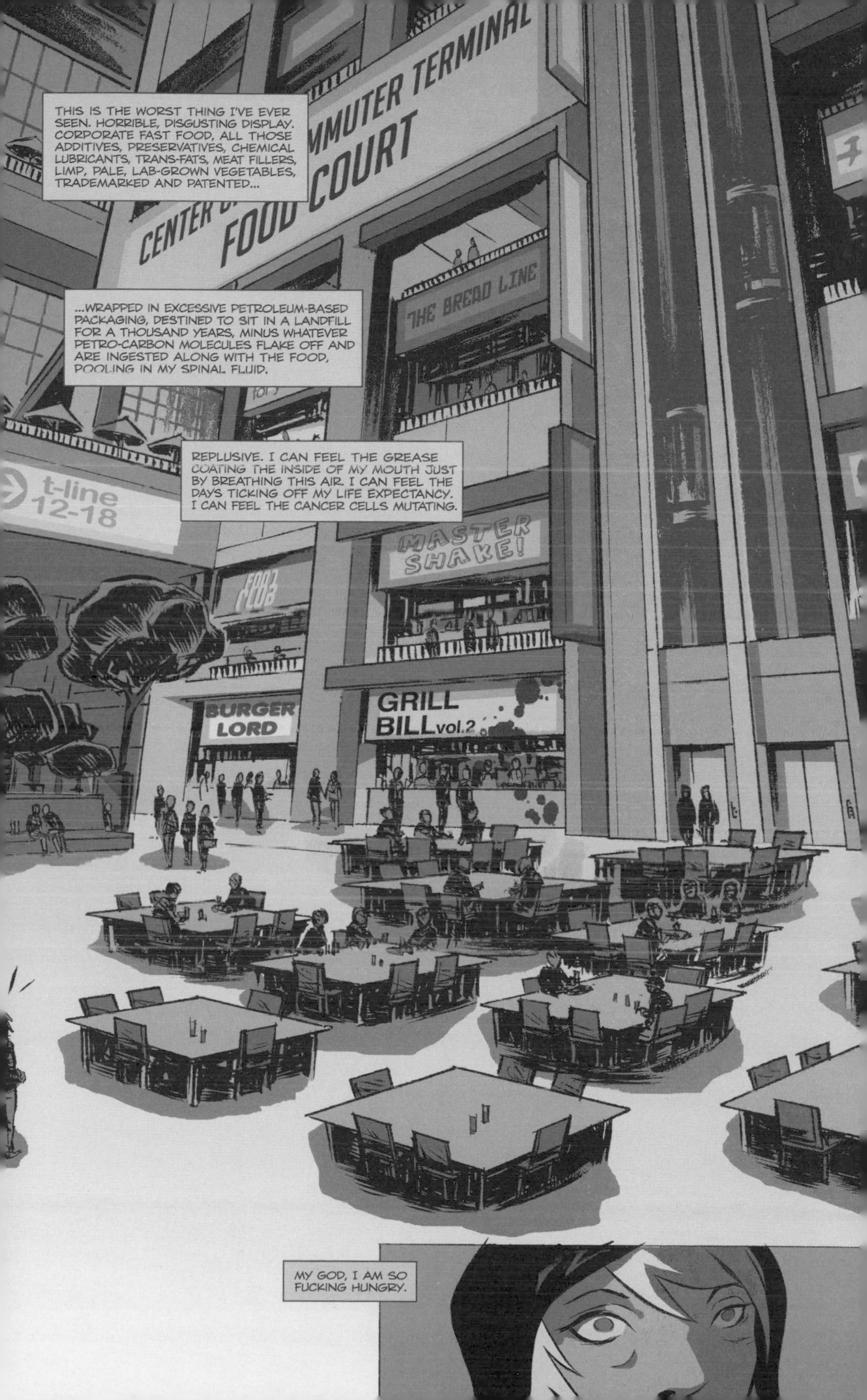
THIS IS THE WORST THING I'VE EVER SEEN. HORRIBLE, DISGUSTING DISPLAY. CORPORATE FAST FOOD, ALL THOSE ADDITIVES, PRESERVATIVES, CHEMICAL LUBRICANTS, TRANS-FATS, MEAT FILLERS, LIMP, PALE, LAB-GROWN VEGETABLES, TRADEMARKED AND PATENTED...
TERMINAL
FOOD COURT
...WRAPPED IN EXCESSIVE PETROLEUM-BASED PACKAGING, DESTINED TO SIT IN A LANDFILL FOR A THOUSAND YEARS, MINUS WHATEVER PETRO-CARBON MOLECULES FLAKE OFF AND ARE INGESTED ALONG WITH THE FOOD, POOLING IN MY SPINAL FLUID.
THE BREAD LINE
REPLUSIVE. I CAN FEEL THE GREASE COATING THE INSIDE OF MY MOUTH JUST BY BREATHING THIS AIR. I CAN FEEL THE DAYS TICKING OFF MY LIFE EXPECTANCY. I CAN FEEL THE CANCER CELLS MUTATING.
t-line 12-18
MASTER SHAKE!
BURGER LORD
GRILL BILL vol.2
MY GOD, I AM SO FUCKING HUNGRY.

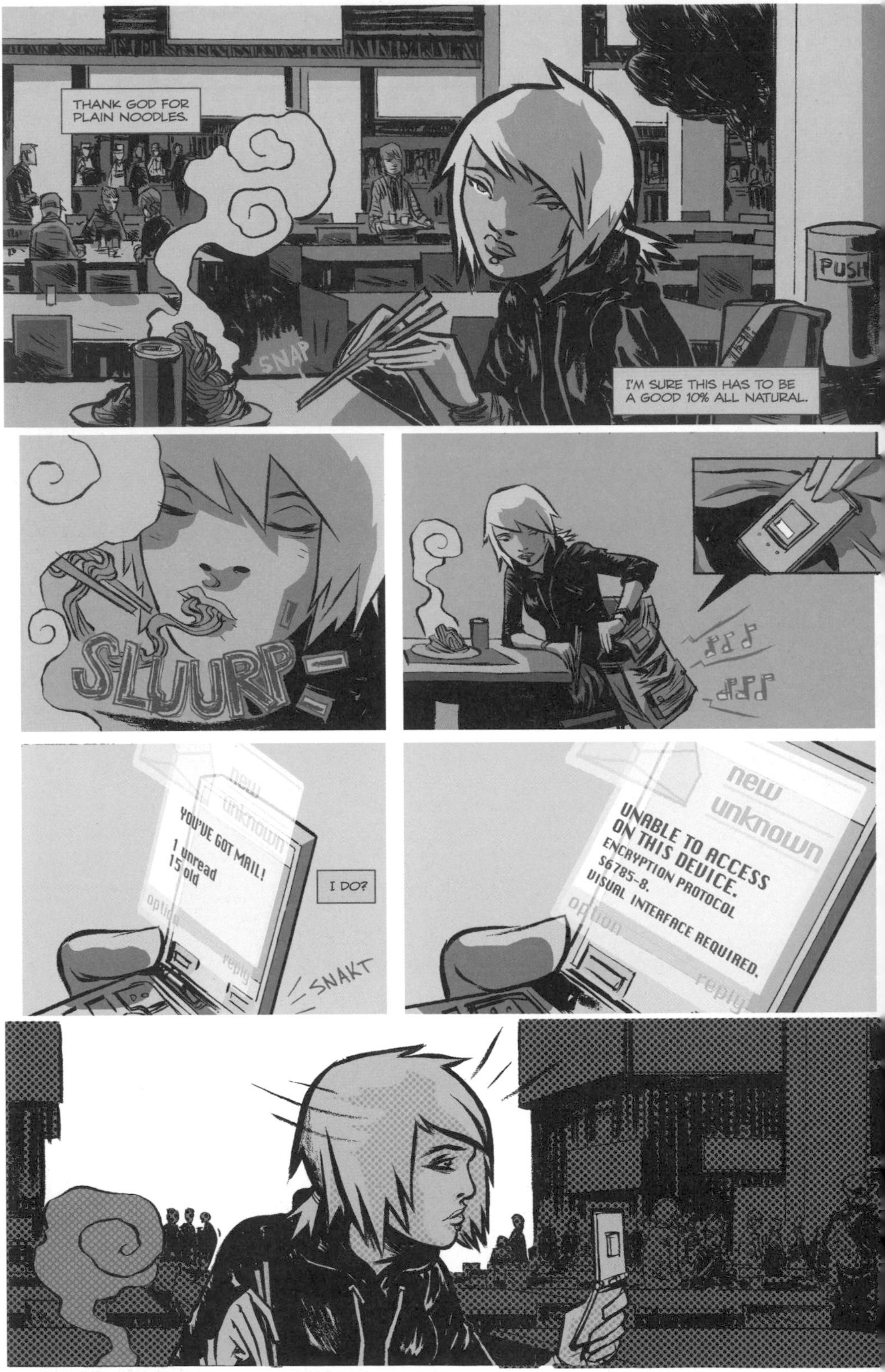
THANK GOD FOR PLAIN NOODLES.
SNAP
I'M SURE THIS HAS TO BE A GOOD 10% ALL NATURAL.
PUSH
SLUURP
YOU'VE GOT MAIL!
1 unread
15 old
new
unknown
option
reply
I DO?
SNAKT
UNABLE TO ACCESS ON THIS DEVICE.
ENCRYPTION PROTOCOL S6785-8.
VISUAL INTERFACE REQUIRED.

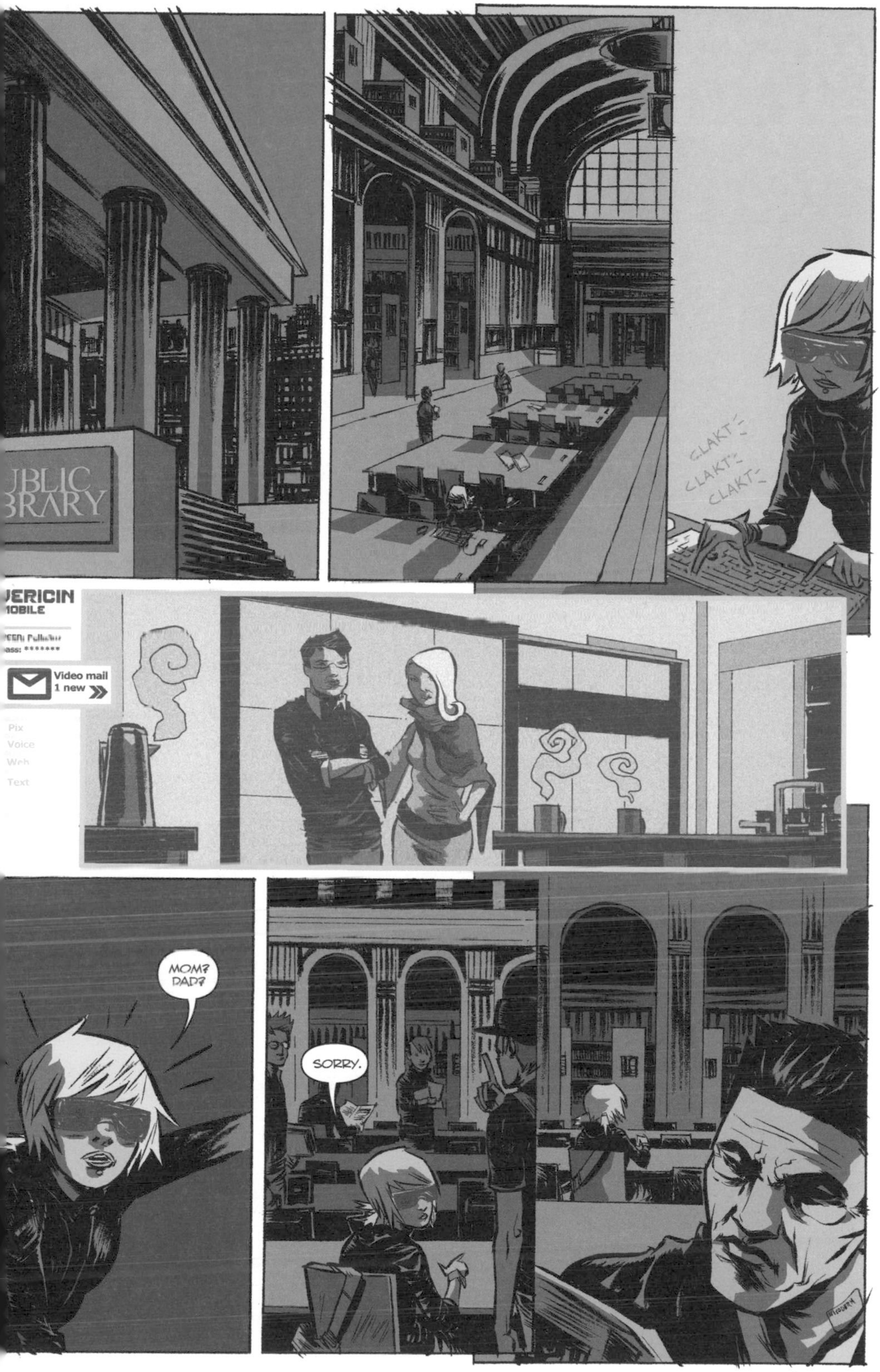
UBLIC
BRARY
CLAKT
CLAKT
CLAKT
VERICIN
MOBILE
Video mail
1 new
Pix
Voice
Web
Text
MOM?
DAD?
SORRY.

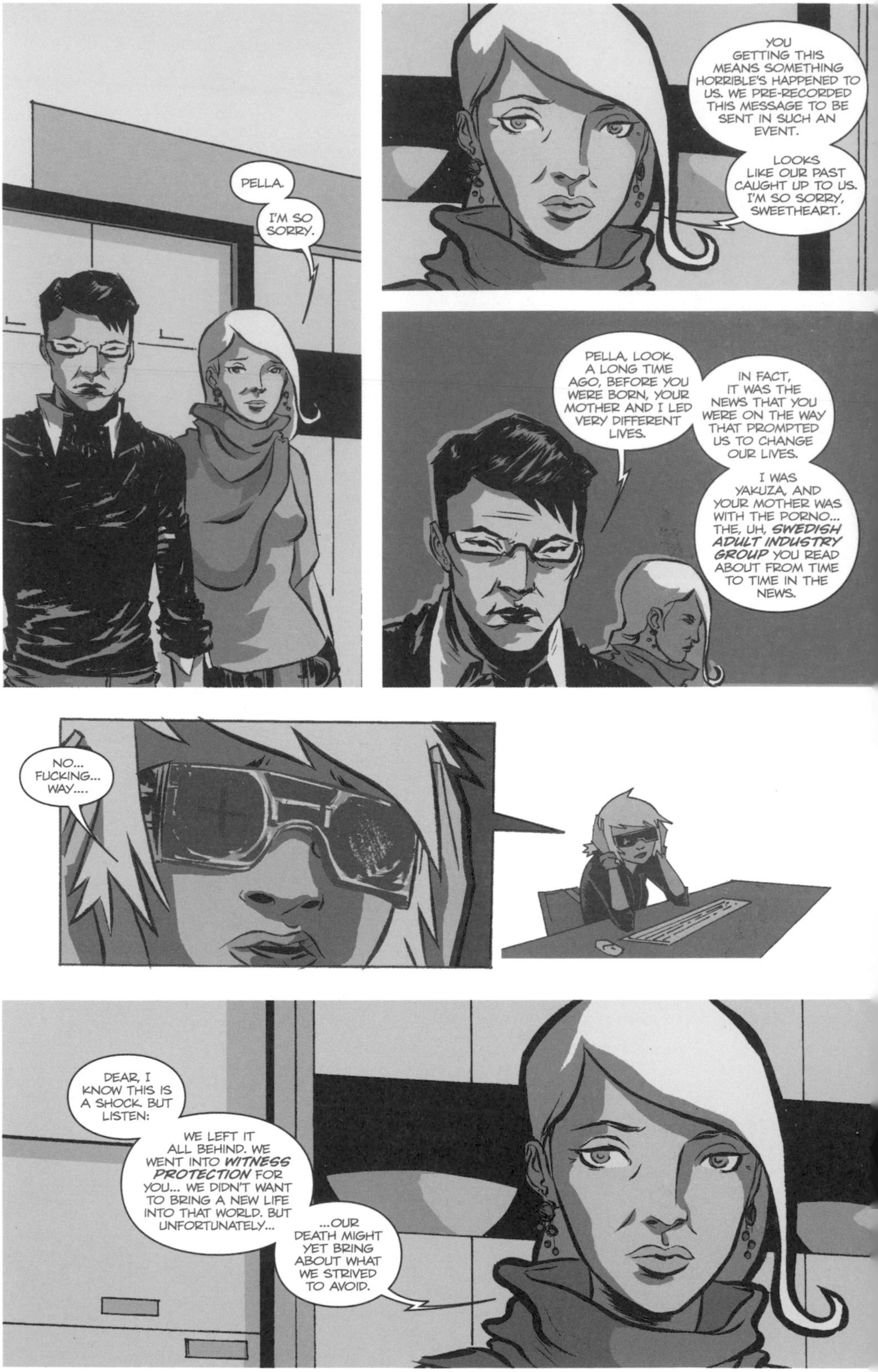
PELLA.
I'M SO SORRY.
YOU GETTING THIS MEANS SOMETHING HORRIBLE'S HAPPENED TO US. WE PRE-RECORDED THIS MESSAGE TO BE SENT IN SUCH AN EVENT.
LOOKS LIKE OUR PAST CAUGHT UP TO US. I'M SO SORRY, SWEETHEART.
PELLA, LOOK. A LONG TIME AGO, BEFORE YOU WERE BORN, YOUR MOTHER AND I LED VERY DIFFERENT LIVES.
IN FACT, IT WAS THE NEWS THAT YOU WERE ON THE WAY THAT PROMPTED US TO CHANGE OUR LIVES.
I WAS YAKUZA, AND YOUR MOTHER WAS WITH THE PORNO... THE, UH, ***SWEDISH ADULT INDUSTRY GROUP*** YOU READ ABOUT FROM TIME TO TIME IN THE NEWS.
NO... FUCKING... WAY....
DEAR, I KNOW THIS IS A SHOCK. BUT LISTEN:
WE LEFT IT ALL BEHIND. WE WENT INTO ***WITNESS PROTECTION*** FOR YOU... WE DIDN'T WANT TO BRING A NEW LIFE INTO THAT WORLD. BUT UNFORTUNATELY...
...OUR DEATH MIGHT YET BRING ABOUT WHAT WE STRIVED TO AVOID.

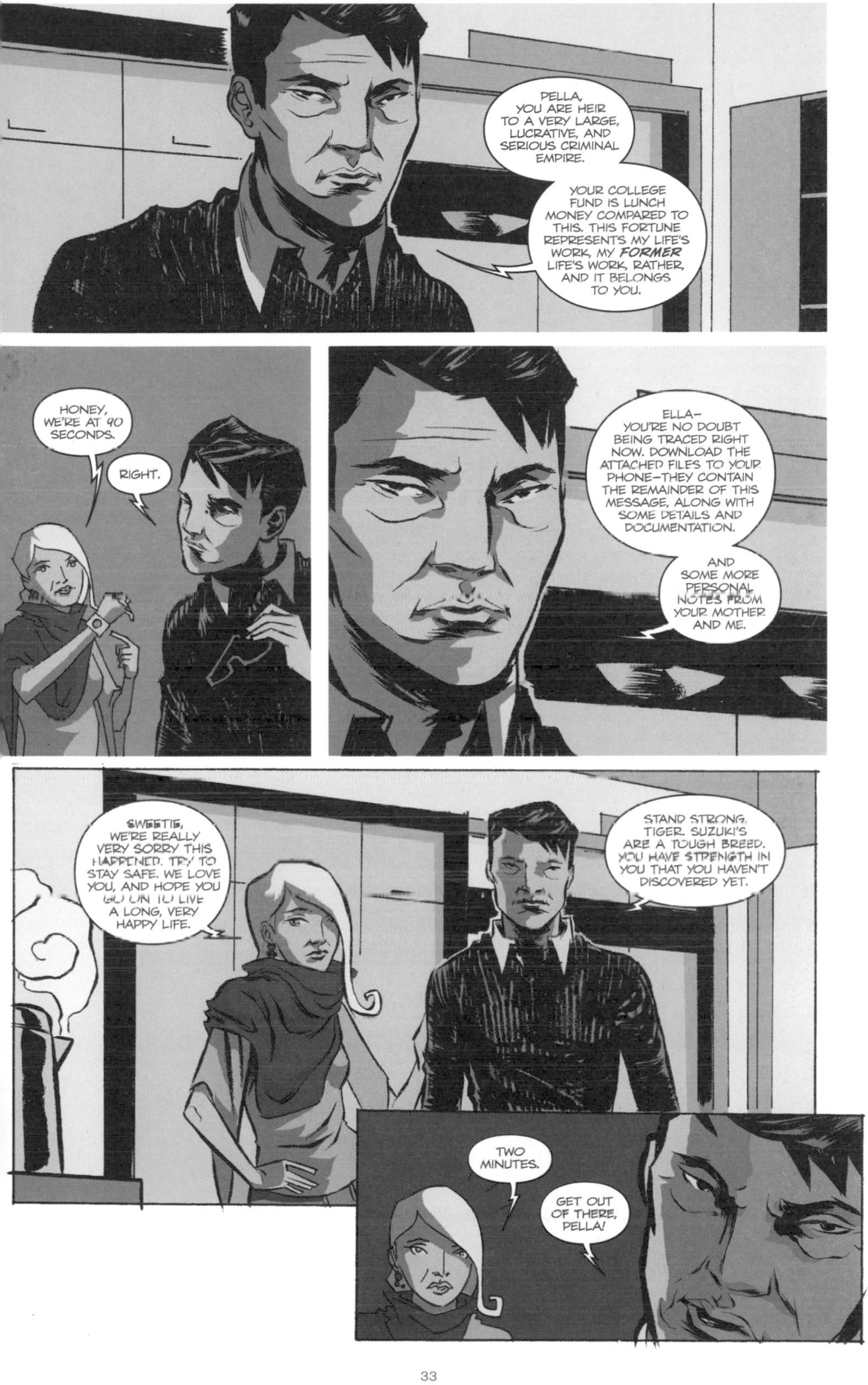
PELLA, YOU ARE HEIR TO A VERY LARGE, LUCRATIVE, AND SERIOUS CRIMINAL EMPIRE.
YOUR COLLEGE FUND IS LUNCH MONEY COMPARED TO THIS. THIS FORTUNE REPRESENTS MY LIFE'S WORK, MY *FORMER* LIFE'S WORK, RATHER, AND IT BELONGS TO YOU.
HONEY, WE'RE AT 90 SECONDS.
RIGHT.
ELLA– YOU'RE NO DOUBT BEING TRACED RIGHT NOW. DOWNLOAD THE ATTACHED FILES TO YOUR PHONE—THEY CONTAIN THE REMAINDER OF THIS MESSAGE, ALONG WITH SOME DETAILS AND DOCUMENTATION.
AND SOME MORE PERSONAL NOTES FROM YOUR MOTHER AND ME.
SWEETIE, WE'RE REALLY VERY SORRY THIS HAPPENED. TRY TO STAY SAFE. WE LOVE YOU, AND HOPE YOU GO ON TO LIVE A LONG, VERY HAPPY LIFE.
STAND STRONG, TIGER. SUZUKI'S ARE A TOUGH BREED. YOU HAVE STRENGTH IN YOU THAT YOU HAVEN'T DISCOVERED YET.
TWO MINUTES.
GET OUT OF THERE, PELLA!

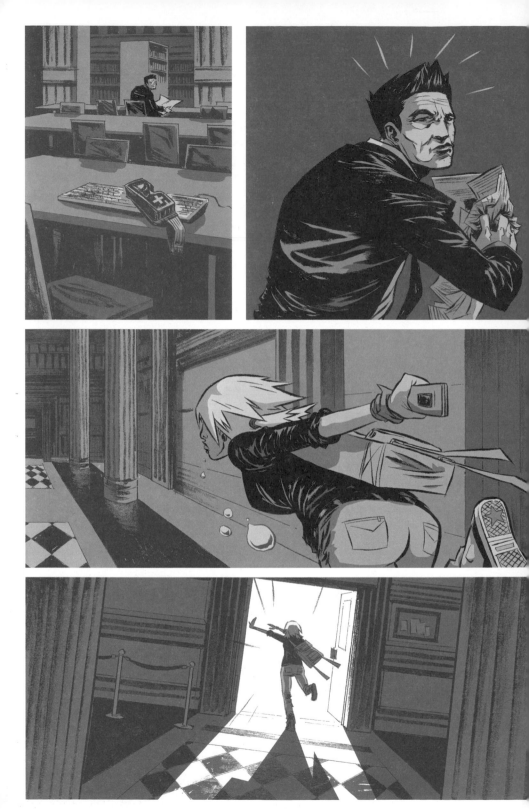

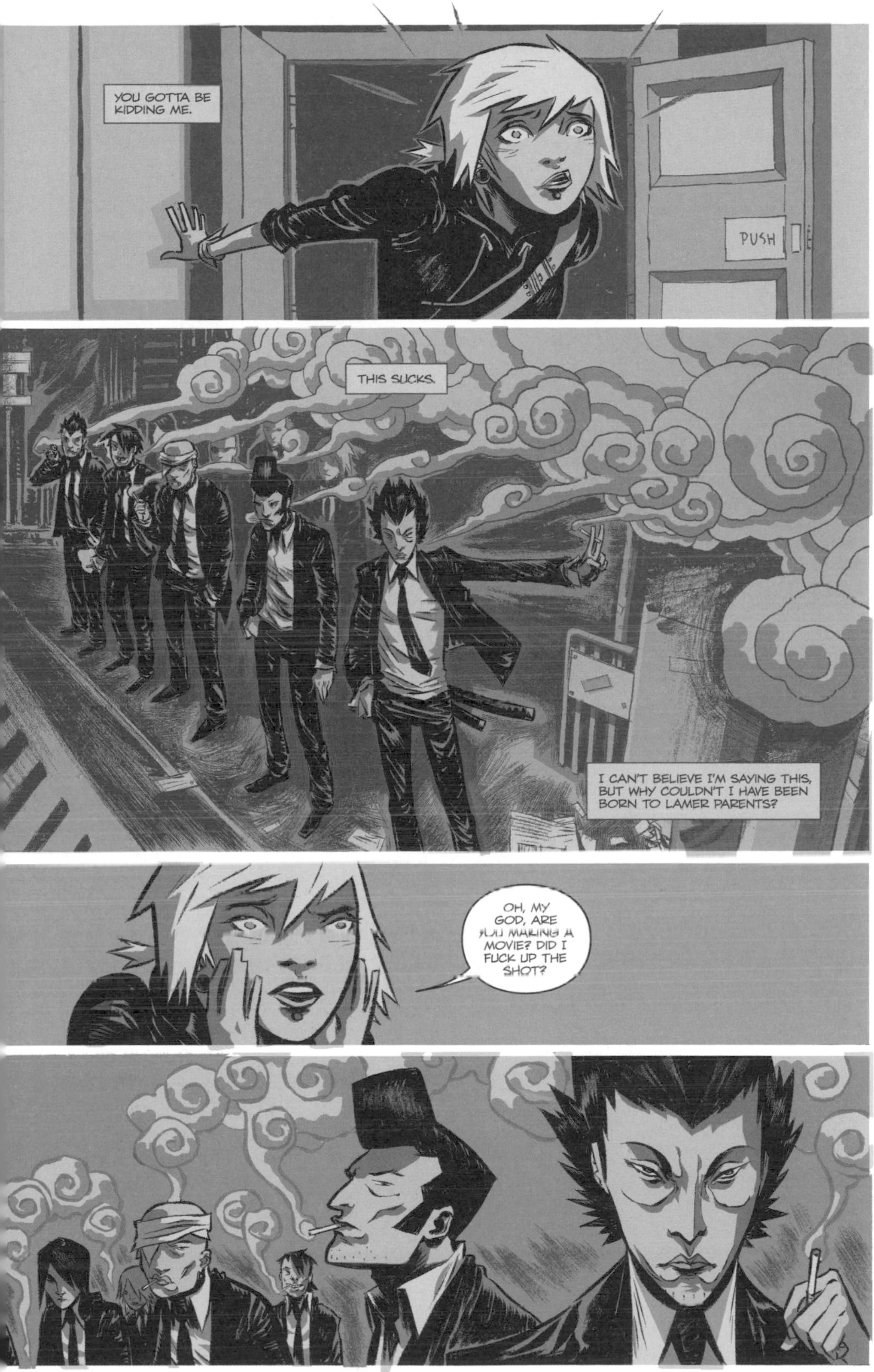
YOU GOTTA BE KIDDING ME.
PUSH
THIS SUCKS.
I CAN'T BELIEVE I'M SAYING THIS, BUT WHY COULDN'T I HAVE BEEN BORN TO LAMER PARENTS?
OH, MY GOD, ARE YOU MAKING A MOVIE? DID I FUCK UP THE SHOT?

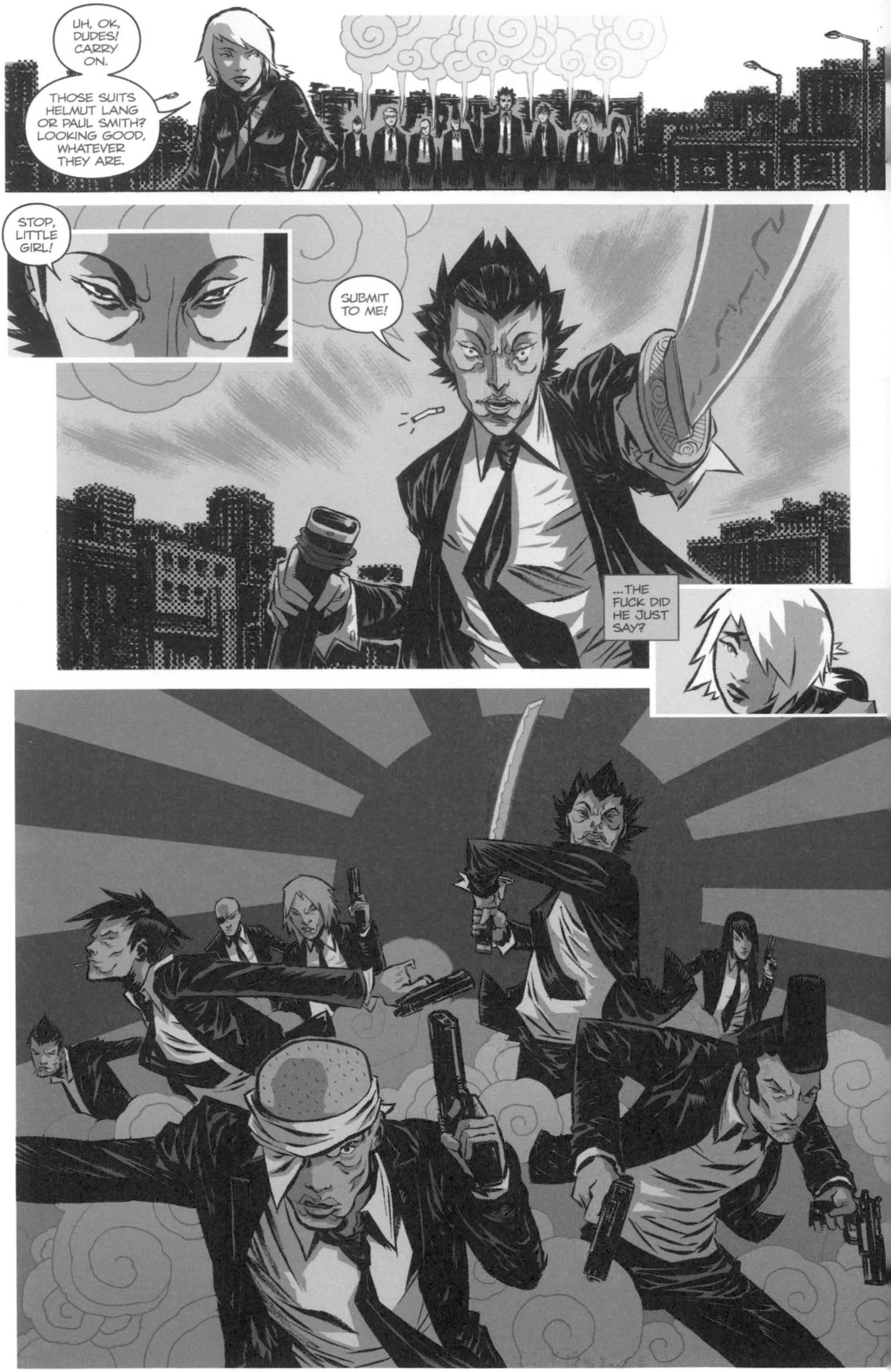
UH, OK, DUDES! CARRY ON.
THOSE SUITS HELMUT LANG OR PAUL SMITH? LOOKING GOOD, WHATEVER THEY ARE.
STOP, LITTLE GIRL!
SUBMIT TO ME!
...THE FUCK DID HE JUST SAY?

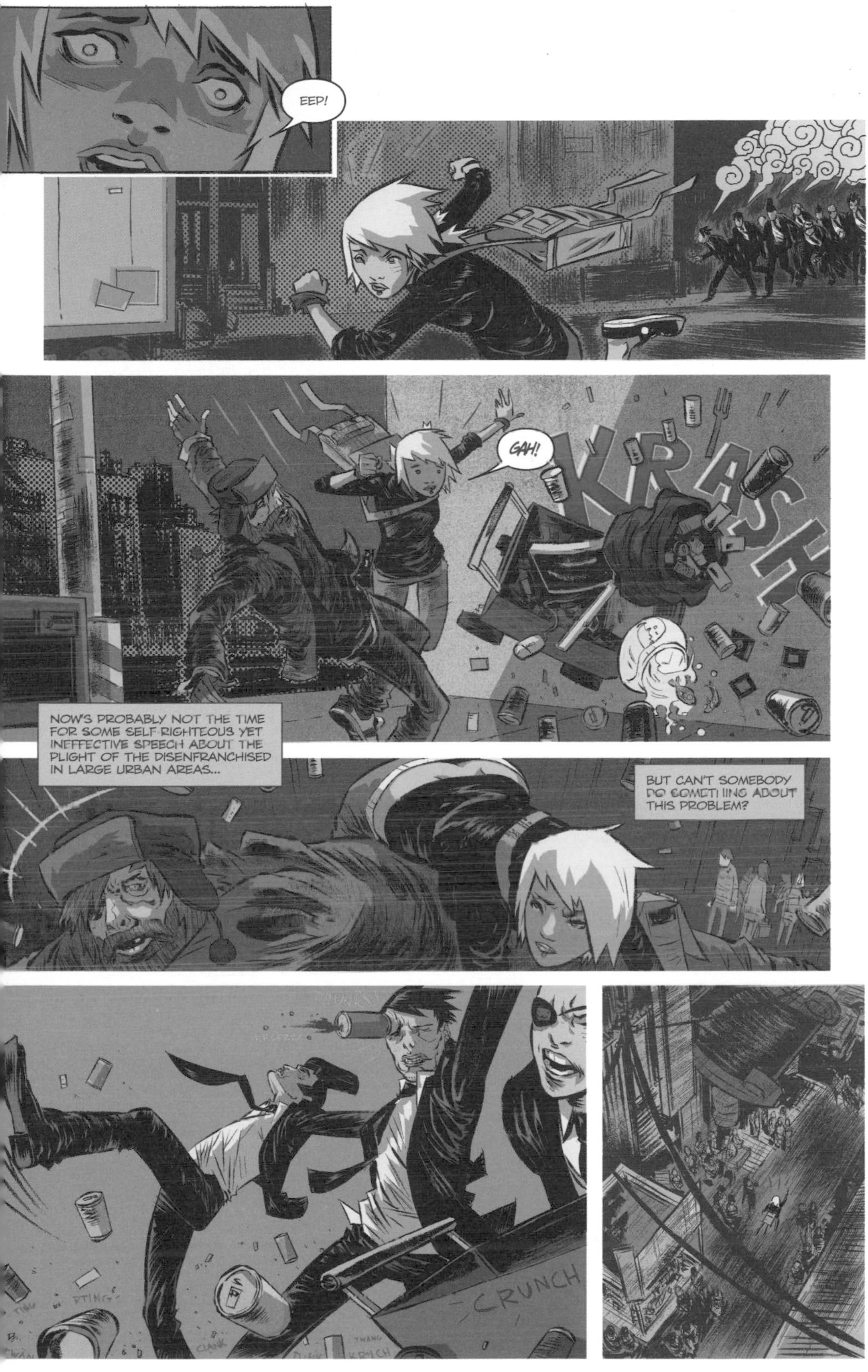
EEP!
GAH!
KRASH
NOW'S PROBABLY NOT THE TIME FOR SOME SELF-RIGHTEOUS YET INEFFECTIVE SPEECH ABOUT THE PLIGHT OF THE DISENFRANCHISED IN LARGE URBAN AREAS...
BUT CAN'T SOMEBODY DO SOMETHING ABOUT THIS PROBLEM?
CRUNCH
DTING
CLANK
TWANG

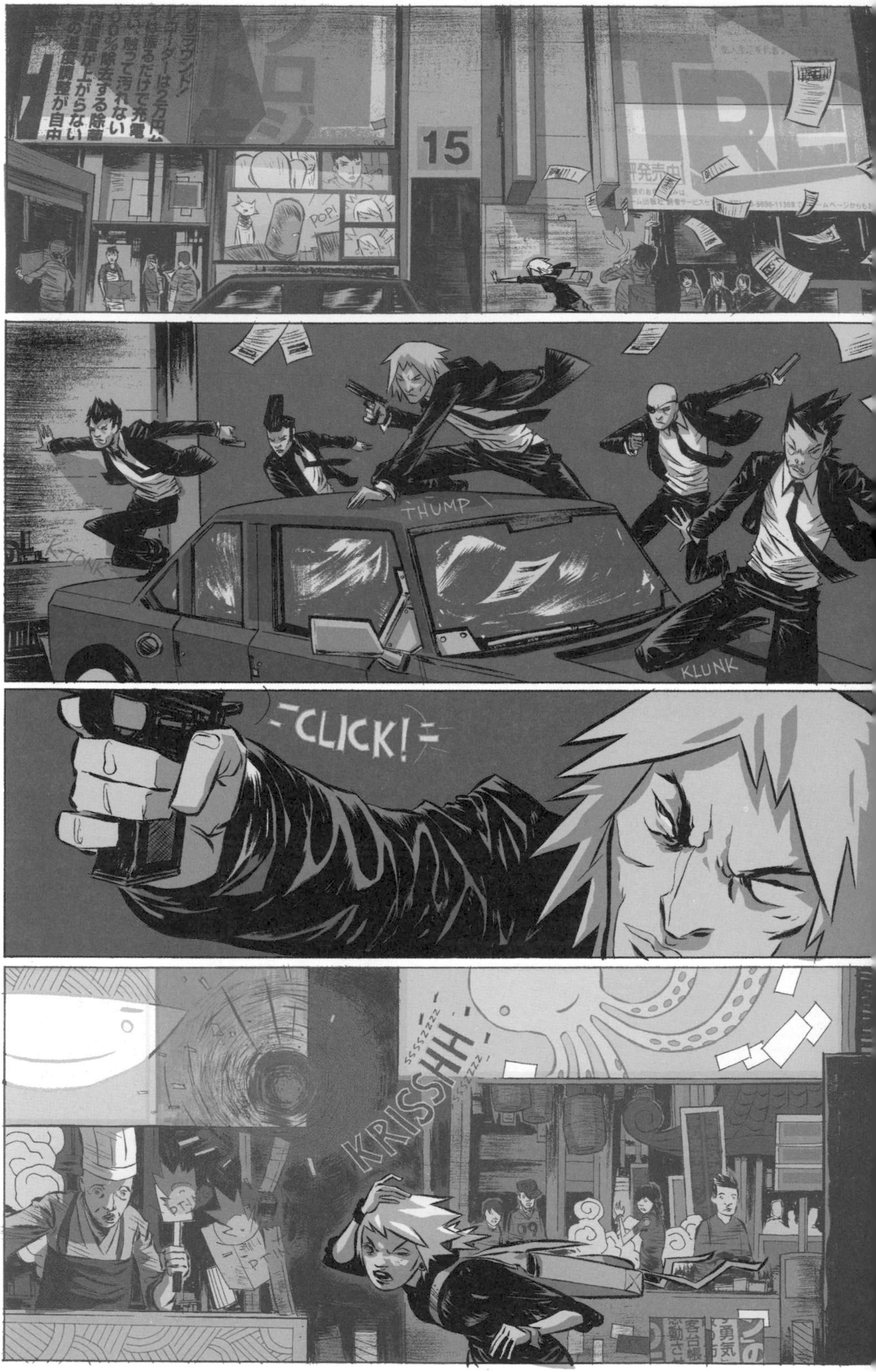
15
POP!
THUMP
K-TONK
KLUNK
CLICK!
KRISSHH
SSSSZZZZ

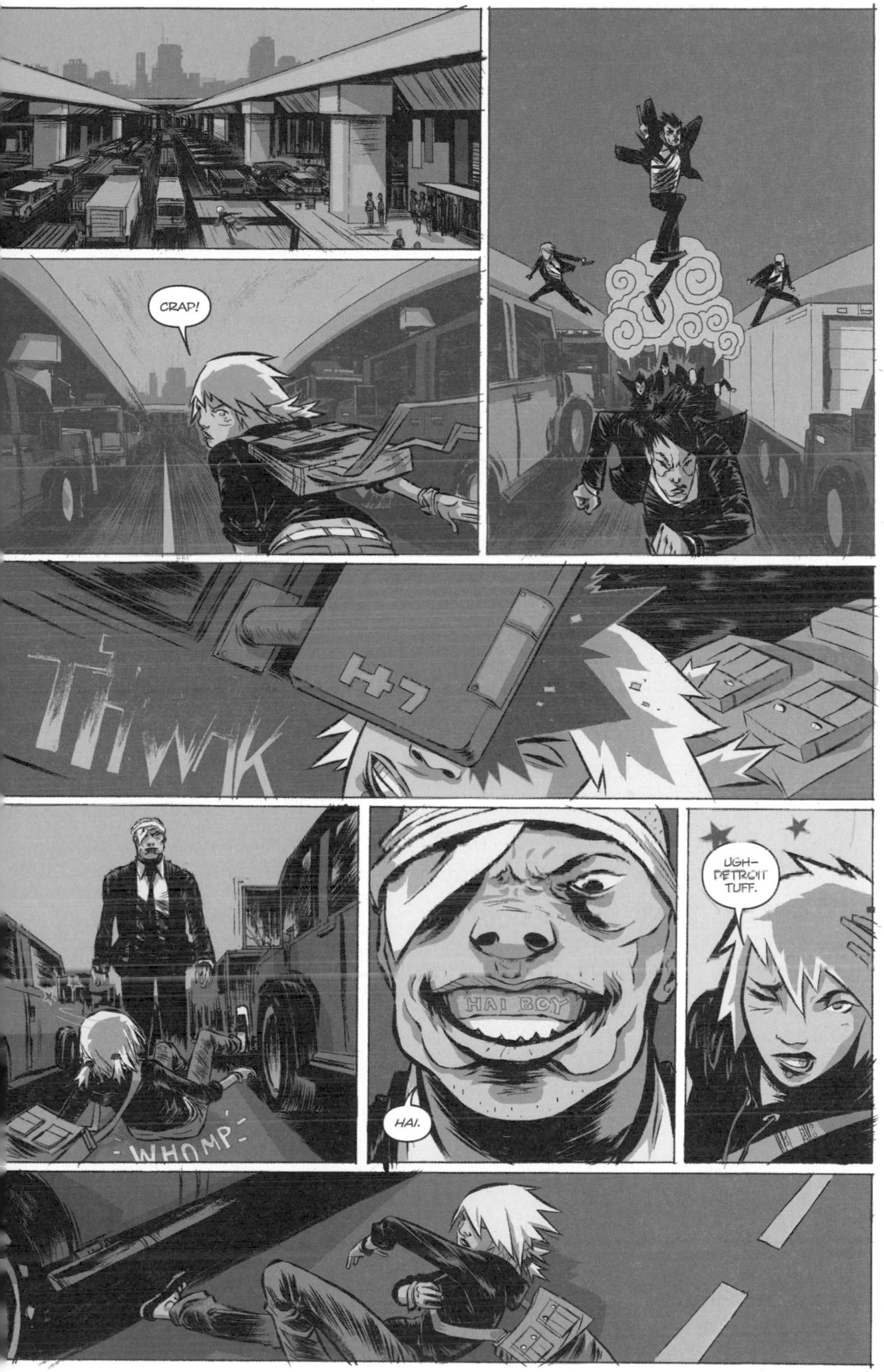
CRAP!
THWK
WHOMP
HAI BOY
HAI.
UGH-
DETROIT
TUFF.

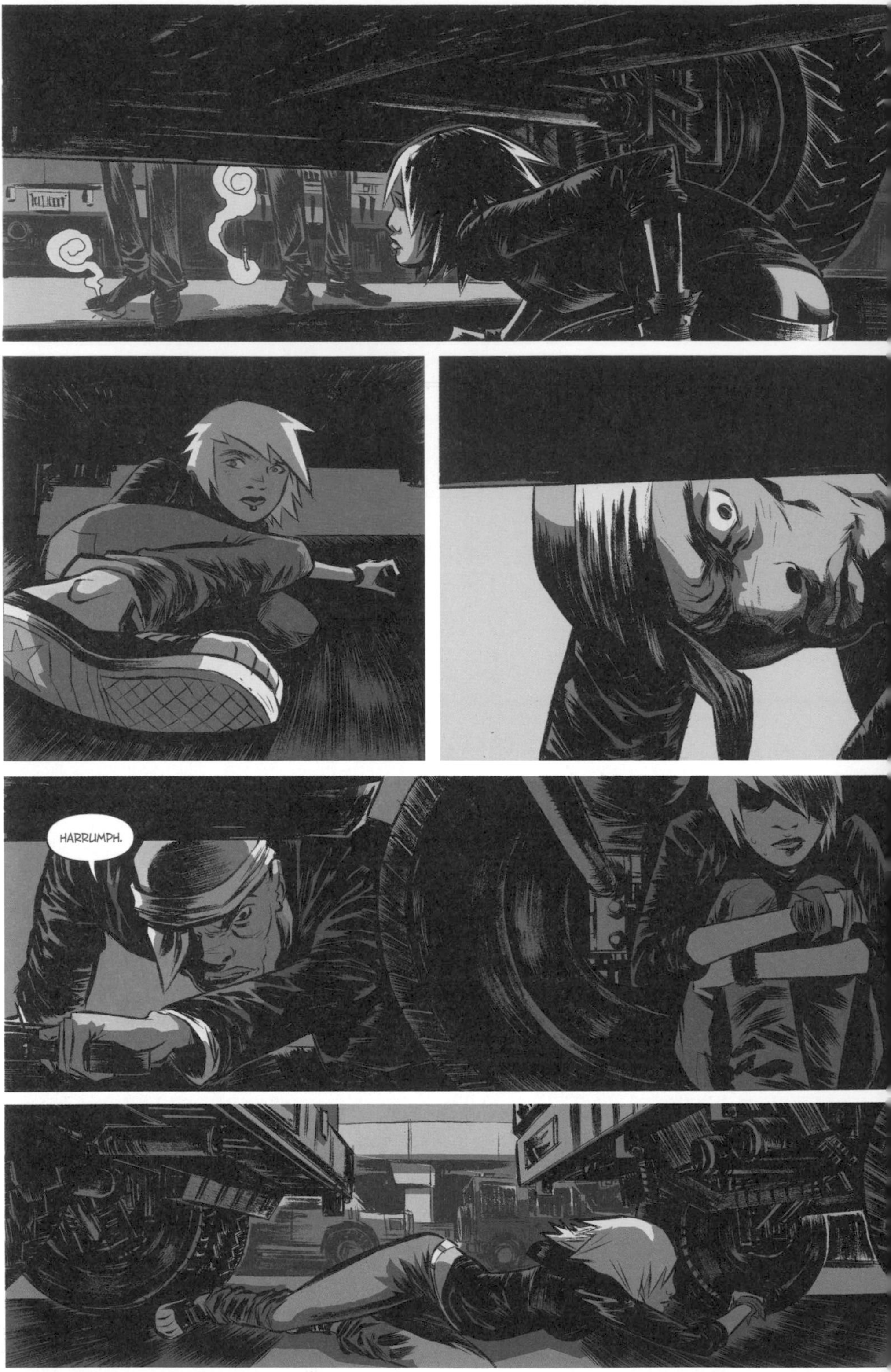
HARRUMPH.

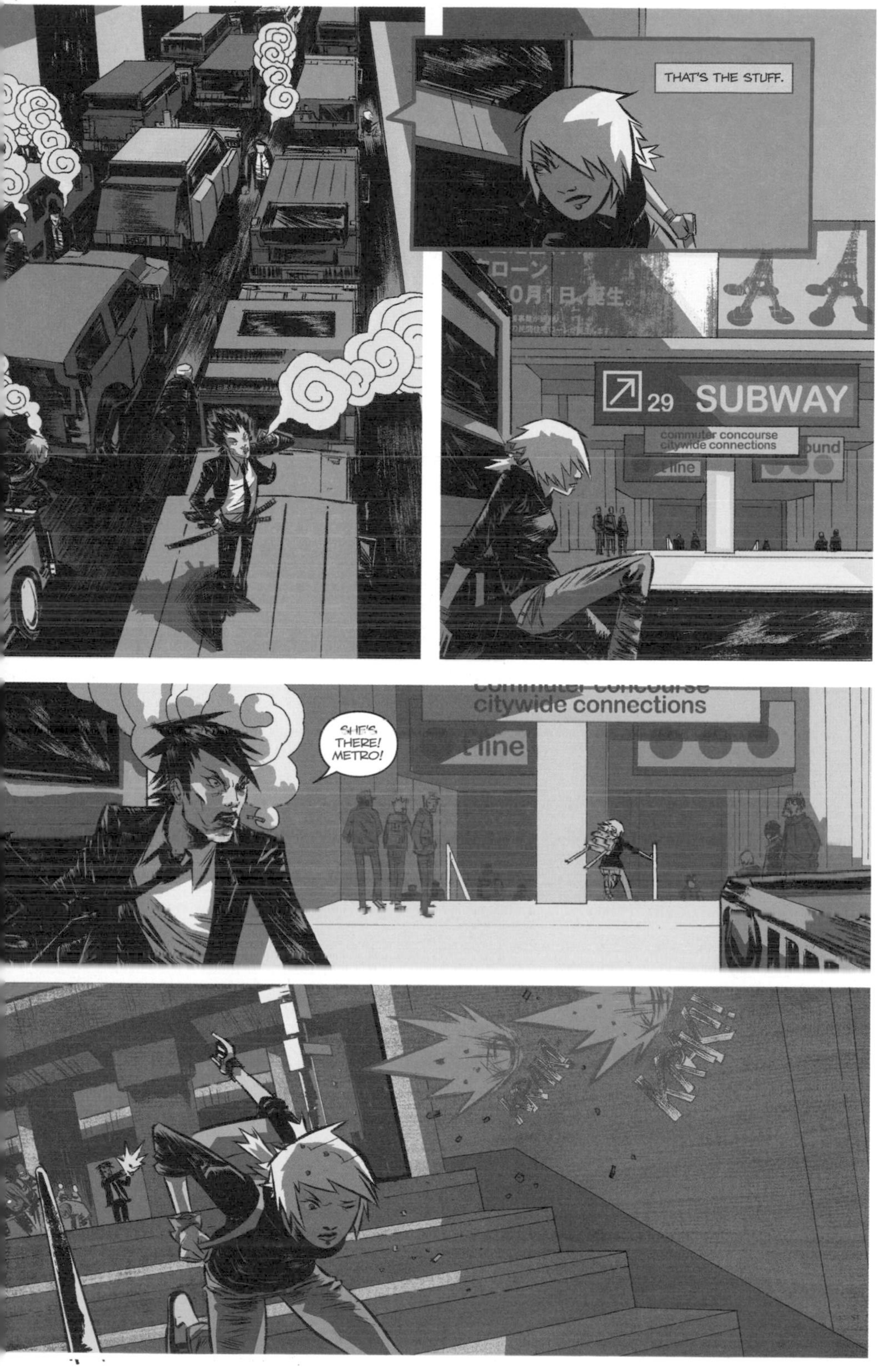
THAT'S THE STUFF.
29 SUBWAY
commuter concourse
citywide connections
SHE'S THERE! METRO!

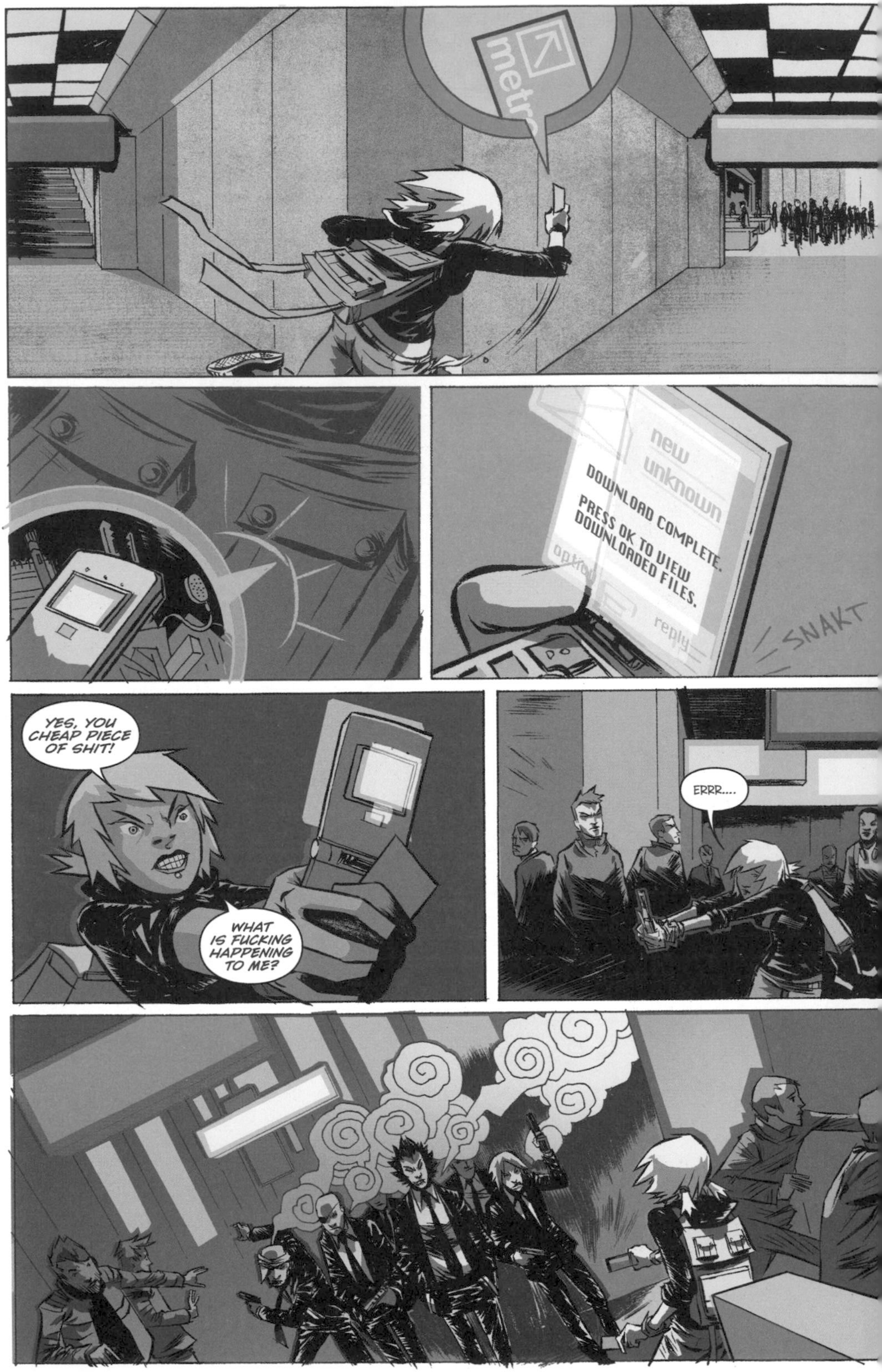
metro
new
unknown
DOWNLOAD COMPLETE.
PRESS OK TO VIEW DOWNLOADED FILES.
option
reply
SNAKT
YES, YOU CHEAP PIECE OF SHIT!
WHAT IS FUCKING HAPPENING TO ME?
ERRR....

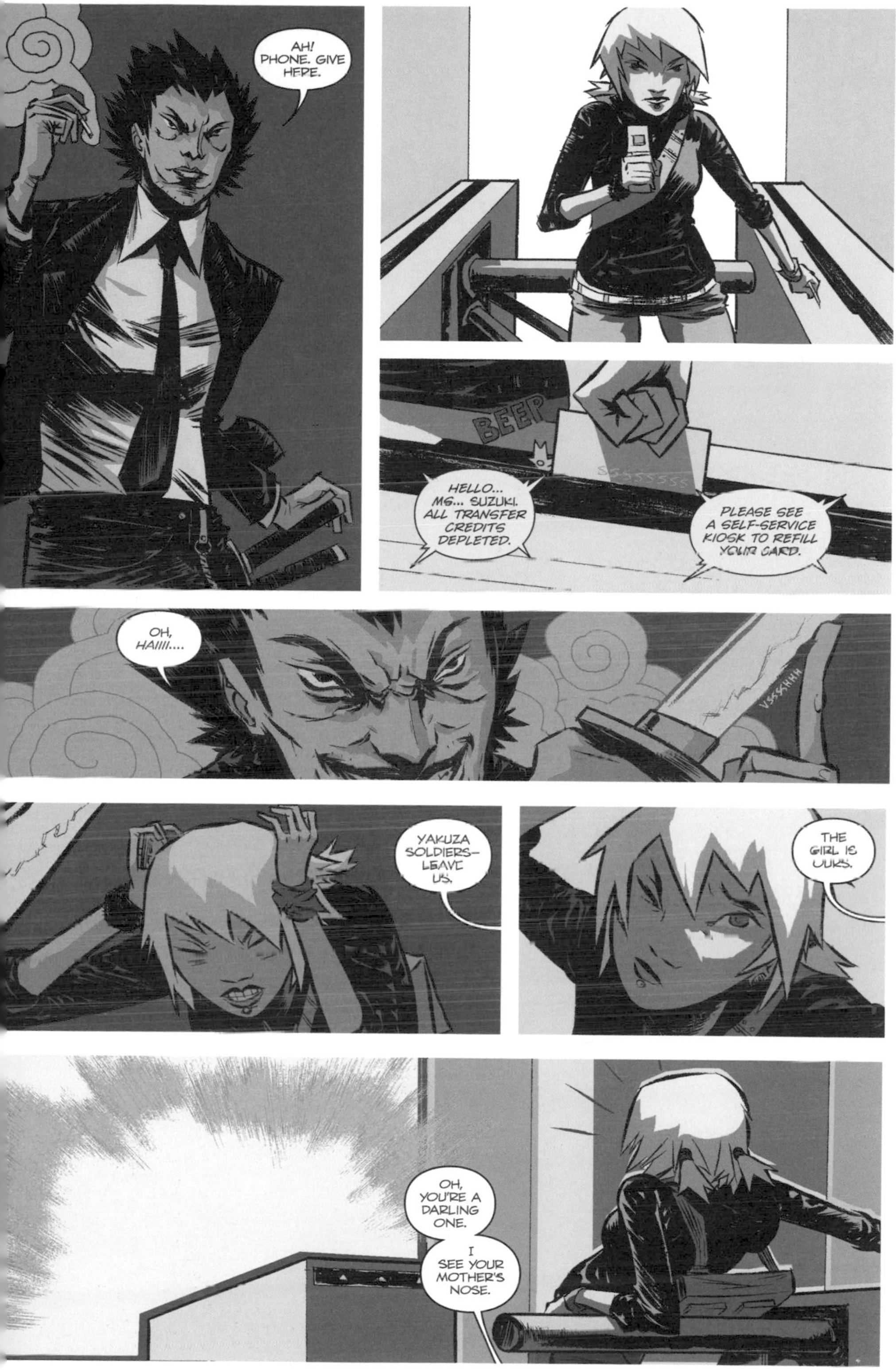
AH! PHONE. GIVE HERE.
BEEP
HELLO... MS... SUZUKI. ALL TRANSFER CREDITS DEPLETED.
PLEASE SEE A SELF-SERVICE KIOSK TO REFILL YOUR CARD.
OH, HAIIII....
YAKUZA SOLDIERS-- LEAVE US.
THE GIRL IS OURS.
OH, YOU'RE A DARLING ONE.
I SEE YOUR MOTHER'S NOSE.

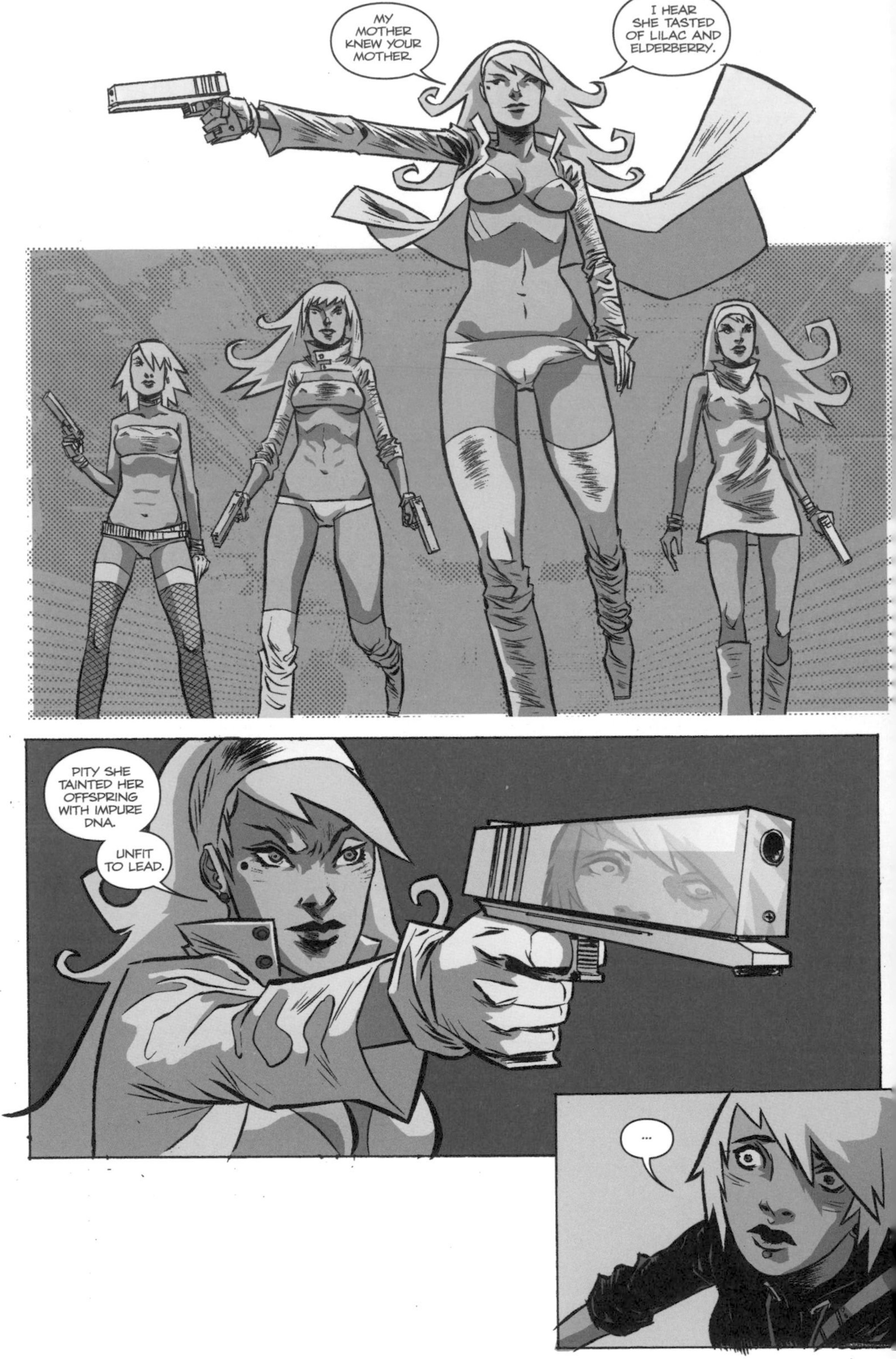
MY MOTHER KNEW YOUR MOTHER.
I HEAR SHE TASTED OF LILAC AND ELDERBERRY.
PITY SHE TAINTED HER OFFSPRING WITH IMPURE DNA.
UNFIT TO LEAD.
...

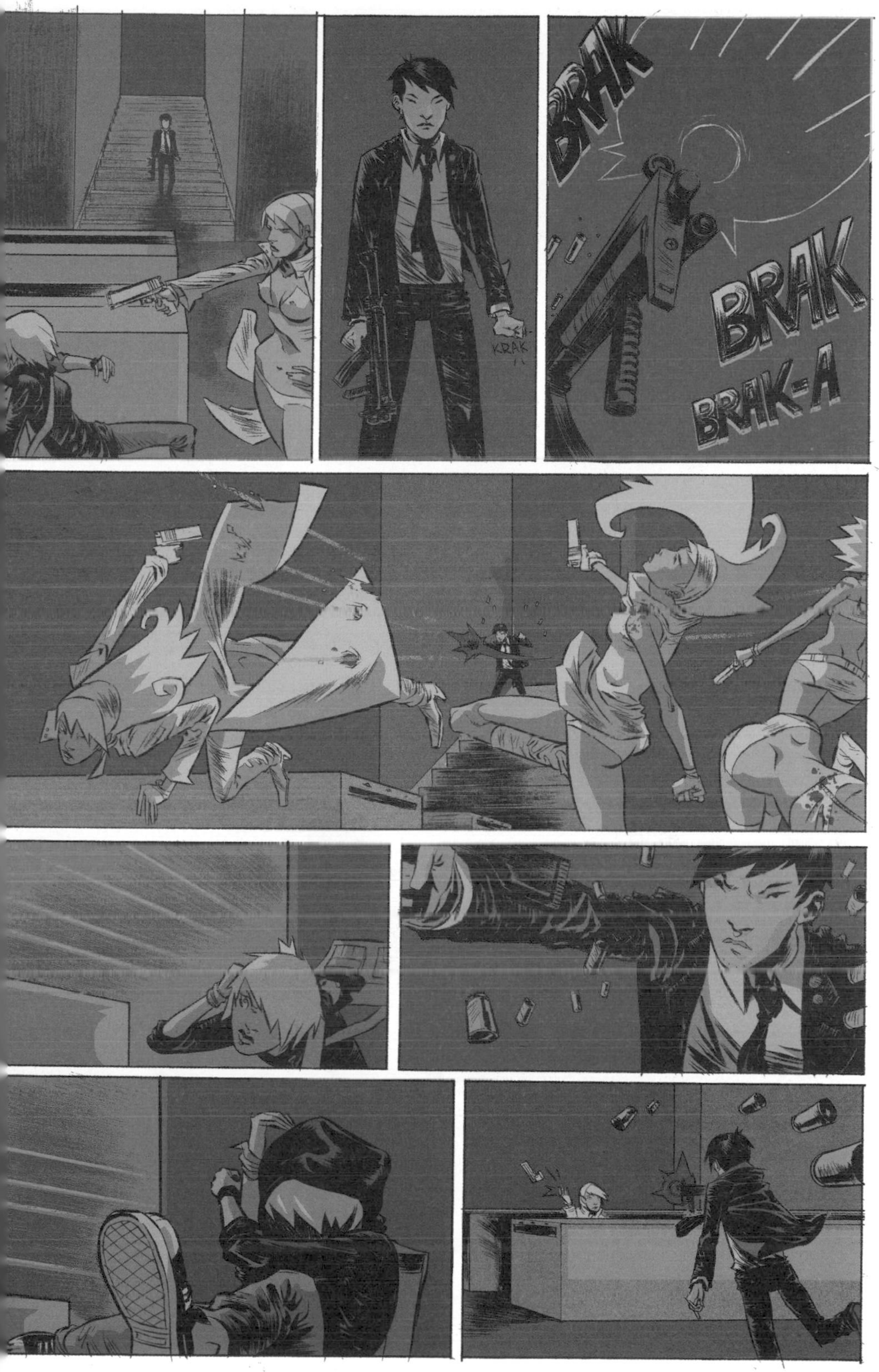
KRAK
BRAK
BRAK
BRAK-A

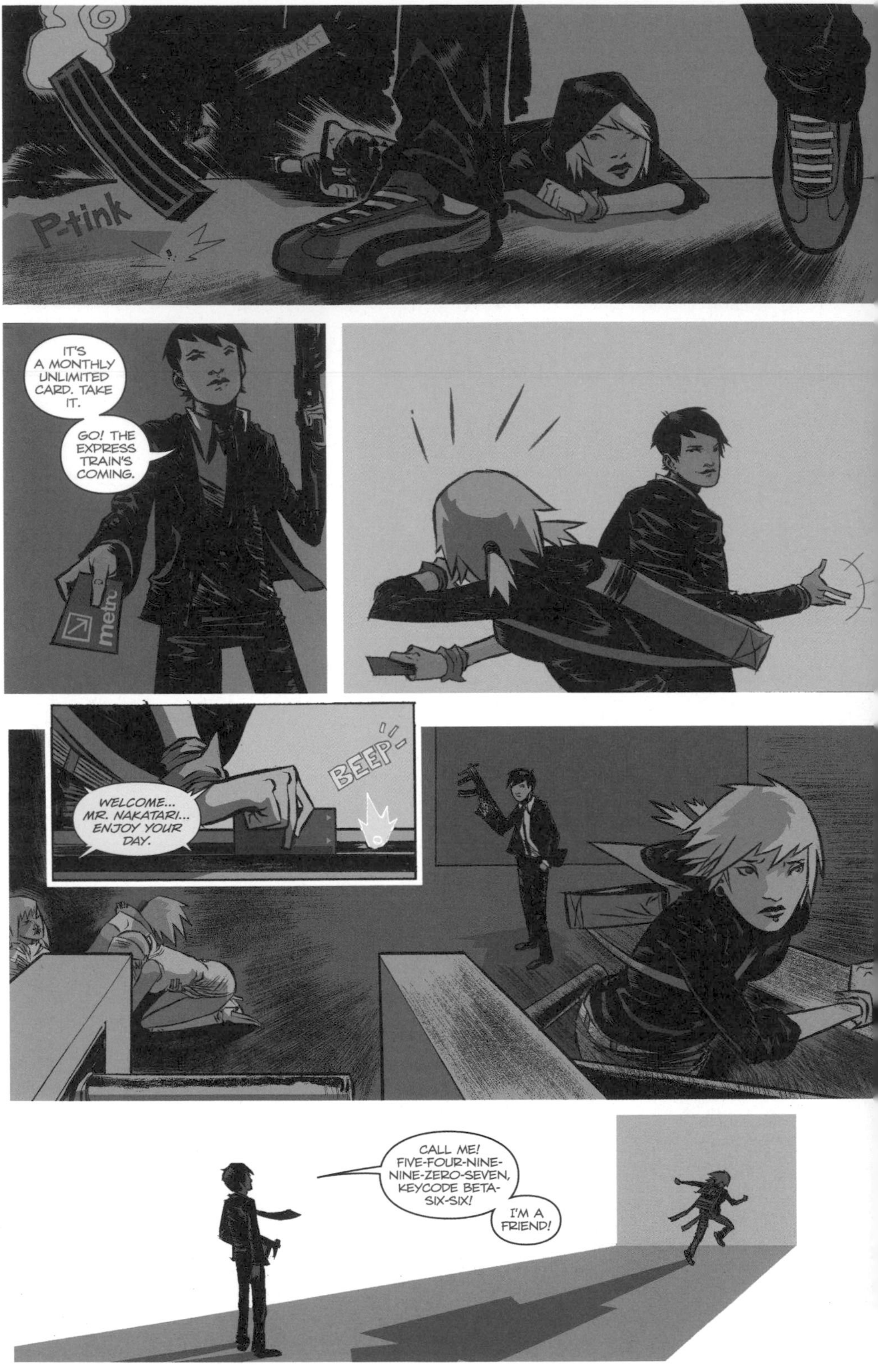
SNAKT
P-tink
IT'S A MONTHLY UNLIMITED CARD. TAKE IT.
GO! THE EXPRESS TRAIN'S COMING.
metro
WELCOME... MR. NAKATARI... ENJOY YOUR DAY.
BEEP
CALL ME! FIVE-FOUR-NINE-NINE-ZERO-SEVEN, KEYCODE BETA-SIX-SIX!
I'M A FRIEND!

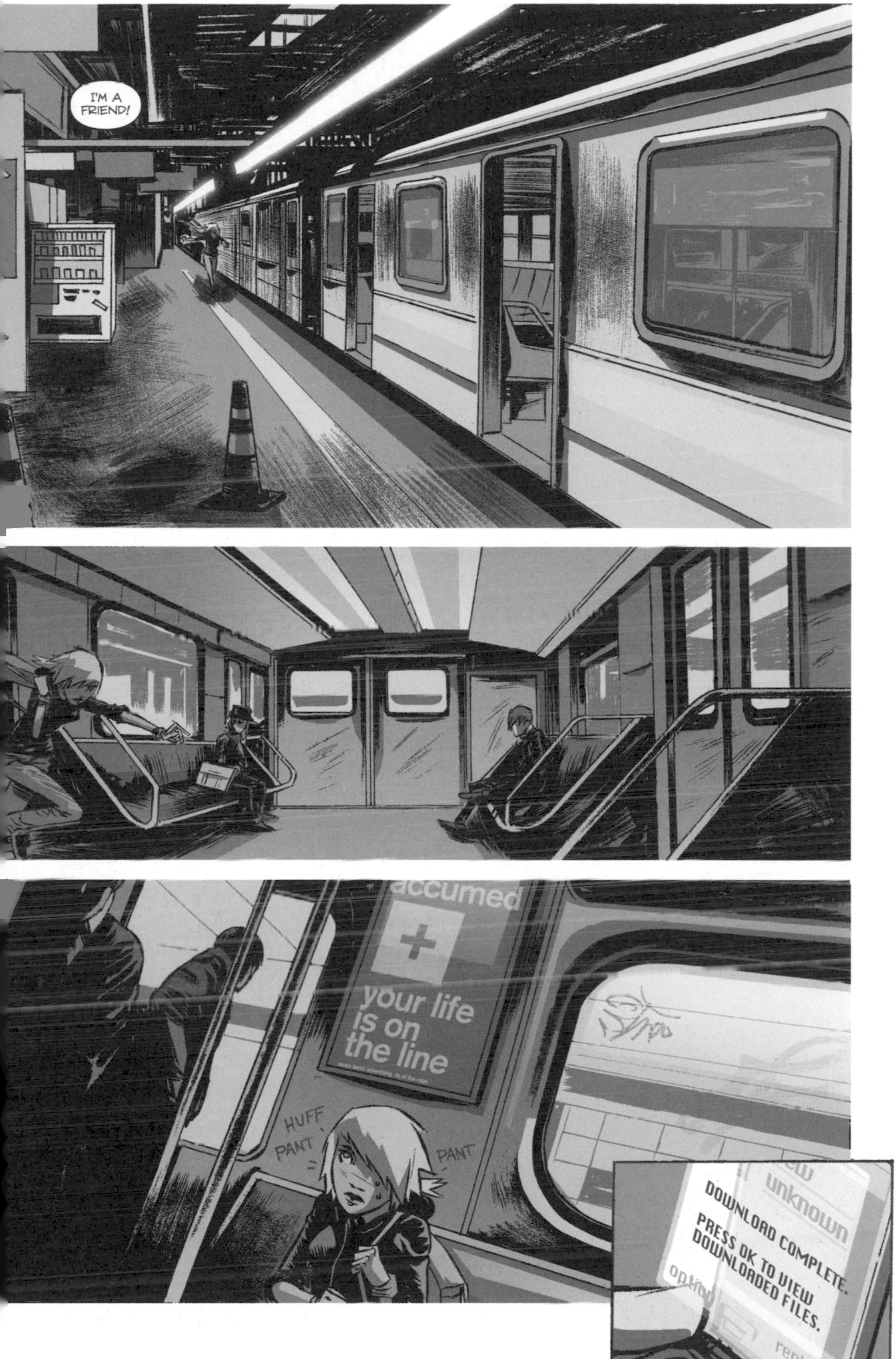
I'M A FRIEND!
accumed
your life is on the line
HUFF
PANT
PANT
unknown
DOWNLOAD COMPLETE.
PRESS OK TO VIEW DOWNLOADED FILES.

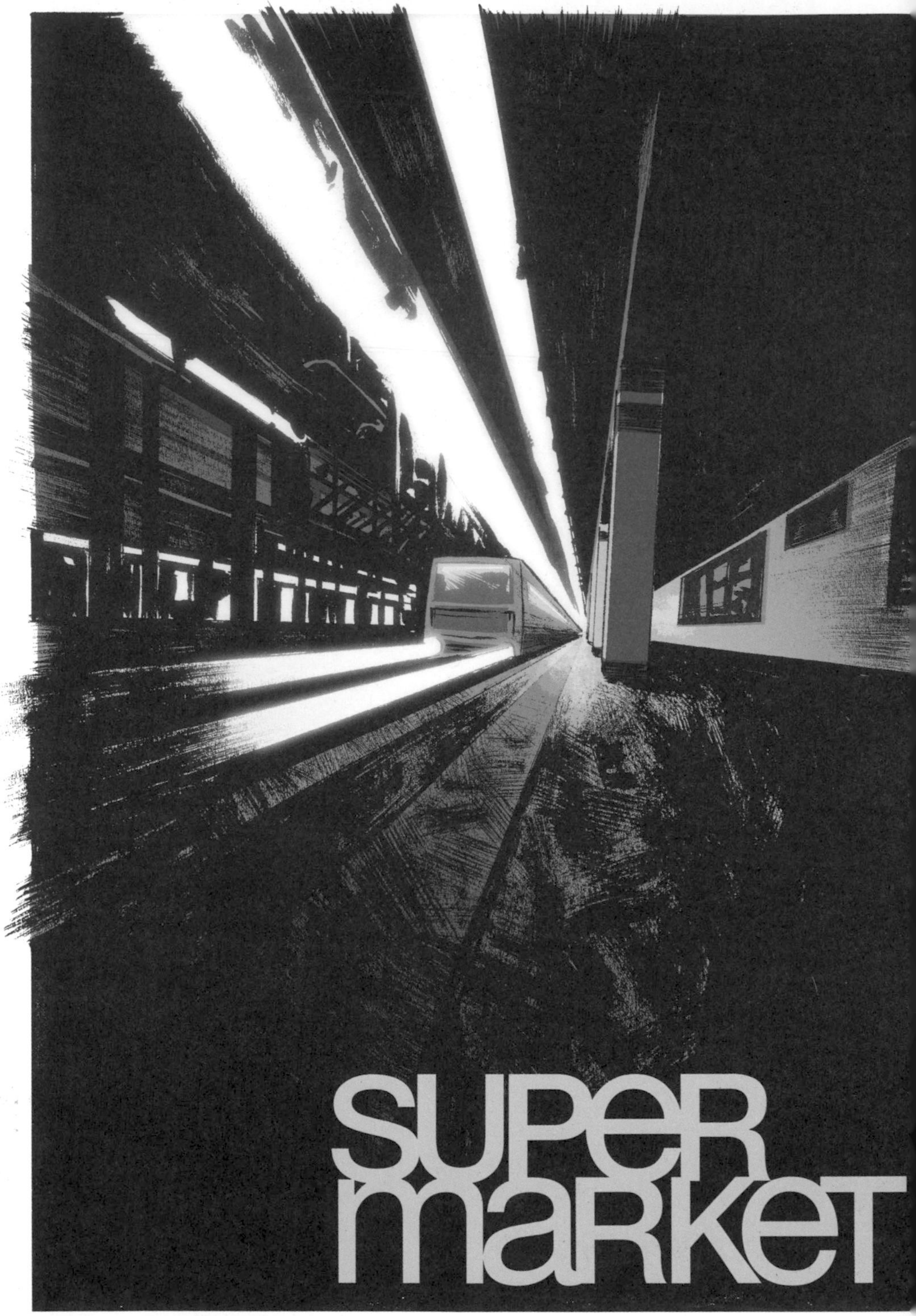
SUPER
market

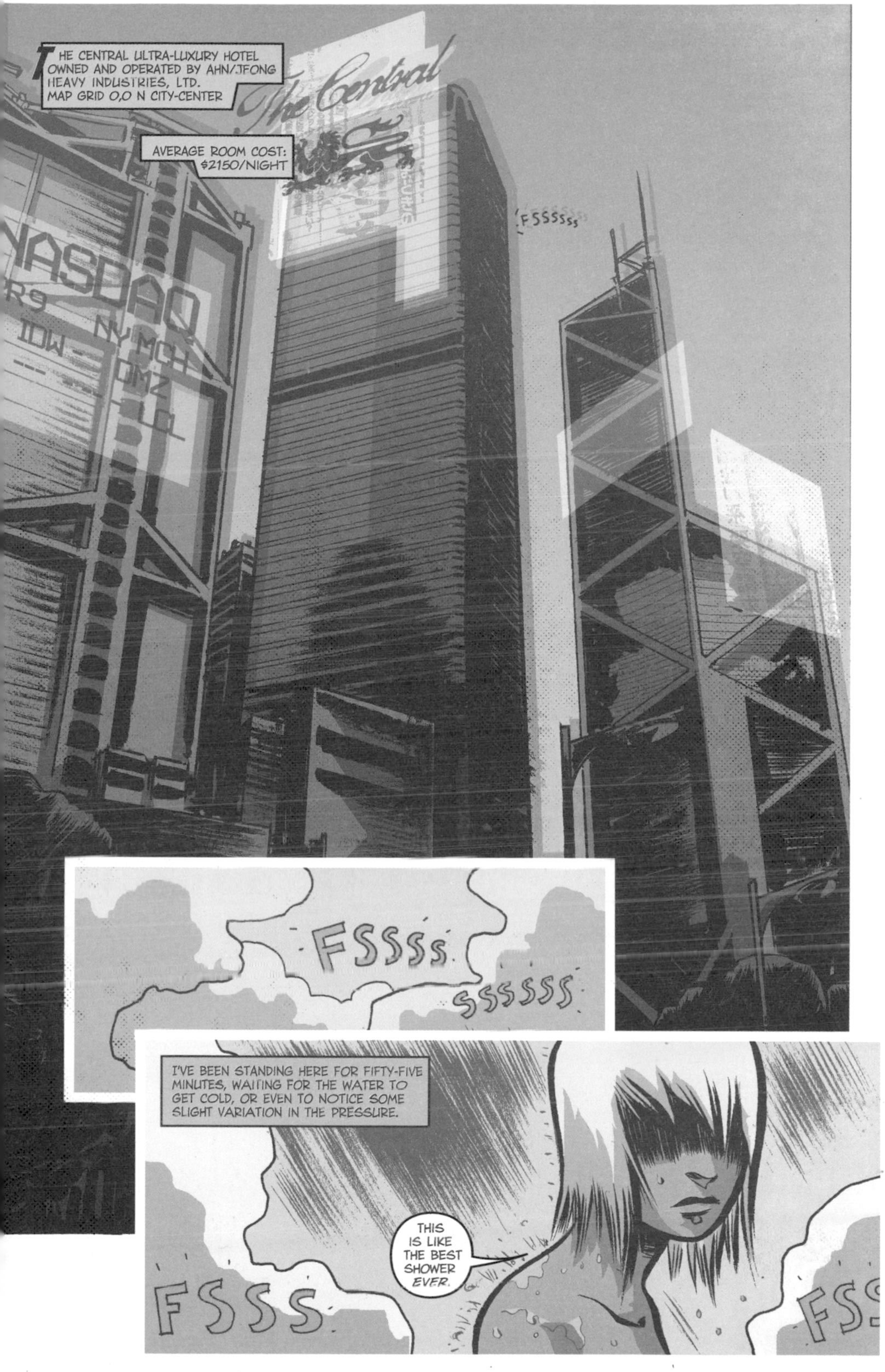
THE CENTRAL ULTRA-LUXURY HOTEL OWNED AND OPERATED BY AHN/JFONG HEAVY INDUSTRIES, LTD. MAP GRID 0,0 N CITY-CENTER
The Central
AVERAGE ROOM COST: $2150/NIGHT
FSSSsss
FSSSs
SSSSSS
I'VE BEEN STANDING HERE FOR FIFTY-FIVE MINUTES, WAITING FOR THE WATER TO GET COLD, OR EVEN TO NOTICE SOME SLIGHT VARIATION IN THE PRESSURE.
THIS IS LIKE THE BEST SHOWER *EVER*.
FSSS

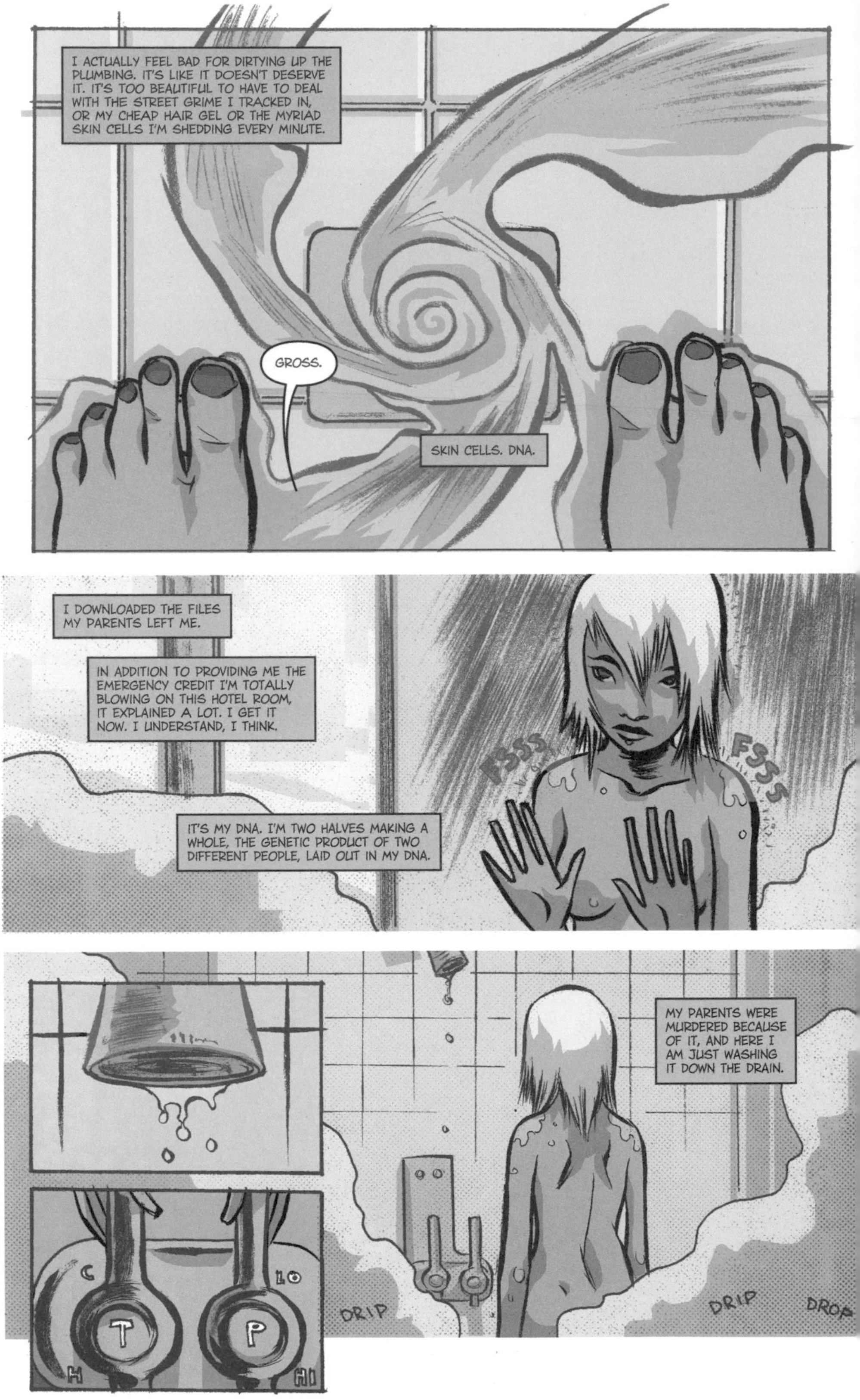

I ACTUALLY FEEL BAD FOR DIRTYING UP THE PLUMBING. IT'S LIKE IT DOESN'T DESERVE IT. IT'S TOO BEAUTIFUL TO HAVE TO DEAL WITH THE STREET GRIME I TRACKED IN, OR MY CHEAP HAIR GEL OR THE MYRIAD SKIN CELLS I'M SHEDDING EVERY MINUTE.
GROSS.
SKIN CELLS. DNA.
I DOWNLOADED THE FILES MY PARENTS LEFT ME.
IN ADDITION TO PROVIDING ME THE EMERGENCY CREDIT I'M TOTALLY BLOWING ON THIS HOTEL ROOM, IT EXPLAINED A LOT. I GET IT NOW. I UNDERSTAND, I THINK.
FSSS
FSSS
IT'S MY DNA. I'M TWO HALVES MAKING A WHOLE, THE GENETIC PRODUCT OF TWO DIFFERENT PEOPLE, LAID OUT IN MY DNA.
MY PARENTS WERE MURDERED BECAUSE OF IT, AND HERE I AM JUST WASHING IT DOWN THE DRAIN.
C
LO
T
P
H
HI
DRIP
DRIP
DROP

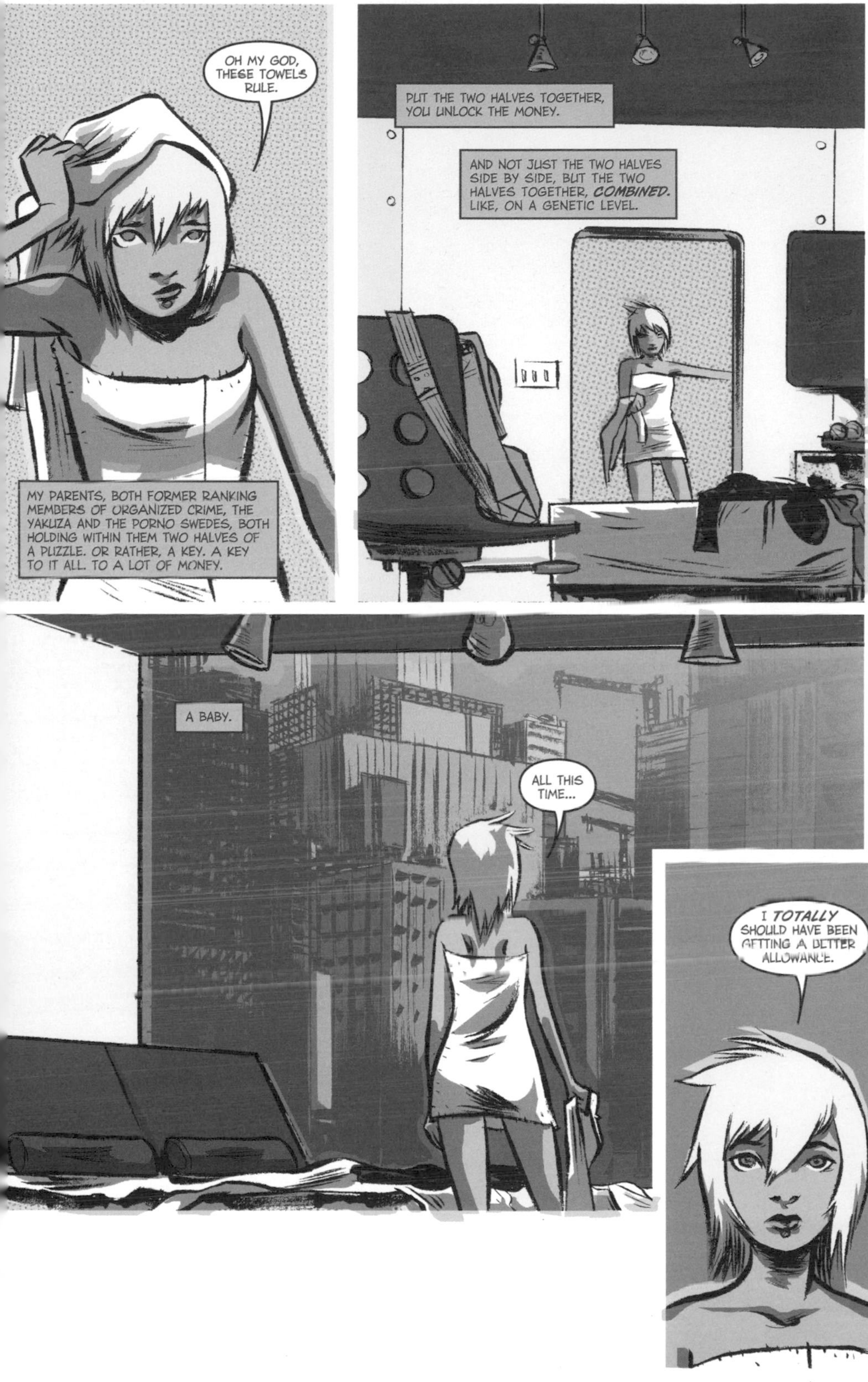
OH MY GOD, THESE TOWELS RULE.
MY PARENTS, BOTH FORMER RANKING MEMBERS OF ORGANIZED CRIME, THE YAKUZA AND THE PORNO SWEDES, BOTH HOLDING WITHIN THEM TWO HALVES OF A PUZZLE. OR RATHER, A KEY. A KEY TO IT ALL. TO A LOT OF MONEY.
PUT THE TWO HALVES TOGETHER, YOU UNLOCK THE MONEY.
AND NOT JUST THE TWO HALVES SIDE BY SIDE, BUT THE TWO HALVES TOGETHER, COMBINED. LIKE, ON A GENETIC LEVEL.
A BABY.
ALL THIS TIME...
I TOTALLY SHOULD HAVE BEEN GETTING A BETTER ALLOWANCE.

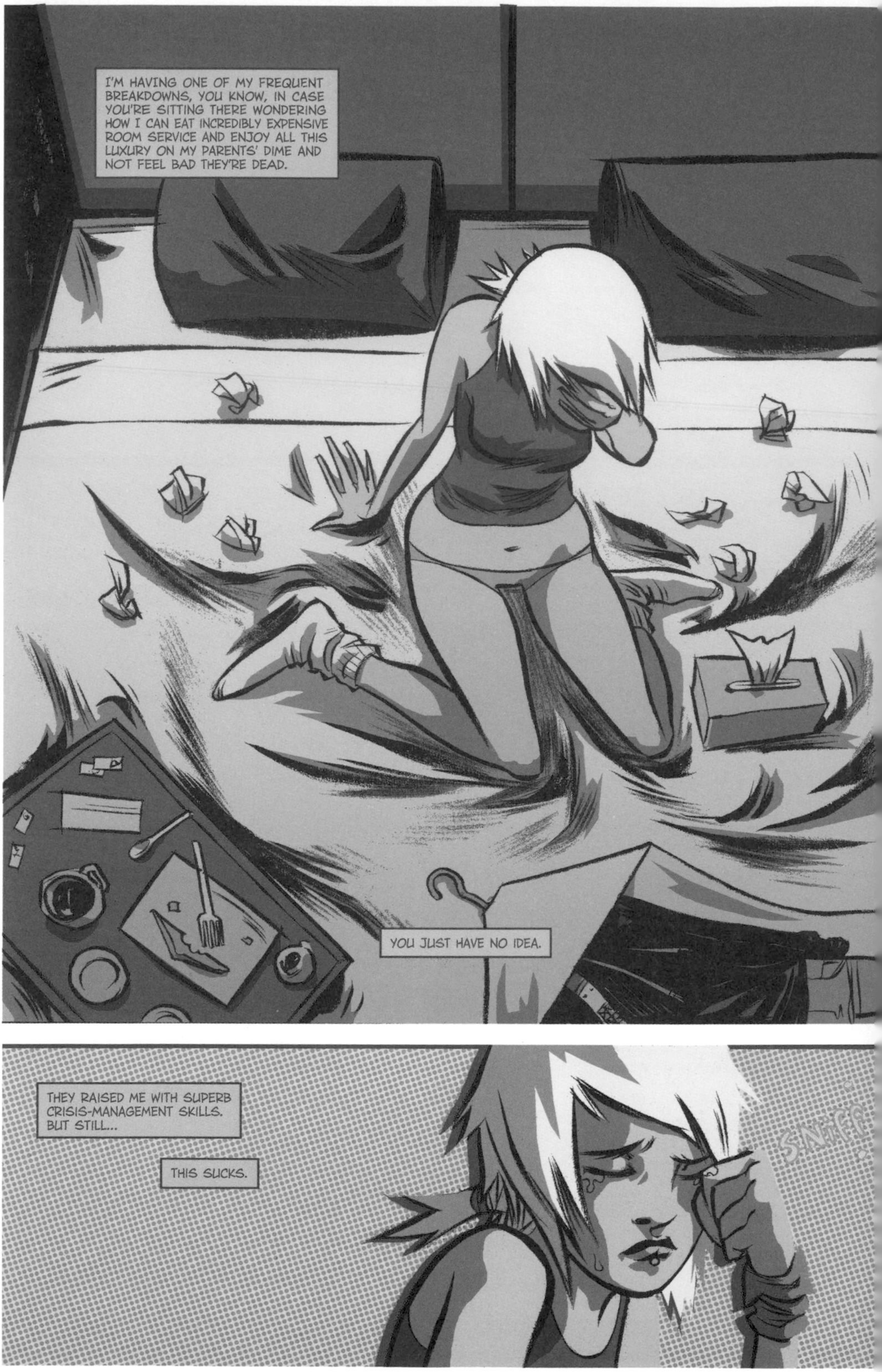
I'M HAVING ONE OF MY FREQUENT BREAKDOWNS, YOU KNOW, IN CASE YOU'RE SITTING THERE WONDERING HOW I CAN EAT INCREDIBLY EXPENSIVE ROOM SERVICE AND ENJOY ALL THIS LUXURY ON MY PARENTS' DIME AND NOT FEEL BAD THEY'RE DEAD.
YOU JUST HAVE NO IDEA.
THEY RAISED ME WITH SUPERB CRISIS-MANAGEMENT SKILLS. BUT STILL...
THIS SUCKS.
SNIFF

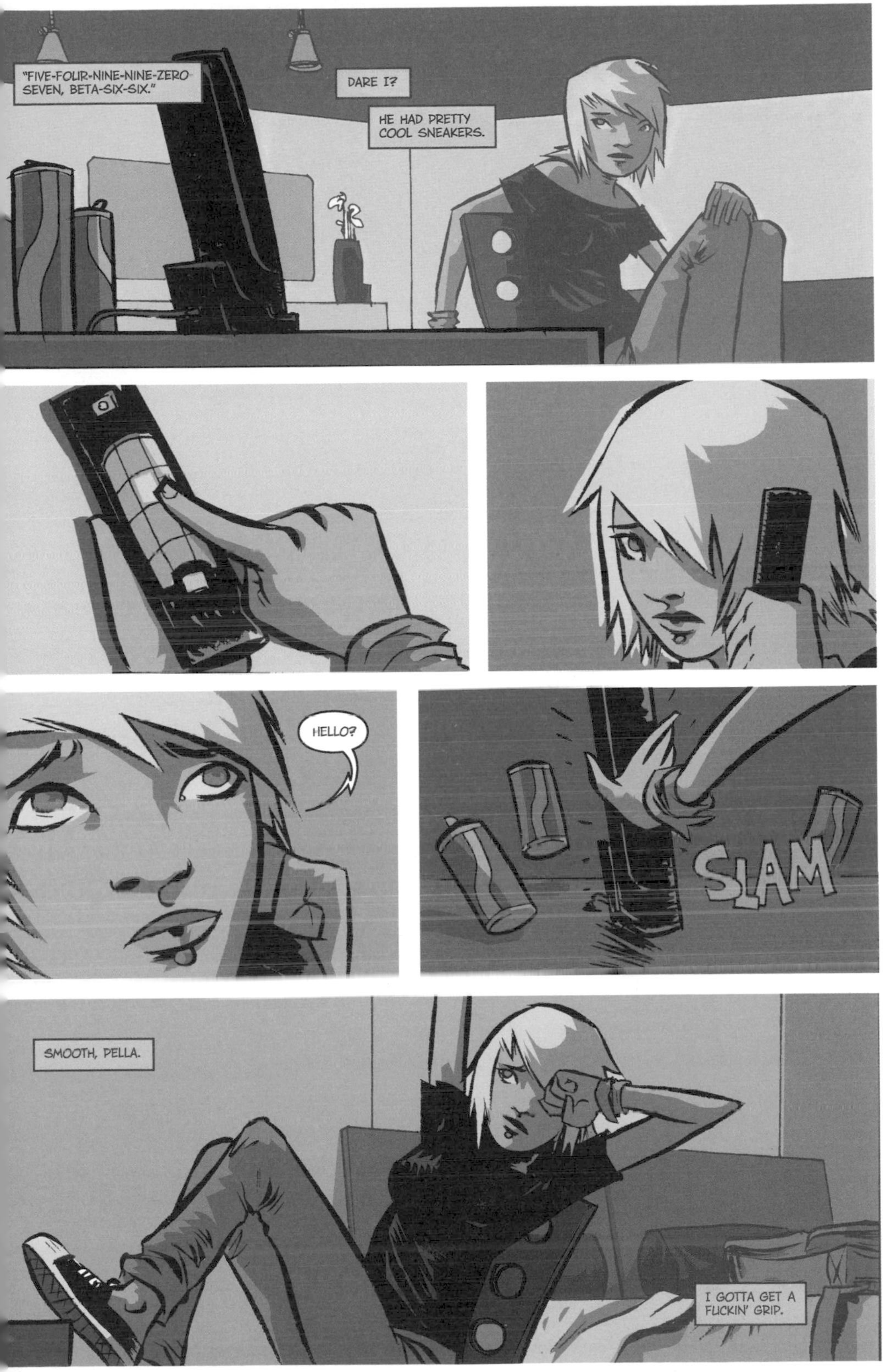
"FIVE-FOUR-NINE-NINE-ZERO SEVEN, BETA-SIX-SIX."
DARE I?
HE HAD PRETTY COOL SNEAKERS.
HELLO?
SLAM
SMOOTH, PELLA.
I GOTTA GET A FUCKIN' GRIP.

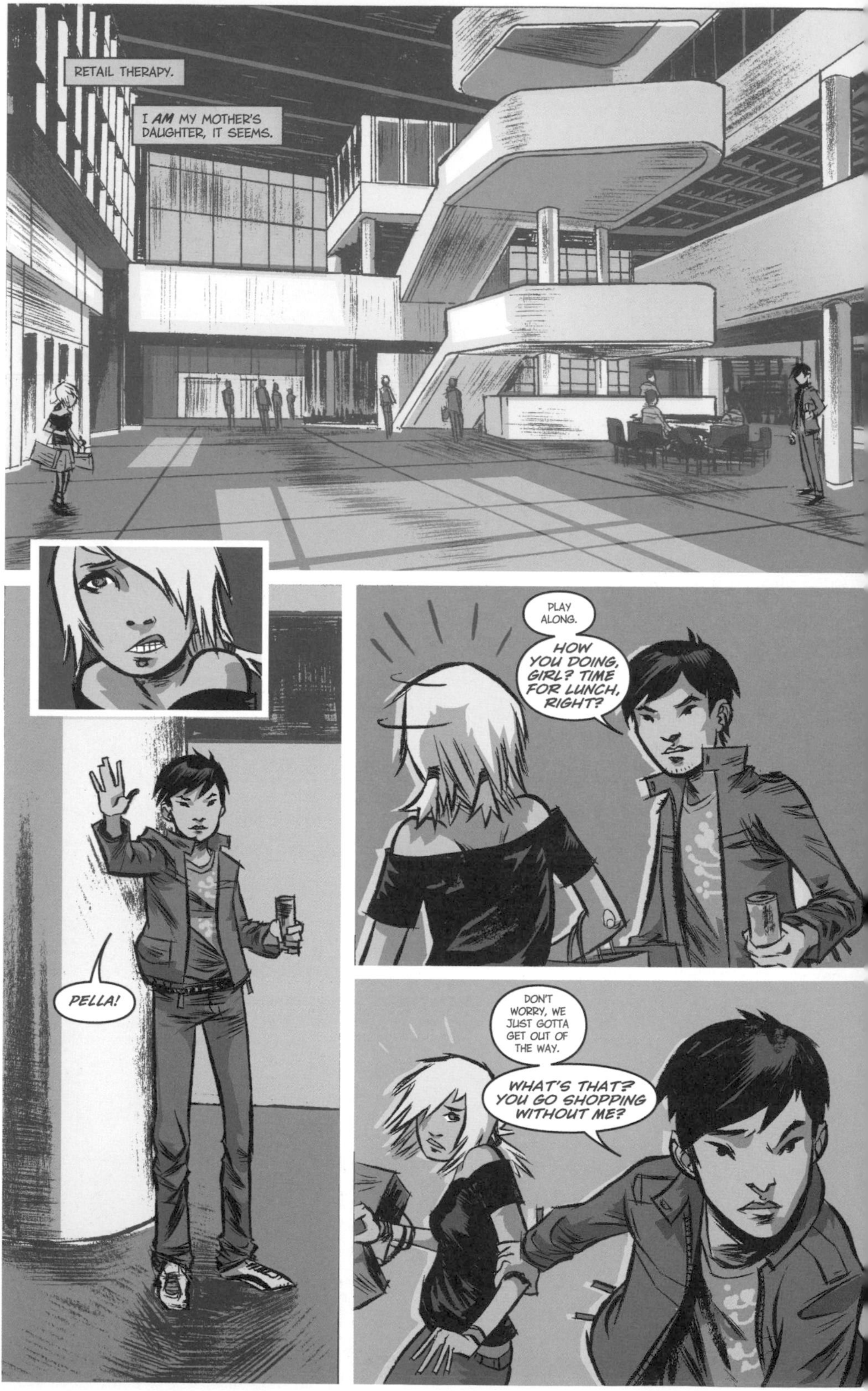
RETAIL THERAPY.
I AM MY MOTHER'S DAUGHTER, IT SEEMS.
PELLA!
PLAY ALONG.
HOW YOU DOING, GIRL? TIME FOR LUNCH, RIGHT?
DON'T WORRY, WE JUST GOTTA GET OUT OF THE WAY.
WHAT'S THAT? YOU GO SHOPPING WITHOUT ME?

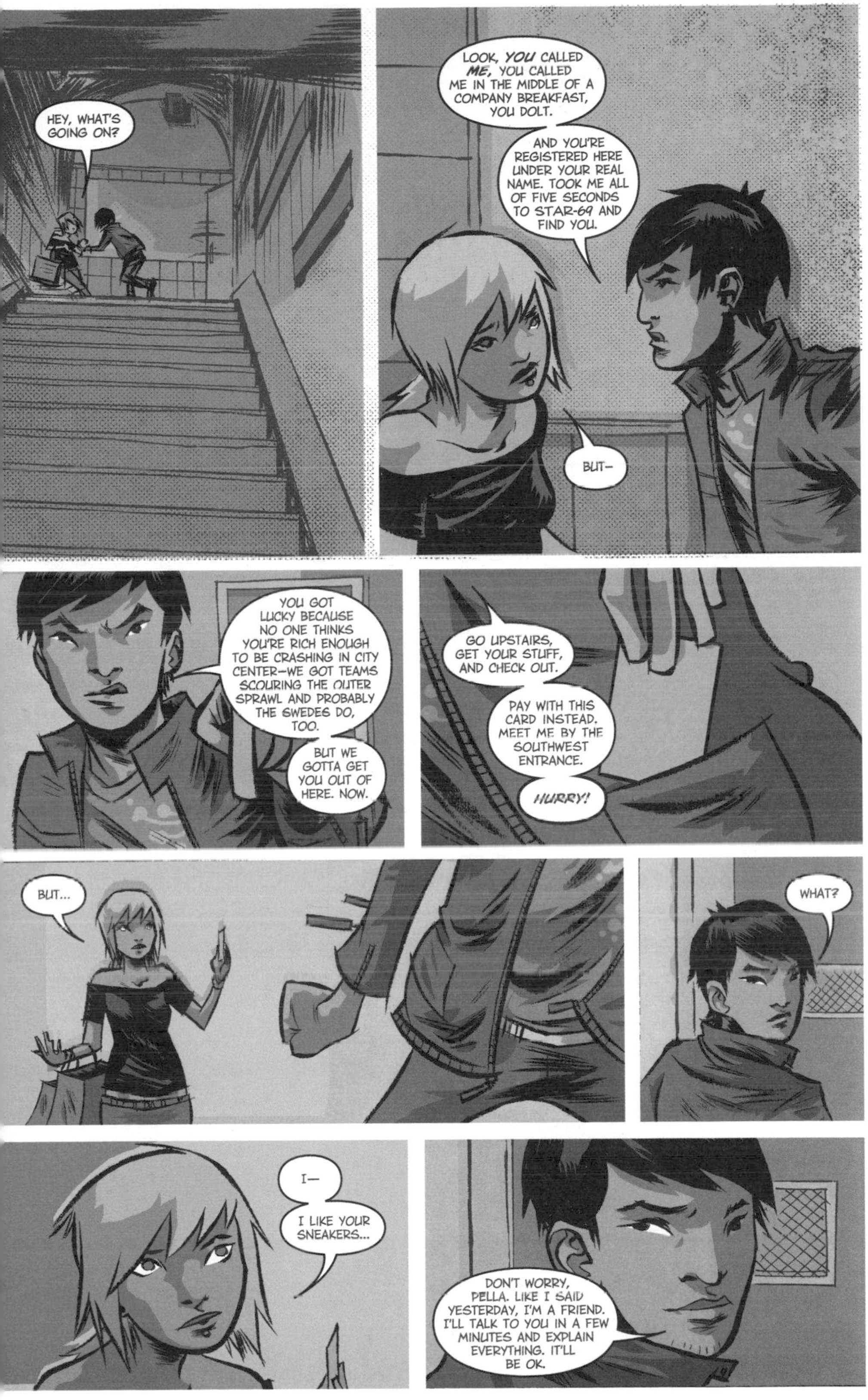
HEY, WHAT'S GOING ON?
LOOK, YOU CALLED ME, YOU CALLED ME IN THE MIDDLE OF A COMPANY BREAKFAST, YOU DOLT.
AND YOU'RE REGISTERED HERE UNDER YOUR REAL NAME. TOOK ME ALL OF FIVE SECONDS TO STAR-69 AND FIND YOU.
BUT–
YOU GOT LUCKY BECAUSE NO ONE THINKS YOU'RE RICH ENOUGH TO BE CRASHING IN CITY CENTER–WE GOT TEAMS SCOURING THE OUTER SPRAWL AND PROBABLY THE SWEDES DO, TOO.
BUT WE GOTTA GET YOU OUT OF HERE. NOW.
GO UPSTAIRS, GET YOUR STUFF, AND CHECK OUT.
PAY WITH THIS CARD INSTEAD. MEET ME BY THE SOUTHWEST ENTRANCE.
HURRY!
BUT...
WHAT?
I–
I LIKE YOUR SNEAKERS...
DON'T WORRY, PELLA. LIKE I SAID YESTERDAY, I'M A FRIEND. I'LL TALK TO YOU IN A FEW MINUTES AND EXPLAIN EVERYTHING. IT'LL BE OK.

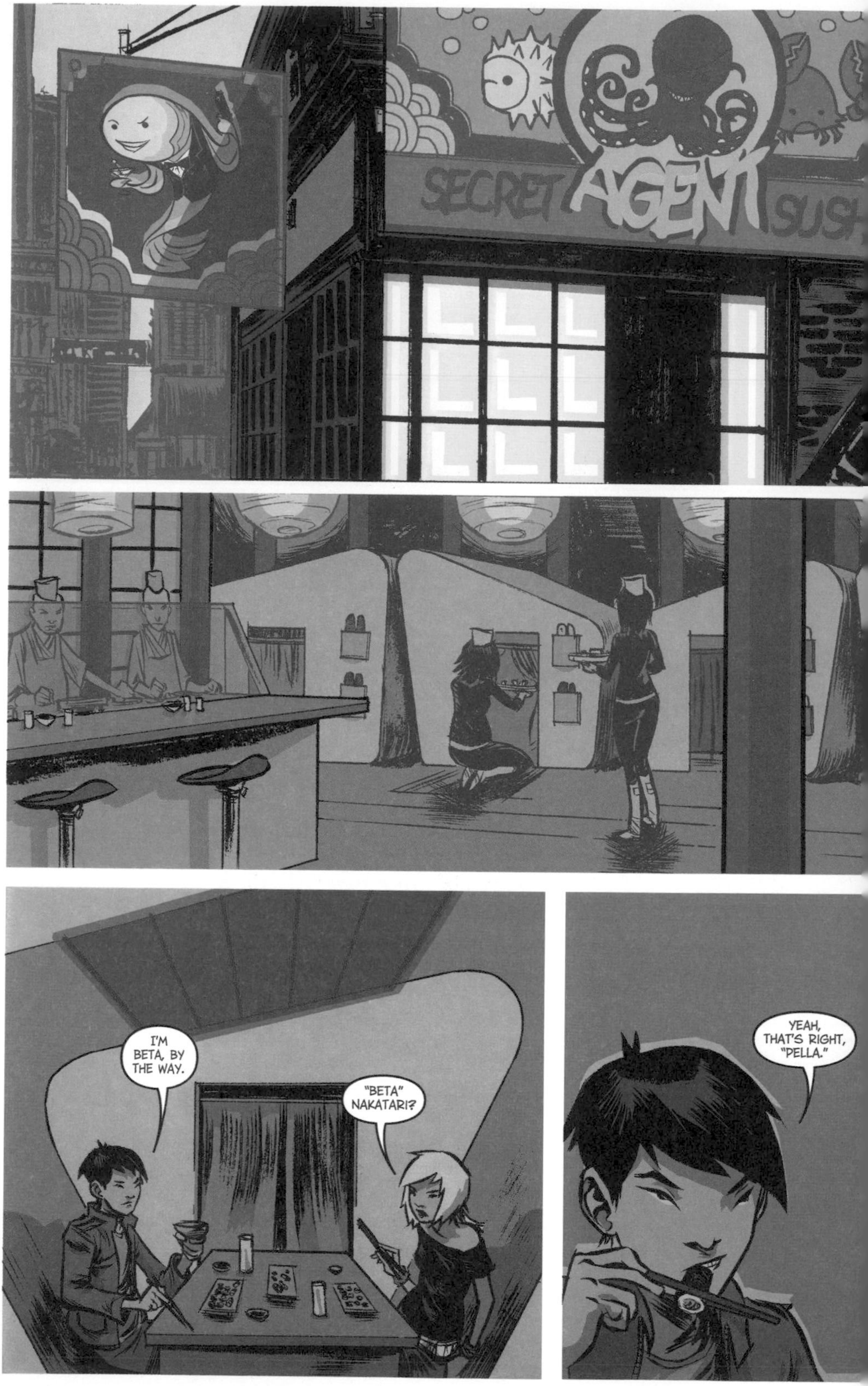
SECRET AGENT
I'M BETA, BY THE WAY.
"BETA" NAKATARI?
YEAH, THAT'S RIGHT, "PELLA."

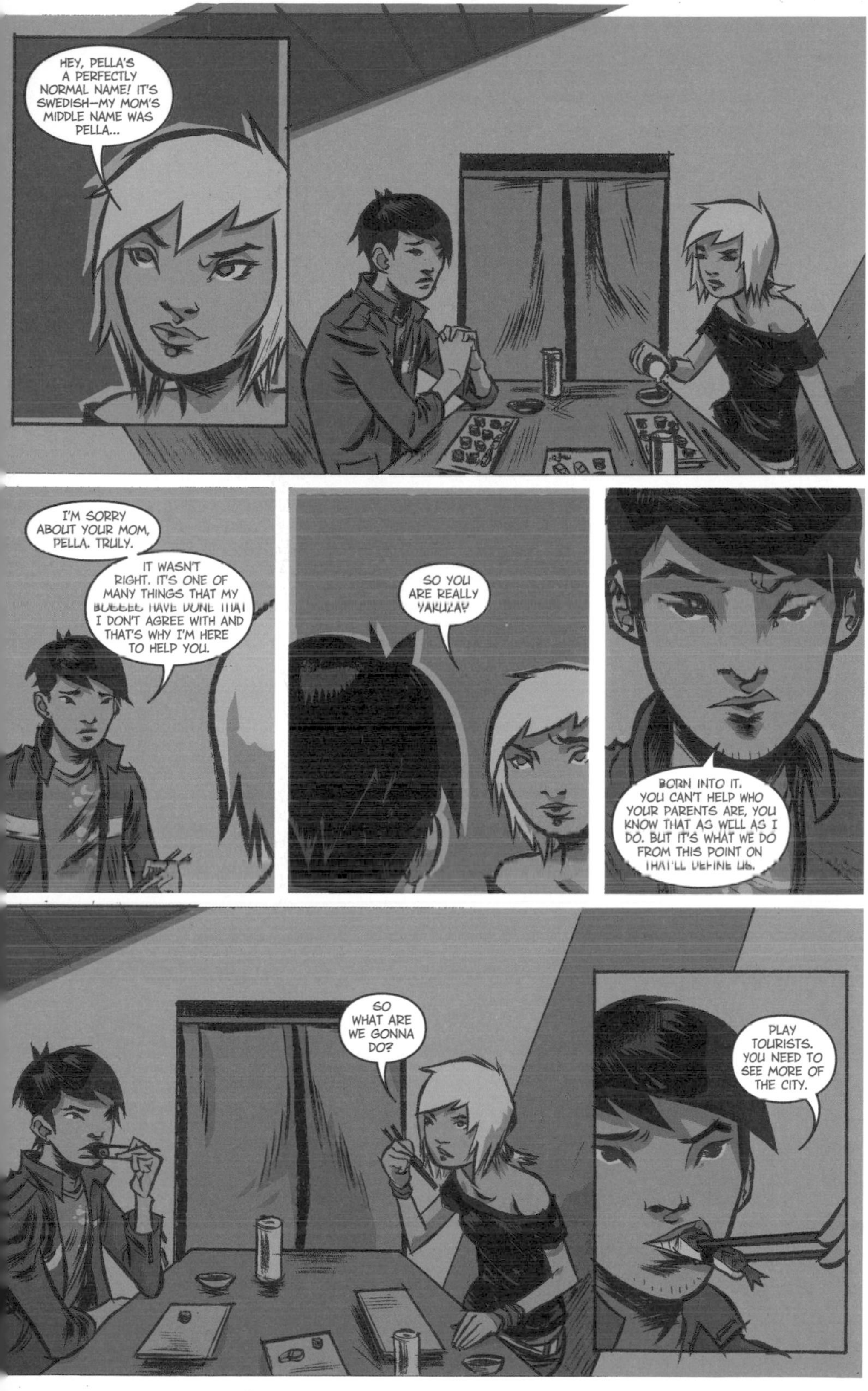
HEY, PELLA'S A PERFECTLY NORMAL NAME! IT'S SWEDISH—MY MOM'S MIDDLE NAME WAS PELLA...
I'M SORRY ABOUT YOUR MOM, PELLA. TRULY.
IT WASN'T RIGHT. IT'S ONE OF MANY THINGS THAT MY BOSSES HAVE DONE THAT I DON'T AGREE WITH AND THAT'S WHY I'M HERE TO HELP YOU.
SO YOU ARE REALLY YAKUZA?
BORN INTO IT. YOU CAN'T HELP WHO YOUR PARENTS ARE, YOU KNOW THAT AS WELL AS I DO. BUT IT'S WHAT WE DO FROM THIS POINT ON THAT'LL DEFINE US.
SO WHAT ARE WE GONNA DO?
PLAY TOURISTS. YOU NEED TO SEE MORE OF THE CITY.

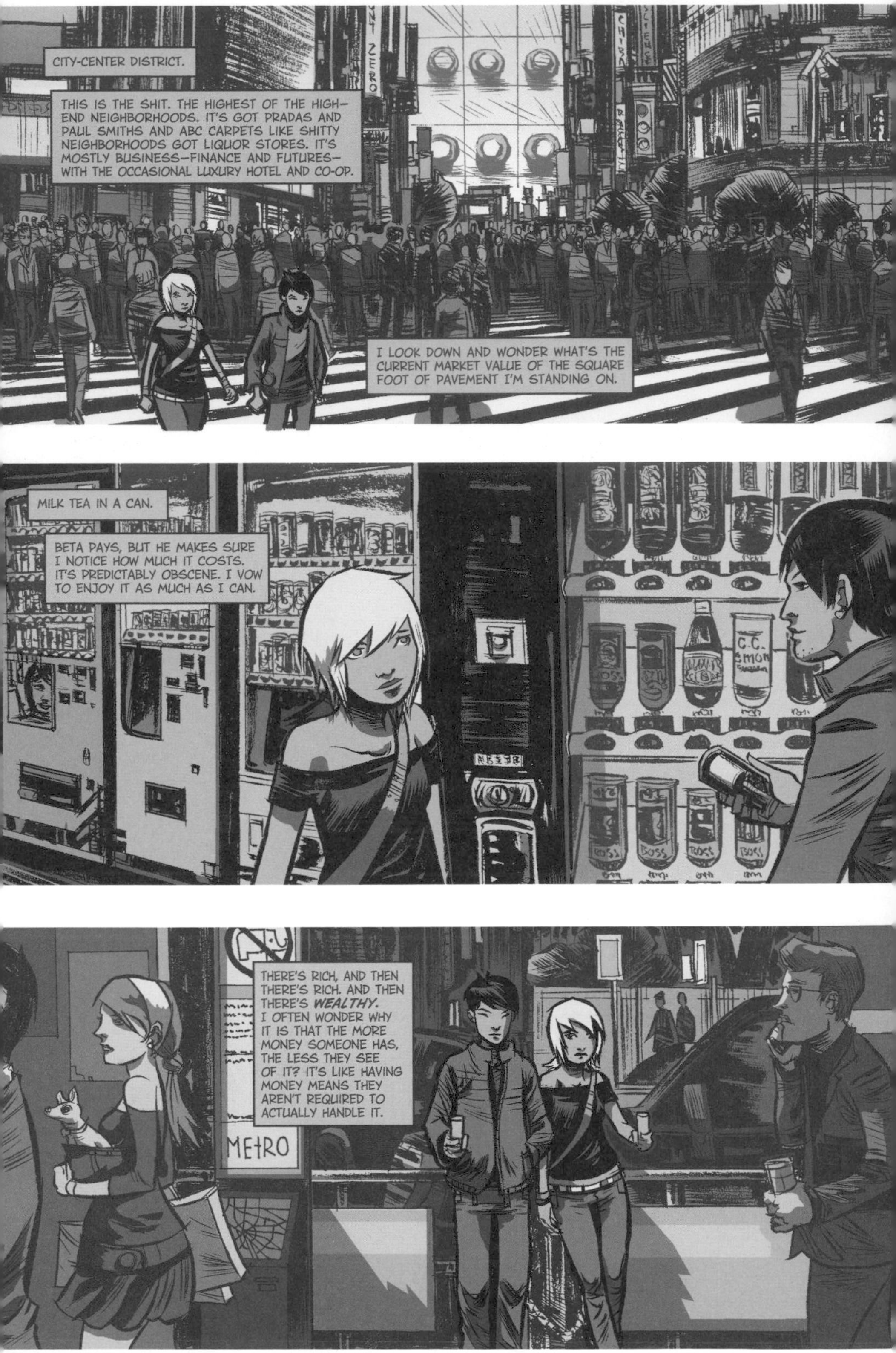
CITY-CENTER DISTRICT.
THIS IS THE SHIT. THE HIGHEST OF THE HIGH-END NEIGHBORHOODS. IT'S GOT PRADAS AND PAUL SMITHS AND ABC CARPETS LIKE SHITTY NEIGHBORHOODS GOT LIQUOR STORES. IT'S MOSTLY BUSINESS—FINANCE AND FUTURES—WITH THE OCCASIONAL LUXURY HOTEL AND CO-OP.
I LOOK DOWN AND WONDER WHAT'S THE CURRENT MARKET VALUE OF THE SQUARE FOOT OF PAVEMENT I'M STANDING ON.
MILK TEA IN A CAN.
BETA PAYS, BUT HE MAKES SURE I NOTICE HOW MUCH IT COSTS. IT'S PREDICTABLY OBSCENE. I VOW TO ENJOY IT AS MUCH AS I CAN.
THERE'S RICH, AND THEN THERE'S RICH. AND THEN THERE'S ***WEALTHY.*** I OFTEN WONDER WHY IT IS THAT THE MORE MONEY SOMEONE HAS, THE LESS THEY SEE OF IT? IT'S LIKE HAVING MONEY MEANS THEY AREN'T REQUIRED TO ACTUALLY HANDLE IT.
METRO

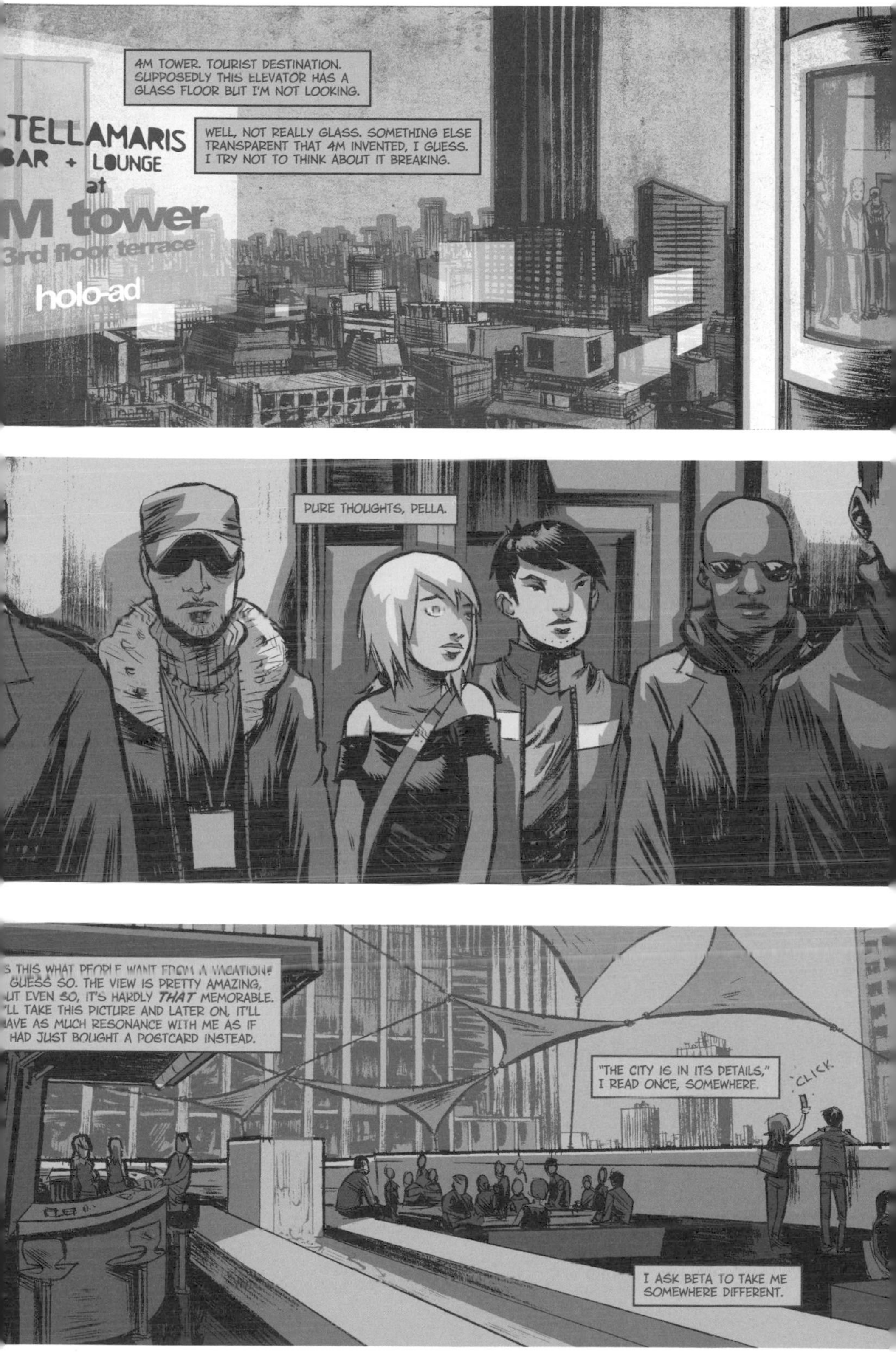
4M TOWER. TOURIST DESTINATION. SUPPOSEDLY THIS ELEVATOR HAS A GLASS FLOOR BUT I'M NOT LOOKING.
TELLAMARIS BAR + LOUNGE at M tower 3rd floor terrace
holo-ad
WELL, NOT REALLY GLASS. SOMETHING ELSE TRANSPARENT THAT 4M INVENTED, I GUESS. I TRY NOT TO THINK ABOUT IT BREAKING.
PURE THOUGHTS, PELLA.
S THIS WHAT PEOPLE WANT FROM A VACATION? GUESS SO. THE VIEW IS PRETTY AMAZING, UT EVEN SO, IT'S HARDLY *THAT* MEMORABLE. 'LL TAKE THIS PICTURE AND LATER ON, IT'LL AVE AS MUCH RESONANCE WITH ME AS IF HAD JUST BOUGHT A POSTCARD INSTEAD.
"THE CITY IS IN ITS DETAILS," I READ ONCE, SOMEWHERE.
CLICK
I ASK BETA TO TAKE ME SOMEWHERE DIFFERENT.

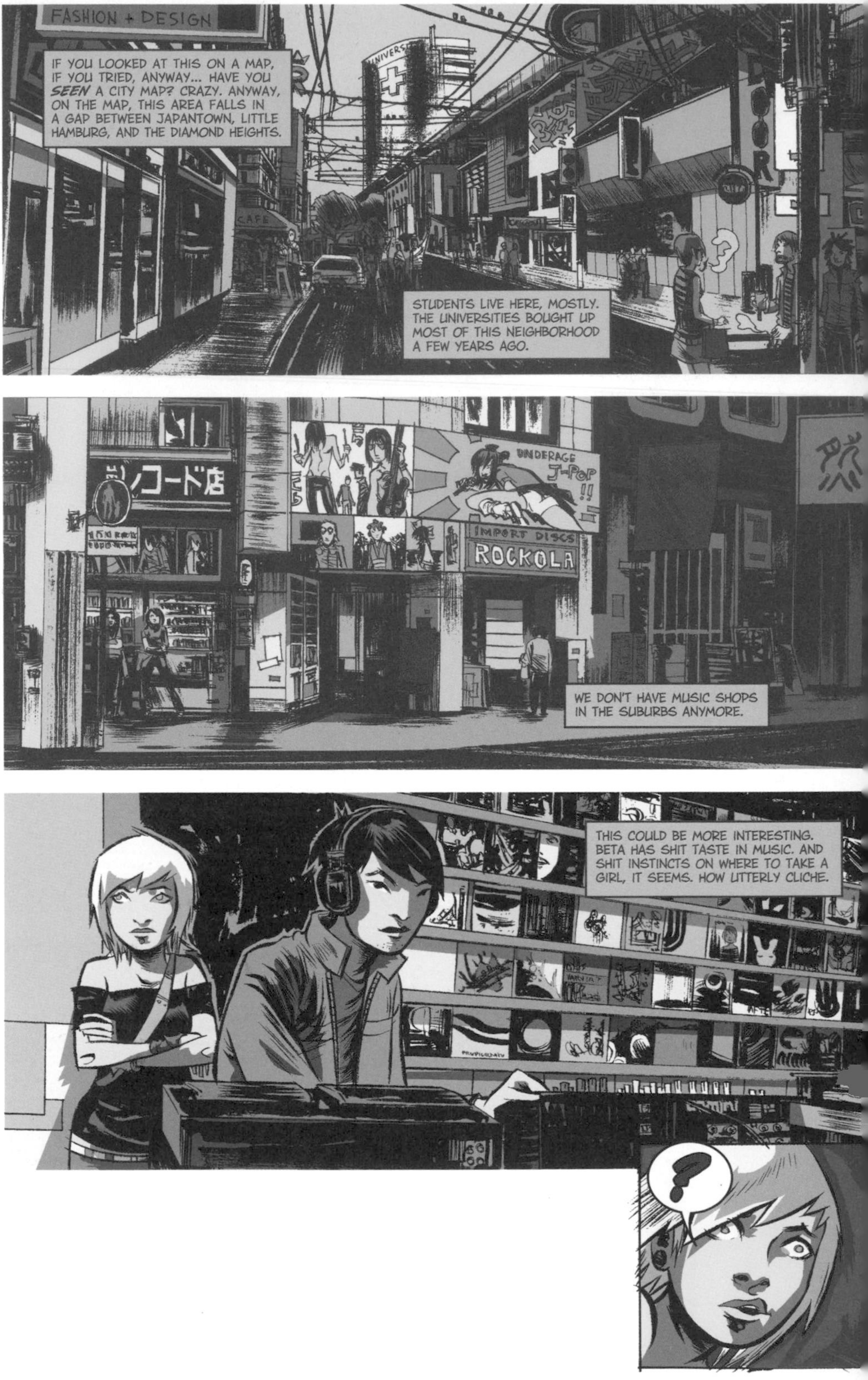
FASHION + DESIGN
IF YOU LOOKED AT THIS ON A MAP, IF YOU TRIED, ANYWAY... HAVE YOU *SEEN* A CITY MAP? CRAZY. ANYWAY, ON THE MAP, THIS AREA FALLS IN A GAP BETWEEN JAPANTOWN, LITTLE HAMBURG, AND THE DIAMOND HEIGHTS.
CAFE
STUDENTS LIVE HERE, MOSTLY. THE UNIVERSITIES BOUGHT UP MOST OF THIS NEIGHBORHOOD A FEW YEARS AGO.
UNDERAGE J-POP !!
IMPORT DISCS
ROCKOLA
WE DON'T HAVE MUSIC SHOPS IN THE SUBURBS ANYMORE.
THIS COULD BE MORE INTERESTING. BETA HAS SHIT TASTE IN MUSIC. AND SHIT INSTINCTS ON WHERE TO TAKE A GIRL, IT SEEMS. HOW UTTERLY CLICHE.
?

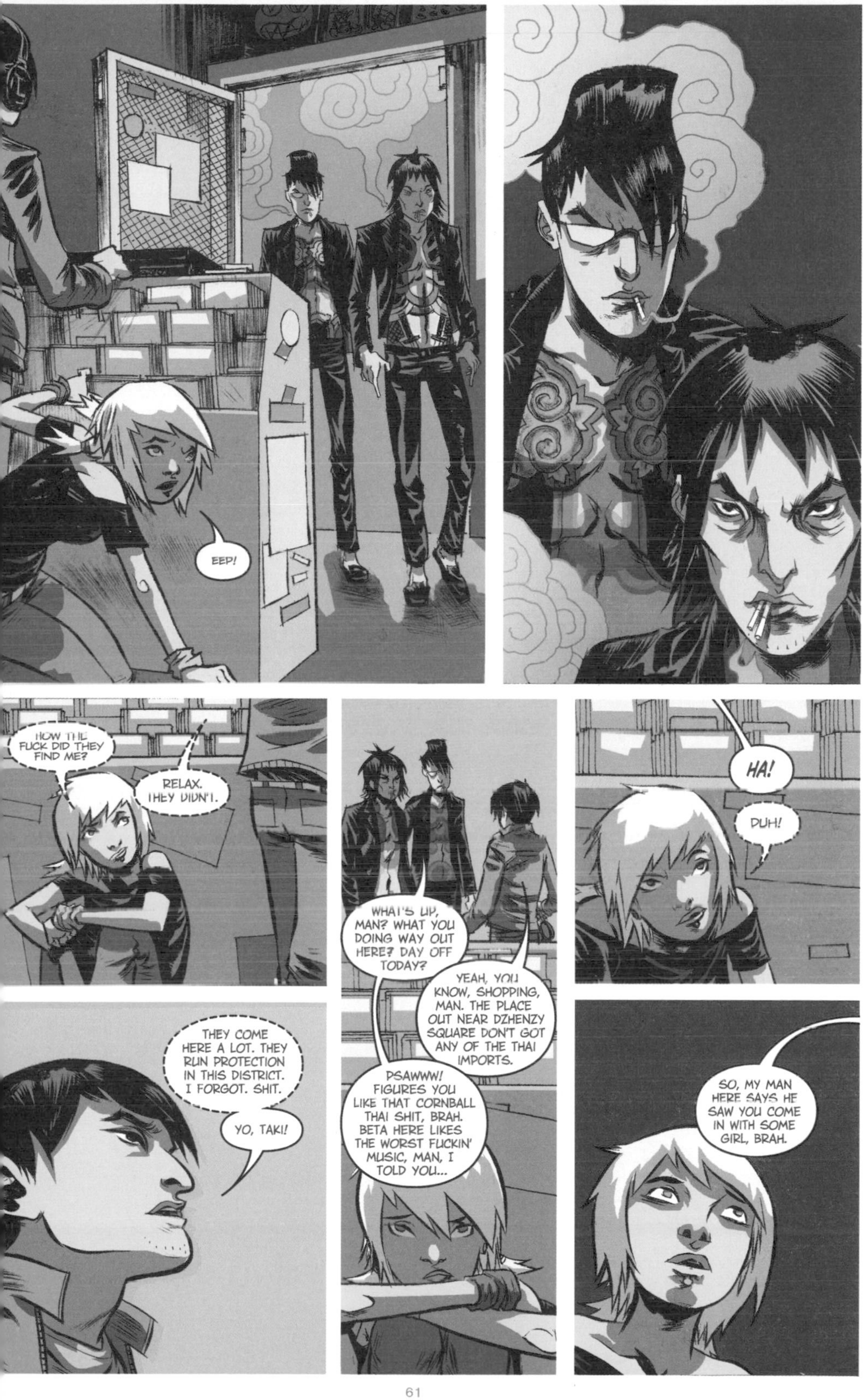
EEP!
HOW THE FUCK DID THEY FIND ME?
RELAX. THEY DIDN'T.
WHAT'S UP, MAN? WHAT YOU DOING WAY OUT HERE? DAY OFF TODAY?
YEAH, YOU KNOW, SHOPPING, MAN. THE PLACE OUT NEAR DZHENZY SQUARE DON'T GOT ANY OF THE THAI IMPORTS.
HA!
DUH!
THEY COME HERE A LOT. THEY RUN PROTECTION IN THIS DISTRICT. I FORGOT. SHIT.
YO, TAKI!
PSAWWW! FIGURES YOU LIKE THAT CORNBALL THAI SHIT, BRAH. BETA HERE LIKES THE WORST FUCKIN' MUSIC, MAN, I TOLD YOU...
SO, MY MAN HERE SAYS HE SAW YOU COME IN WITH SOME GIRL, BRAH.

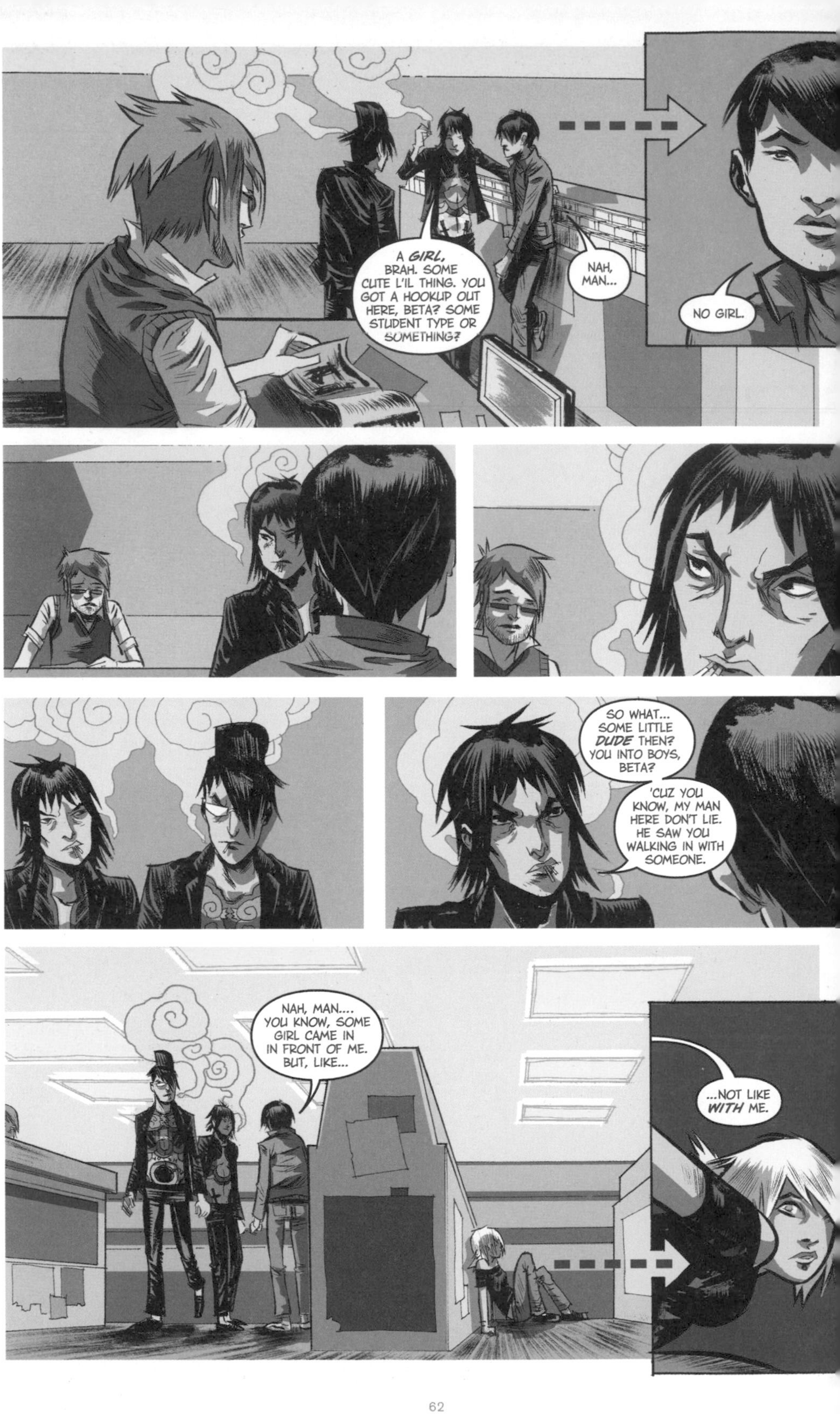
A GIRL, BRAH. SOME CUTE L'IL THING. YOU GOT A HOOKUP OUT HERE, BETA? SOME STUDENT TYPE OR SOMETHING?
NAH, MAN...
NO GIRL.
SO WHAT... SOME LITTLE DUDE THEN? YOU INTO BOYS, BETA?
'CUZ YOU KNOW, MY MAN HERE DON'T LIE. HE SAW YOU WALKING IN WITH SOMEONE.
NAH, MAN.... YOU KNOW, SOME GIRL CAME IN IN FRONT OF ME. BUT, LIKE...
...NOT LIKE WITH ME.

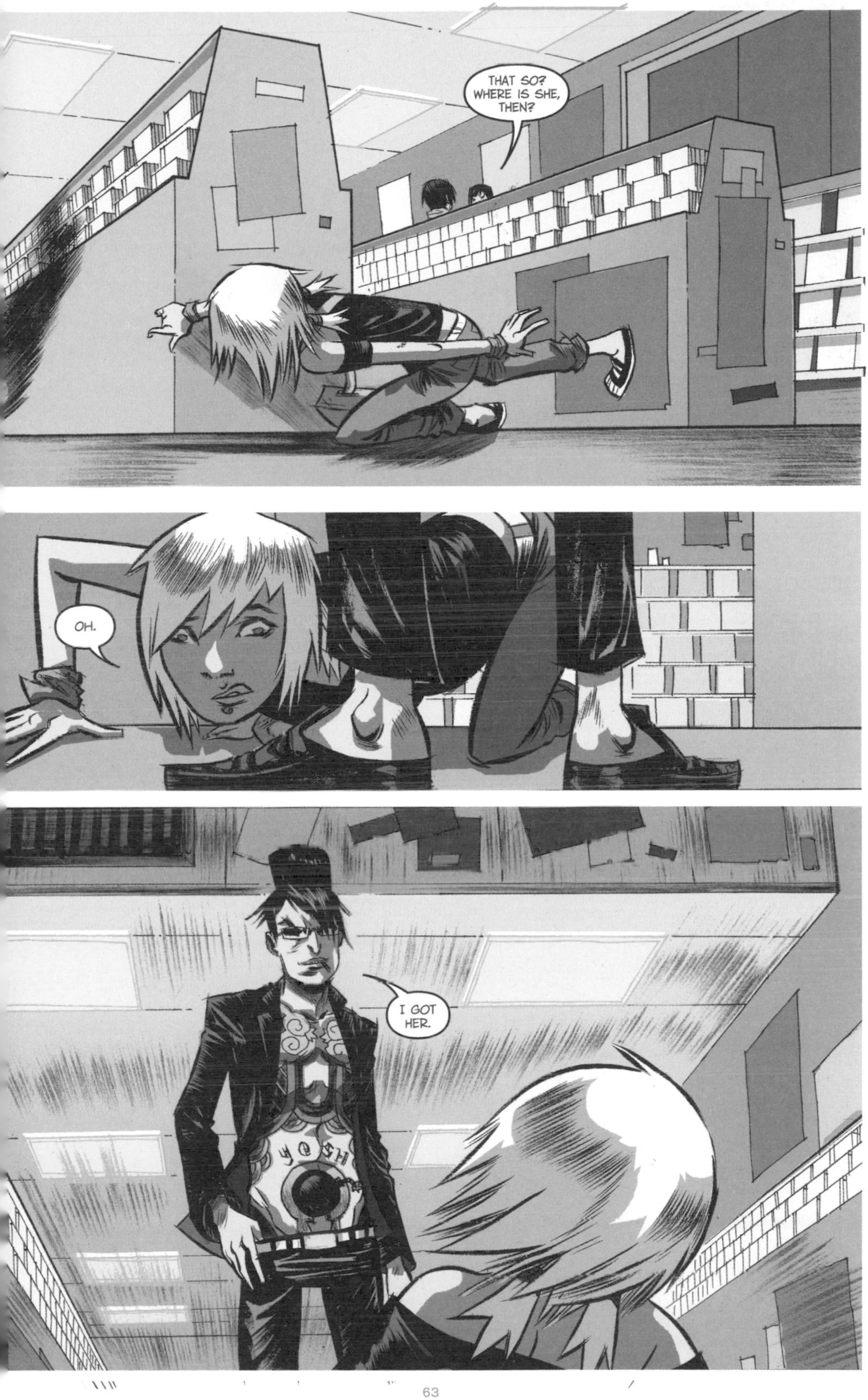
THAT SO? WHERE IS SHE, THEN?
OH.
I GOT HER.

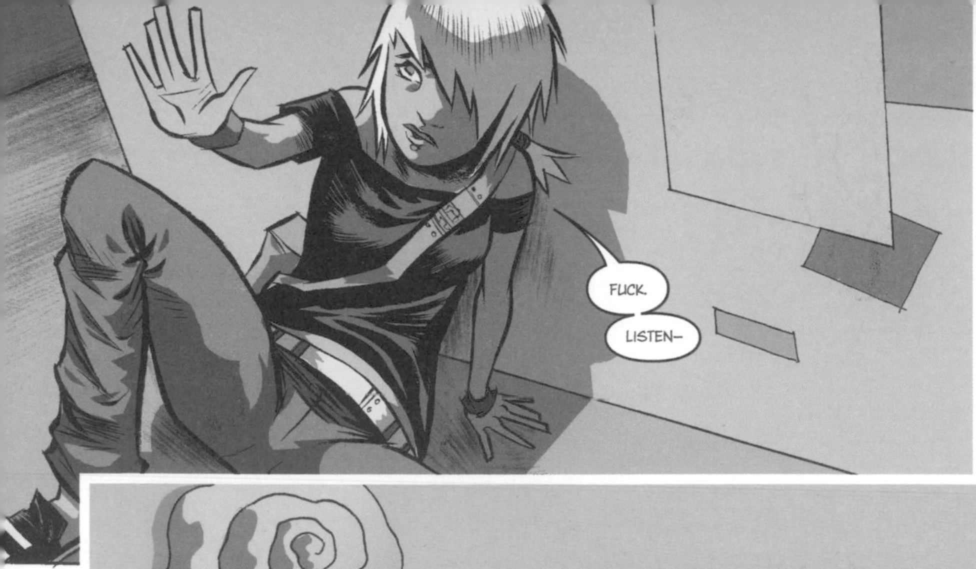
FUCK.
LISTEN–
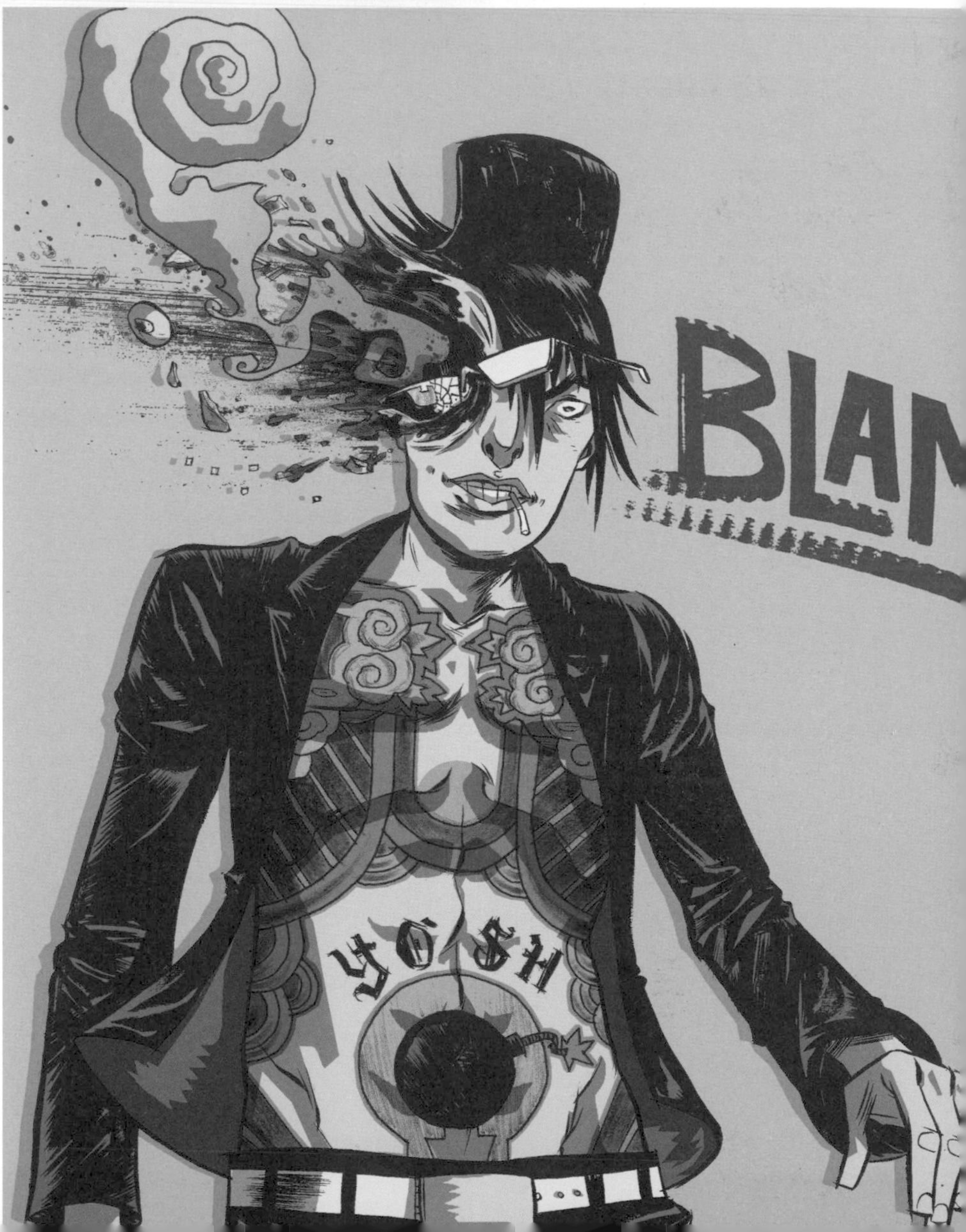
BLAM
YOSH

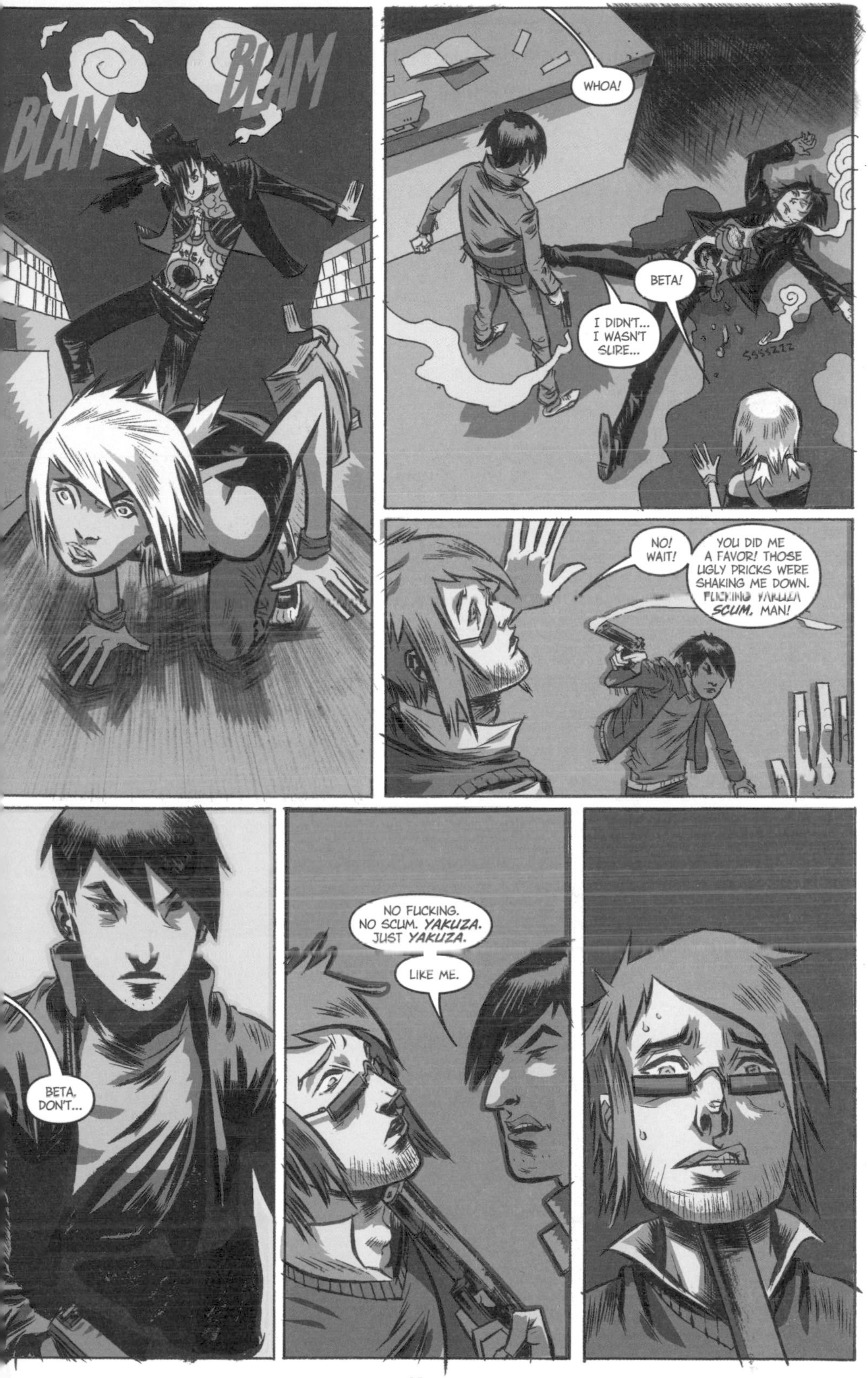
BLAM
BLAM
WHOA!
BETA!
I DIDN'T... I WASN'T SURE...
SSSSZZZ
NO! WAIT!
YOU DID ME A FAVOR! THOSE UGLY PRICKS WERE SHAKING ME DOWN. FUCKING YAKUZA SCUM, MAN!
BETA, DON'T...
NO FUCKING. NO SCUM. YAKUZA. JUST YAKUZA.
LIKE ME.

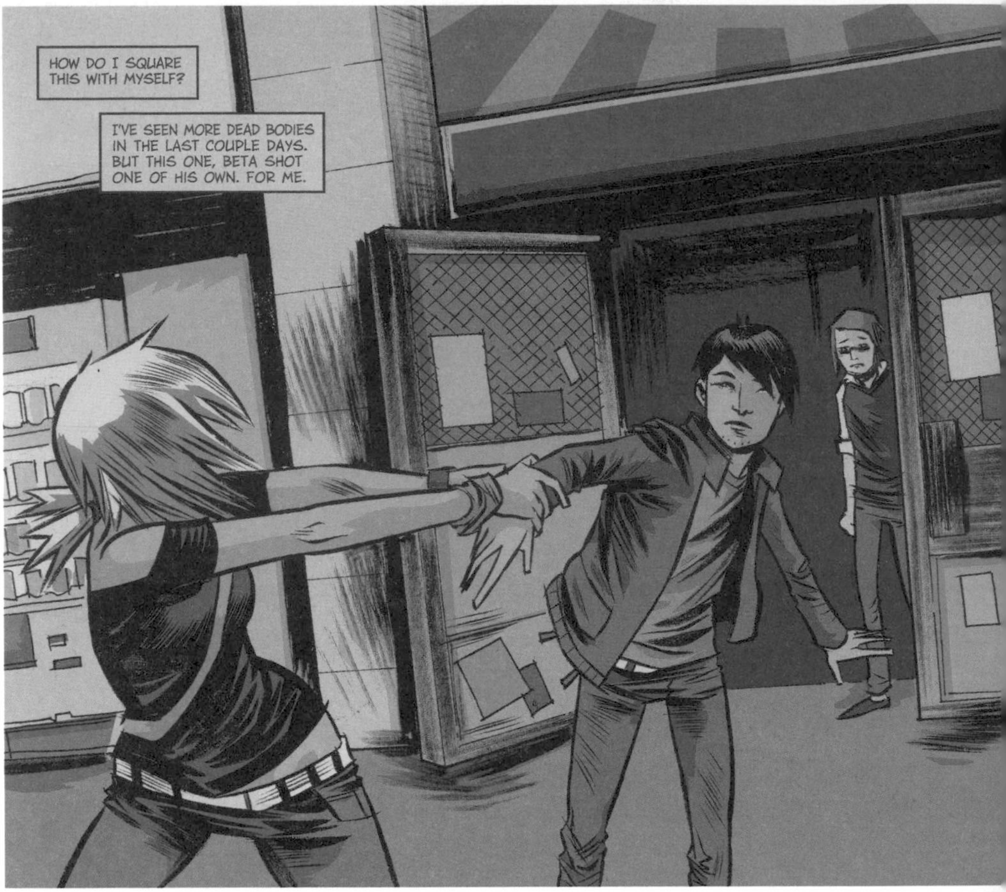
HOW DO I SQUARE THIS WITH MYSELF?
I'VE SEEN MORE DEAD BODIES IN THE LAST COUPLE DAYS. BUT THIS ONE, BETA SHOT ONE OF HIS OWN. FOR ME.

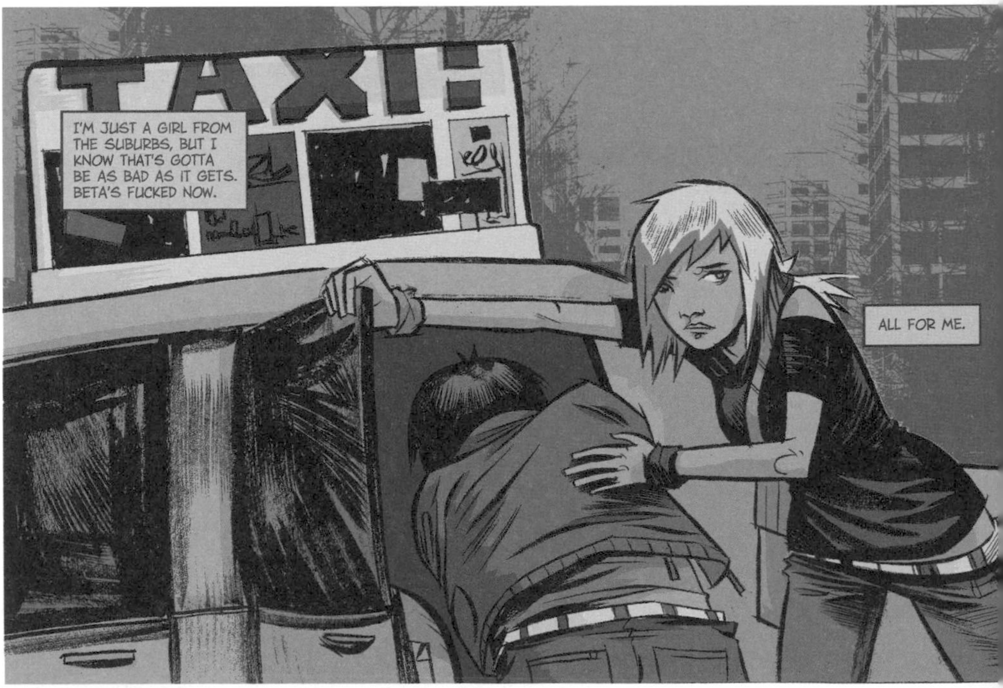
TAXI
I'M JUST A GIRL FROM THE SUBURBS, BUT I KNOW THAT'S GOTTA BE AS BAD AS IT GETS. BETA'S FUCKED NOW.
ALL FOR ME.

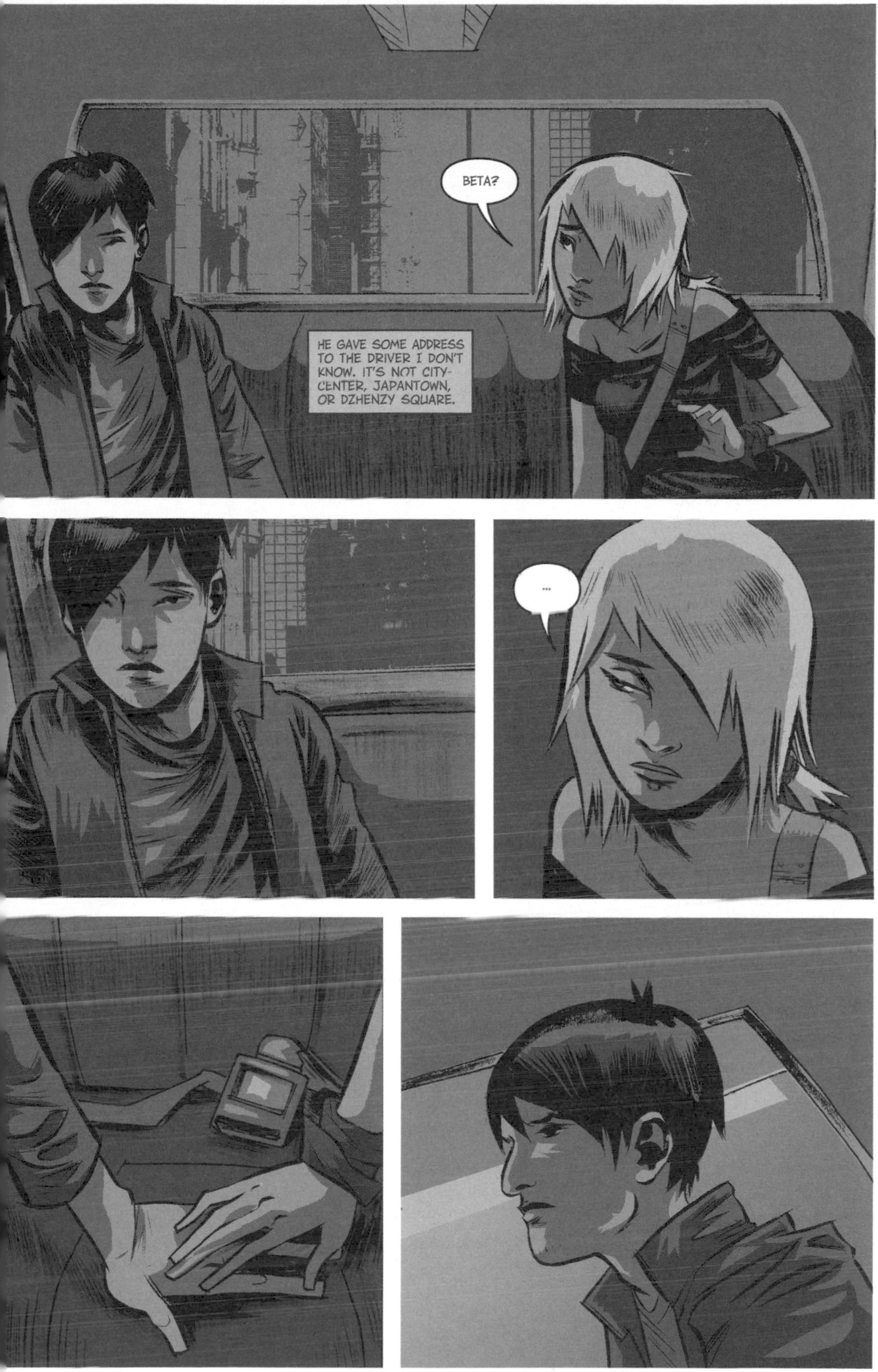
BETA?
HE GAVE SOME ADDRESS TO THE DRIVER I DON'T KNOW. IT'S NOT CITY-CENTER, JAPANTOWN, OR DZHENZY SQUARE.
...

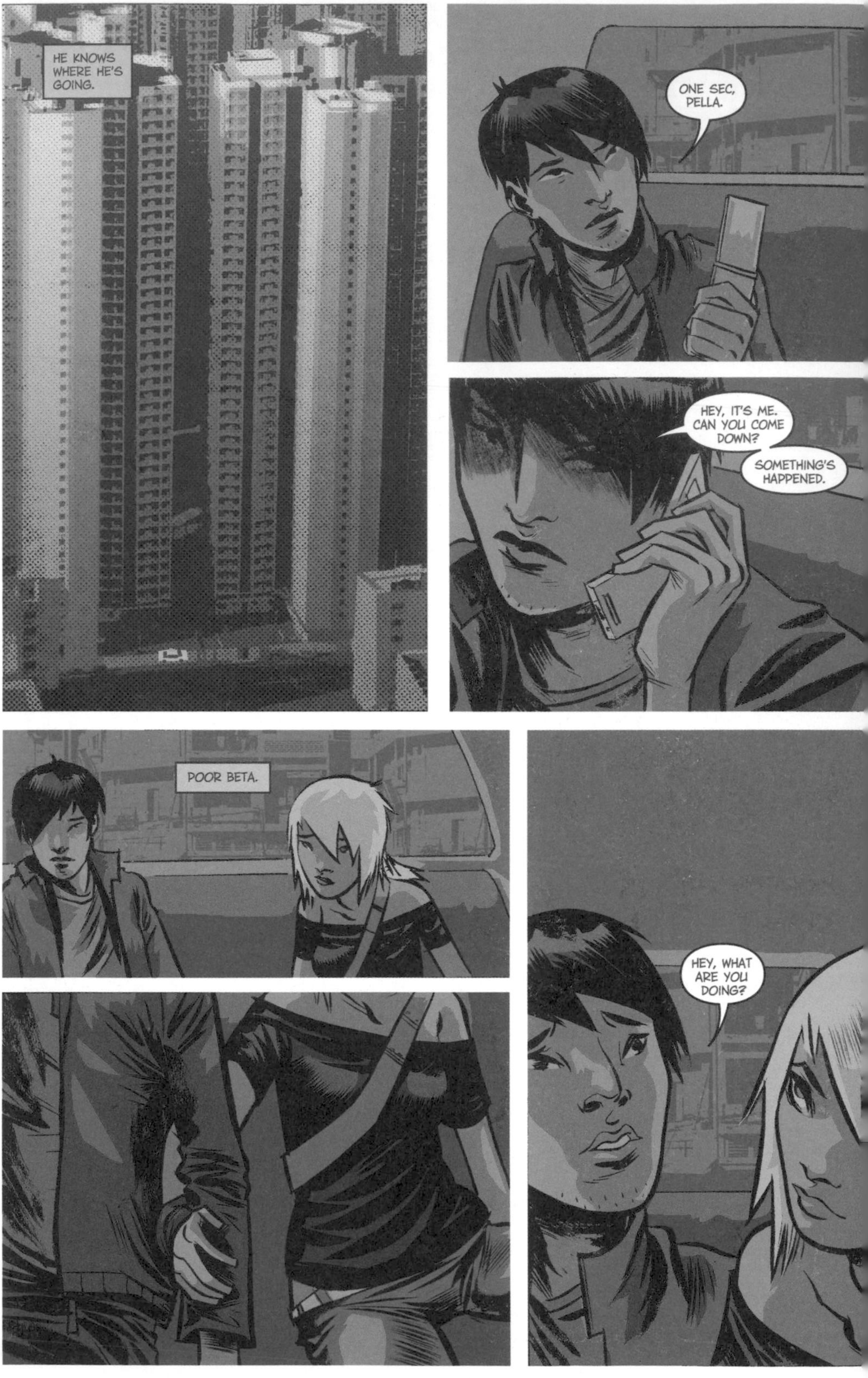
HE KNOWS WHERE HE'S GOING.
ONE SEC, PELLA.
HEY, IT'S ME. CAN YOU COME DOWN?
SOMETHING'S HAPPENED.
POOR BETA.
HEY, WHAT ARE YOU DOING?

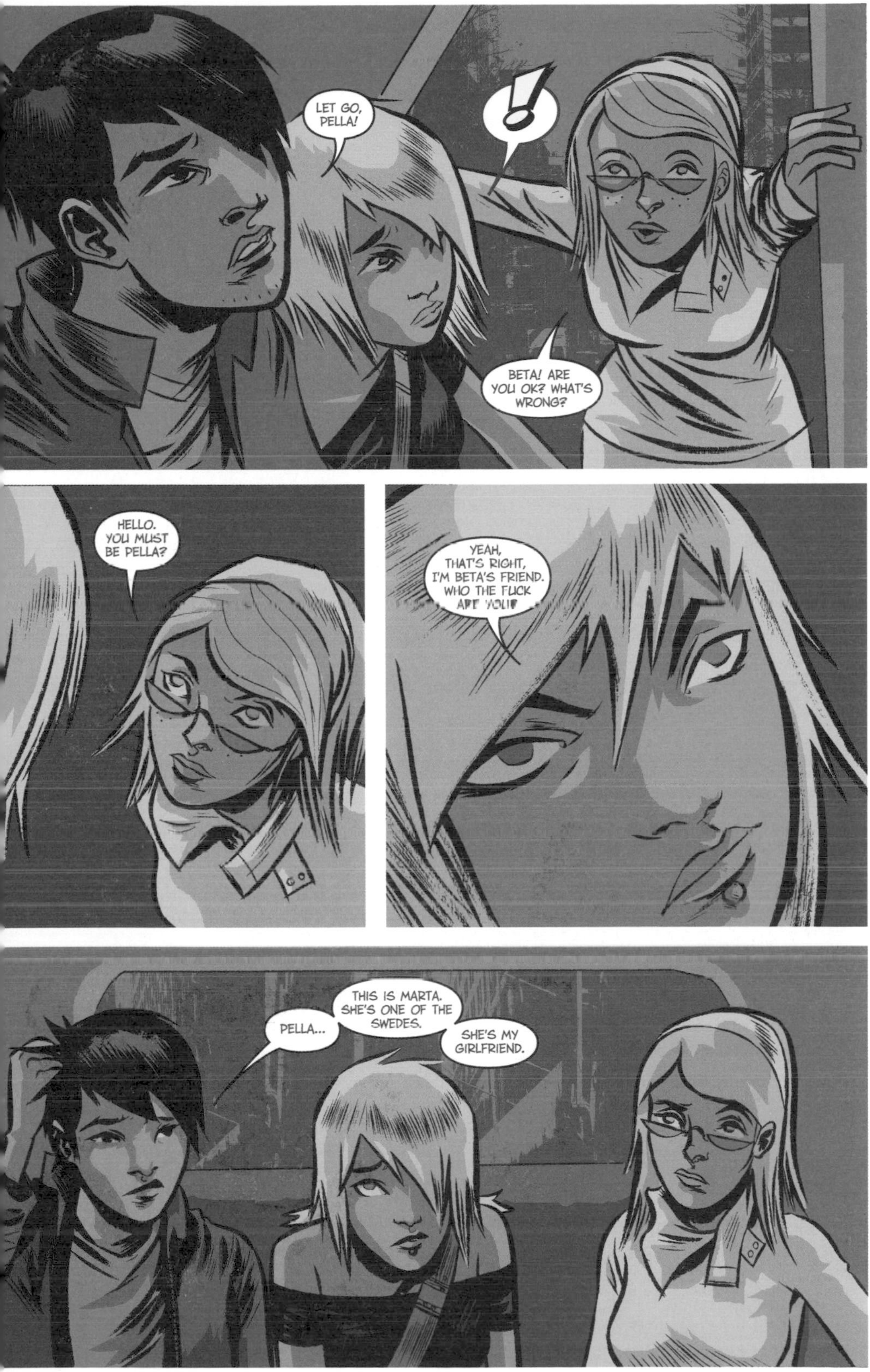
LET GO, PELLA!
!
BETA! ARE YOU OK? WHAT'S WRONG?
HELLO. YOU MUST BE PELLA?
YEAH, THAT'S RIGHT, I'M BETA'S FRIEND. WHO THE FUCK ARE YOU?
PELLA...
THIS IS MARTA. SHE'S ONE OF THE SWEDES.
SHE'S MY GIRLFRIEND.

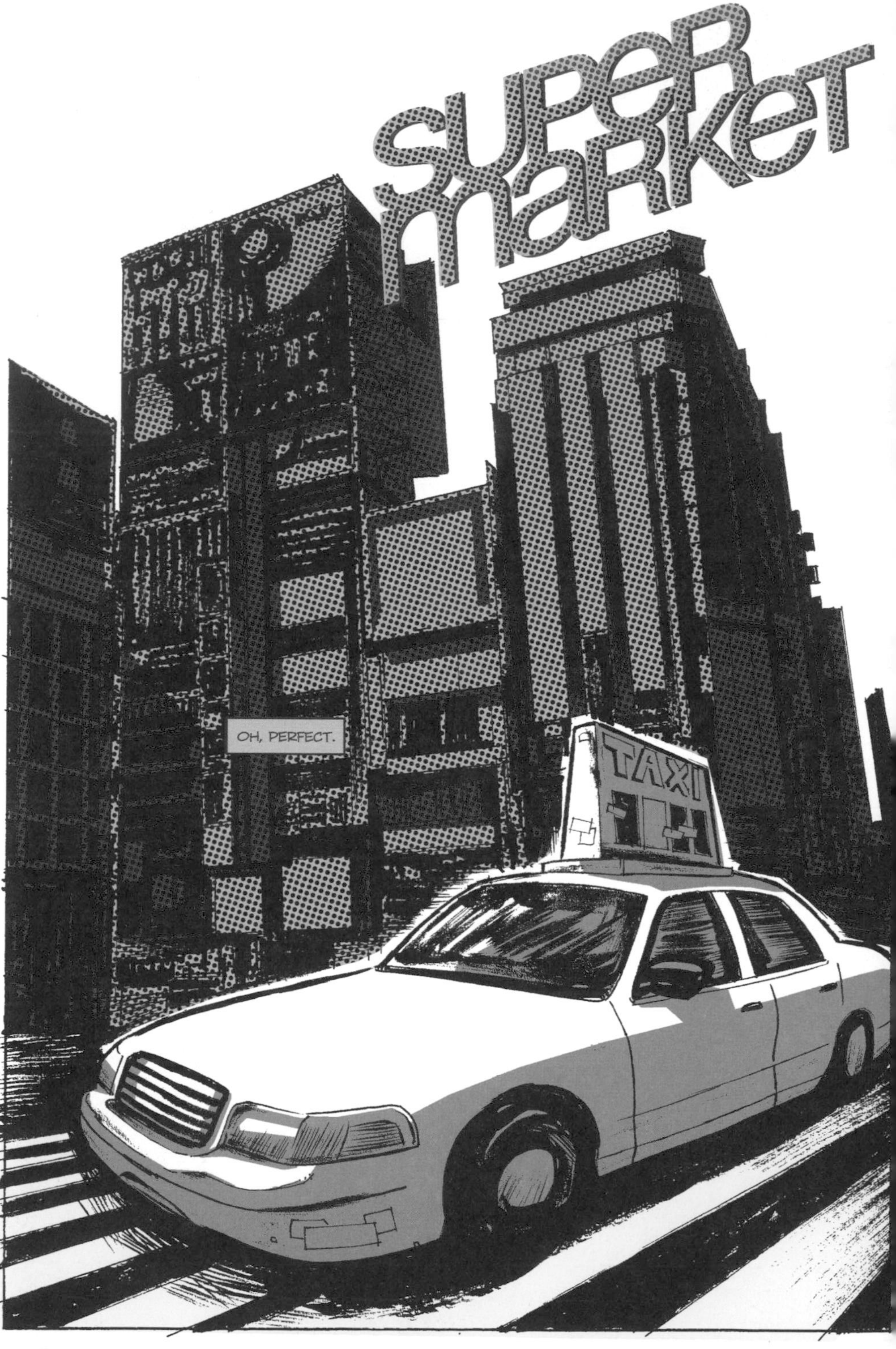
SUPER MARKET
OH, PERFECT.
TAXI

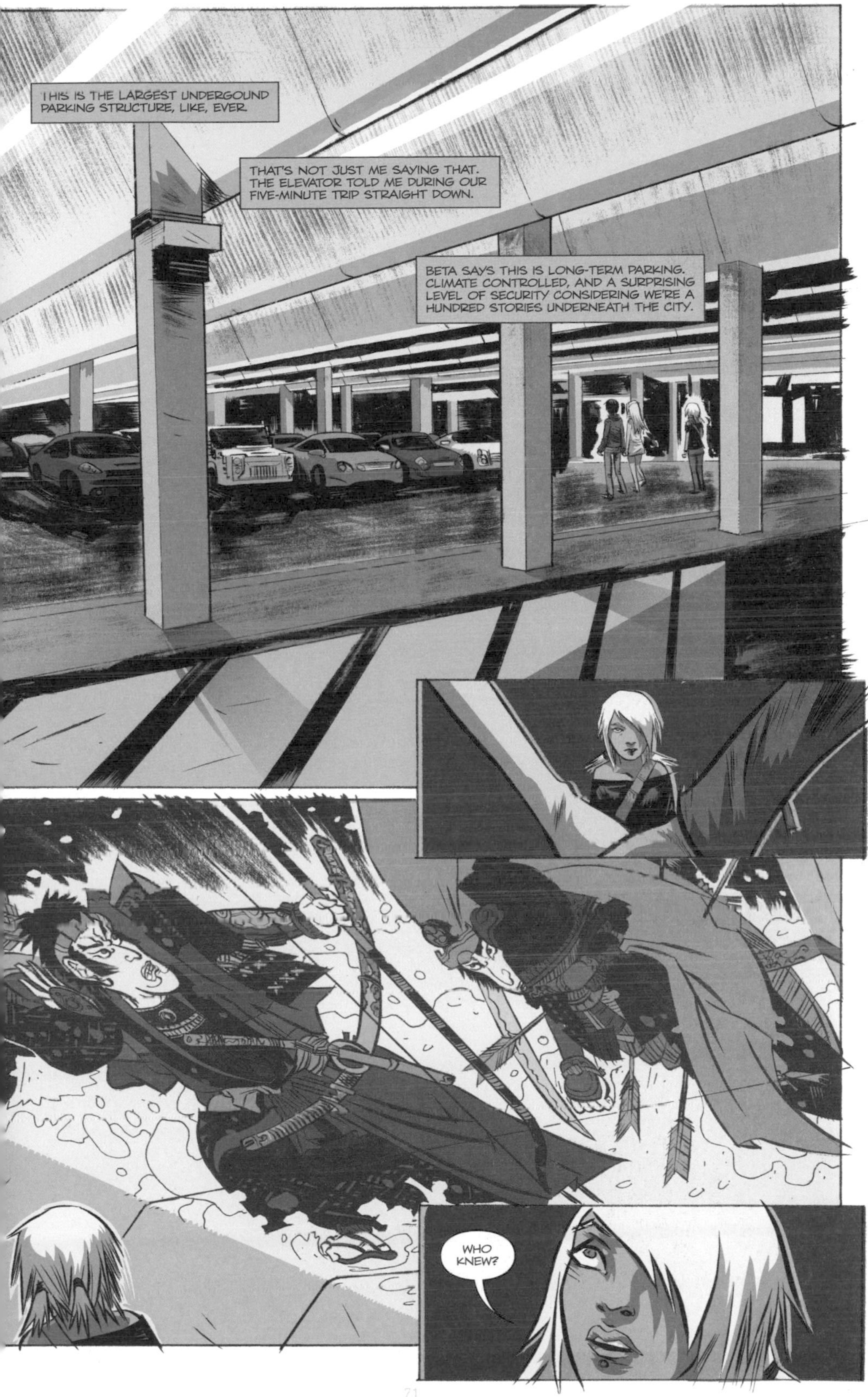
THIS IS THE LARGEST UNDERGOUND PARKING STRUCTURE, LIKE, EVER
THAT'S NOT JUST ME SAYING THAT. THE ELEVATOR TOLD ME DURING OUR FIVE-MINUTE TRIP STRAIGHT DOWN.
BETA SAYS THIS IS LONG-TERM PARKING. CLIMATE CONTROLLED, AND A SURPRISING LEVEL OF SECURITY CONSIDERING WE'RE A HUNDRED STORIES UNDERNEATH THE CITY.
WHO KNEW?

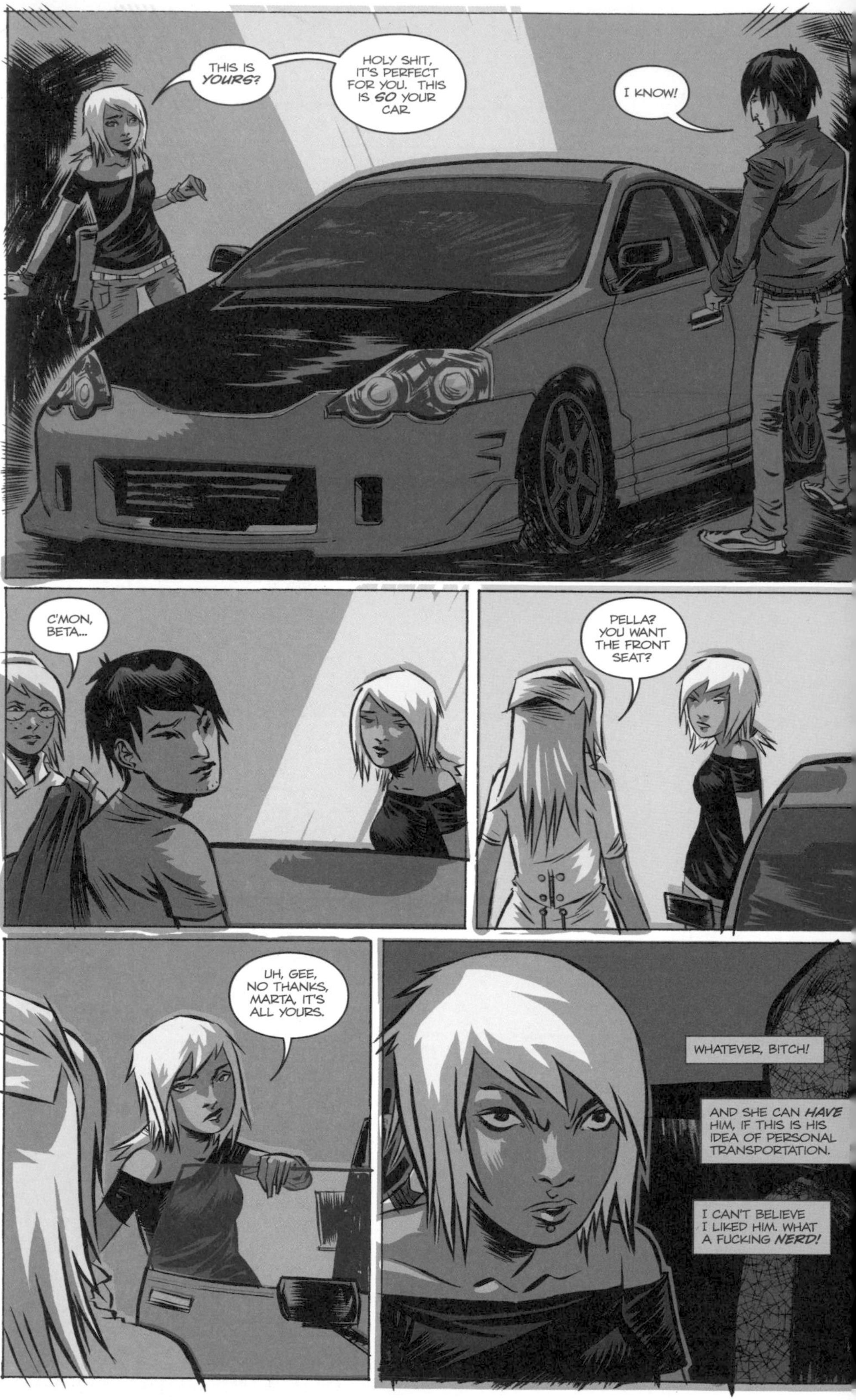
THIS IS YOURS?
HOLY SHIT, IT'S PERFECT FOR YOU. THIS IS SO YOUR CAR
I KNOW!
C'MON, BETA...
PELLA? YOU WANT THE FRONT SEAT?
UH, GEE, NO THANKS, MARTA, IT'S ALL YOURS.
WHATEVER, BITCH!
AND SHE CAN HAVE HIM, IF THIS IS HIS IDEA OF PERSONAL TRANSPORTATION.
I CAN'T BELIEVE I LIKED HIM. WHAT A FUCKING NERD!

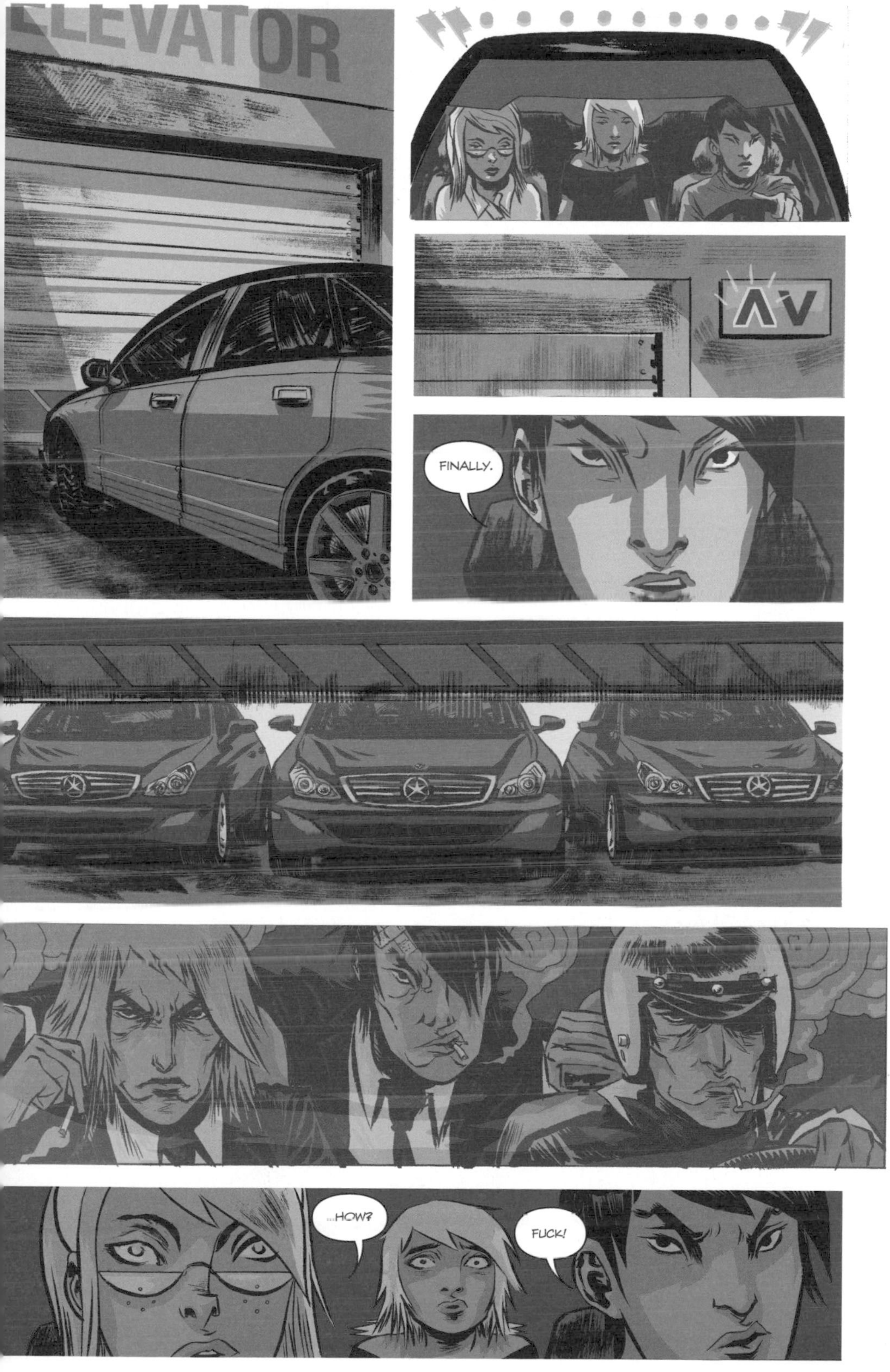
ELEVATOR
FINALLY.
...HOW?
FUCK!

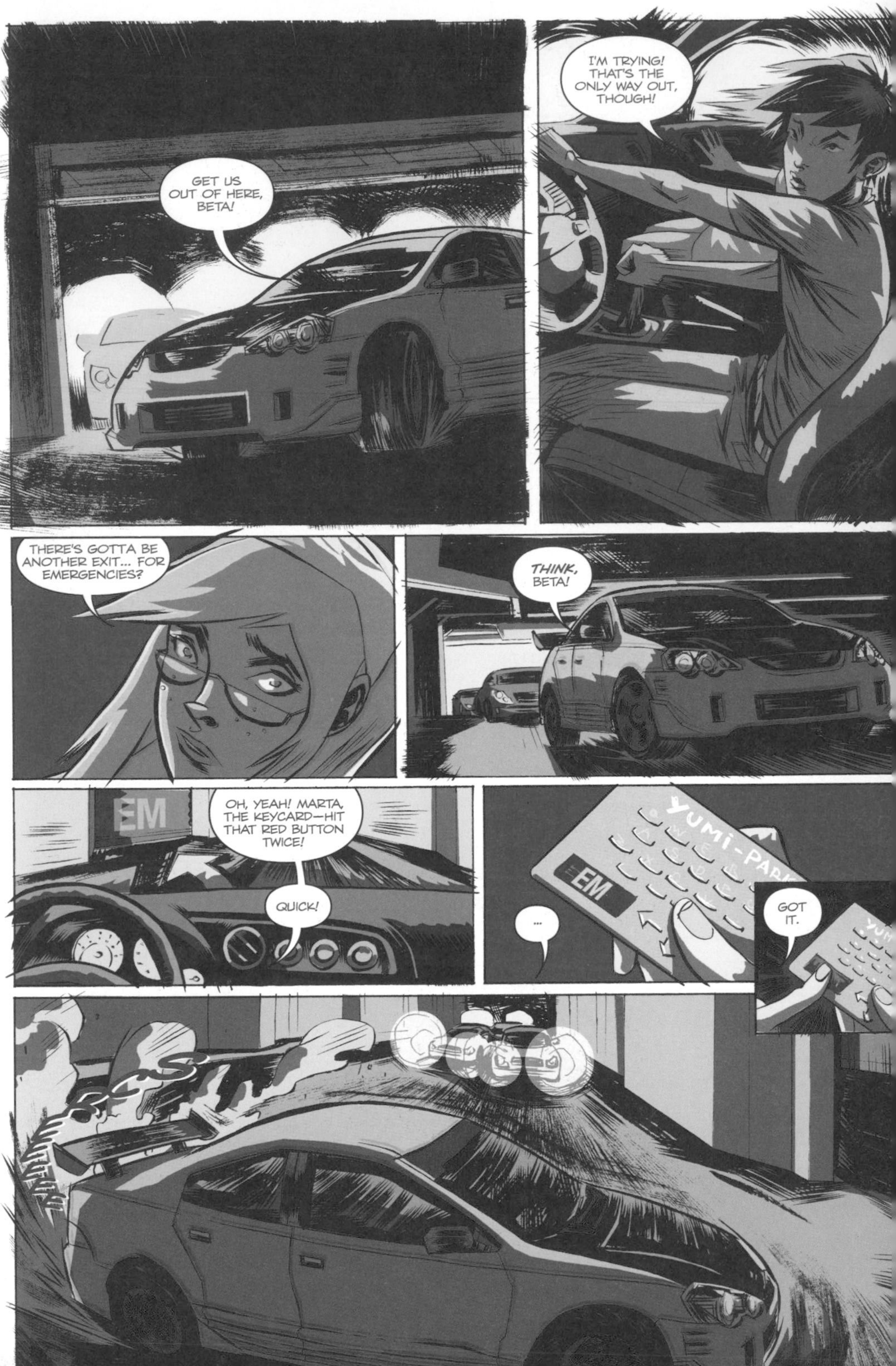
GET US OUT OF HERE, BETA!
I'M TRYING! THAT'S THE ONLY WAY OUT, THOUGH!
THERE'S GOTTA BE ANOTHER EXIT... FOR EMERGENCIES?
THINK, BETA!
EM
OH, YEAH! MARTA, THE KEYCARD—HIT THAT RED BUTTON TWICE!
QUICK!
EM
...
GOT IT.

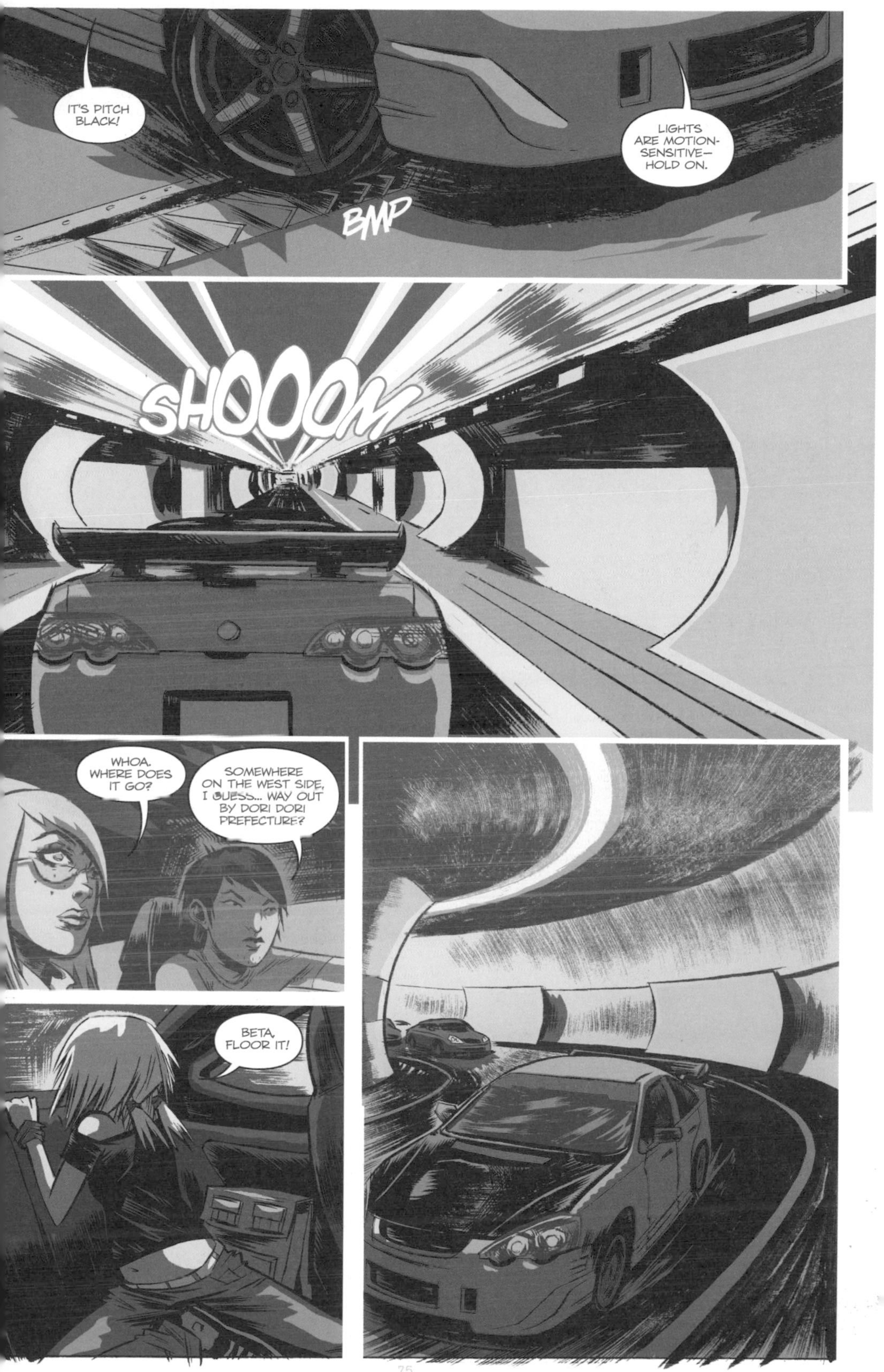
IT'S PITCH BLACK!
LIGHTS ARE MOTION-SENSITIVE—HOLD ON.
BMP
SHOOOM
WHOA. WHERE DOES IT GO?
SOMEWHERE ON THE WEST SIDE, I GUESS... WAY OUT BY DORI DORI PREFECTURE?
BETA, FLOOR IT!

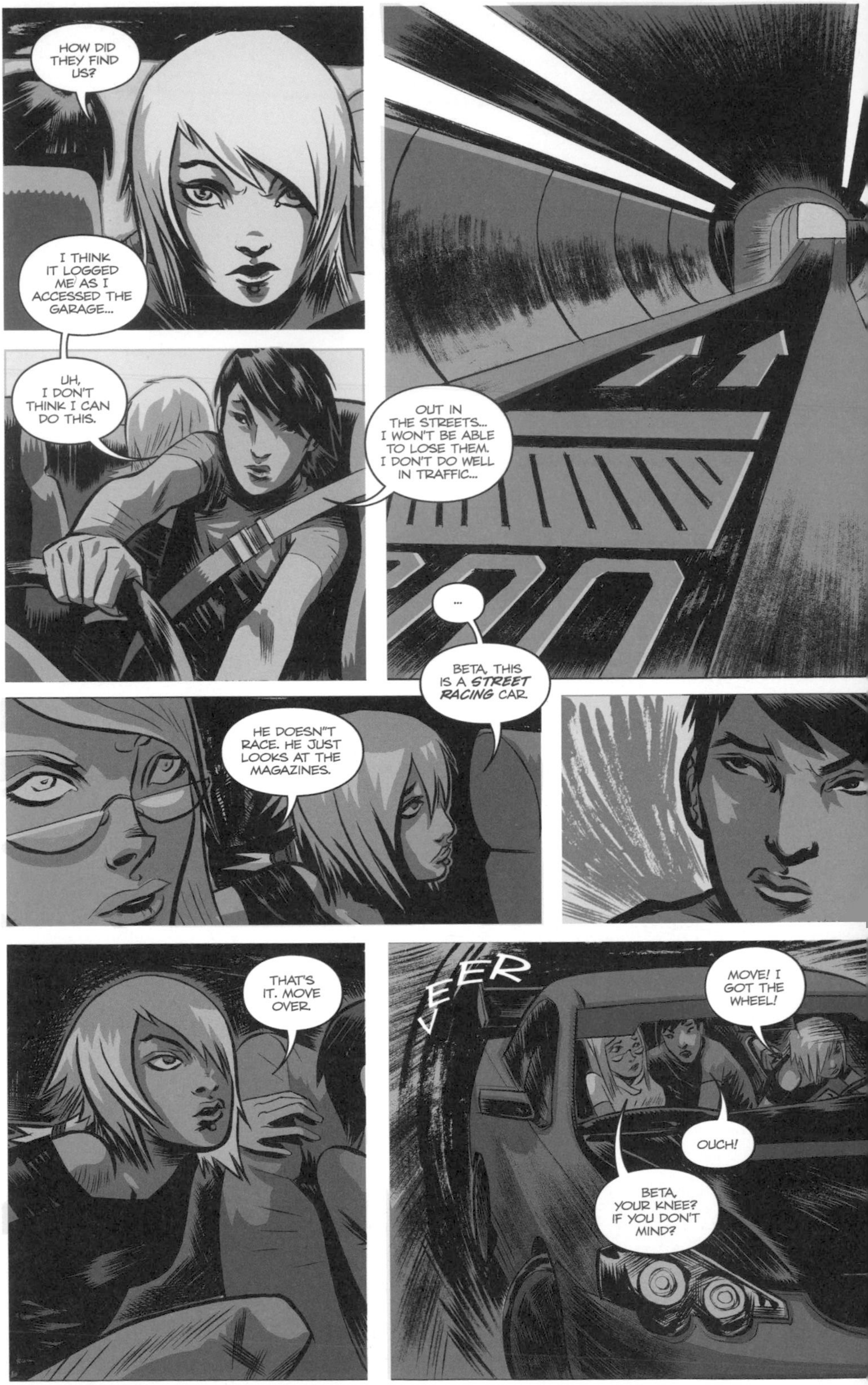
HOW DID THEY FIND US?
I THINK IT LOGGED ME AS I ACCESSED THE GARAGE...
UH, I DON'T THINK I CAN DO THIS.
OUT IN THE STREETS... I WON'T BE ABLE TO LOSE THEM. I DON'T DO WELL IN TRAFFIC...
...
BETA, THIS IS A STREET RACING CAR.
HE DOESN'T RACE. HE JUST LOOKS AT THE MAGAZINES.
THAT'S IT. MOVE OVER.
VEER
MOVE! I GOT THE WHEEL!
OUCH!
BETA, YOUR KNEE? IF YOU DON'T MIND?

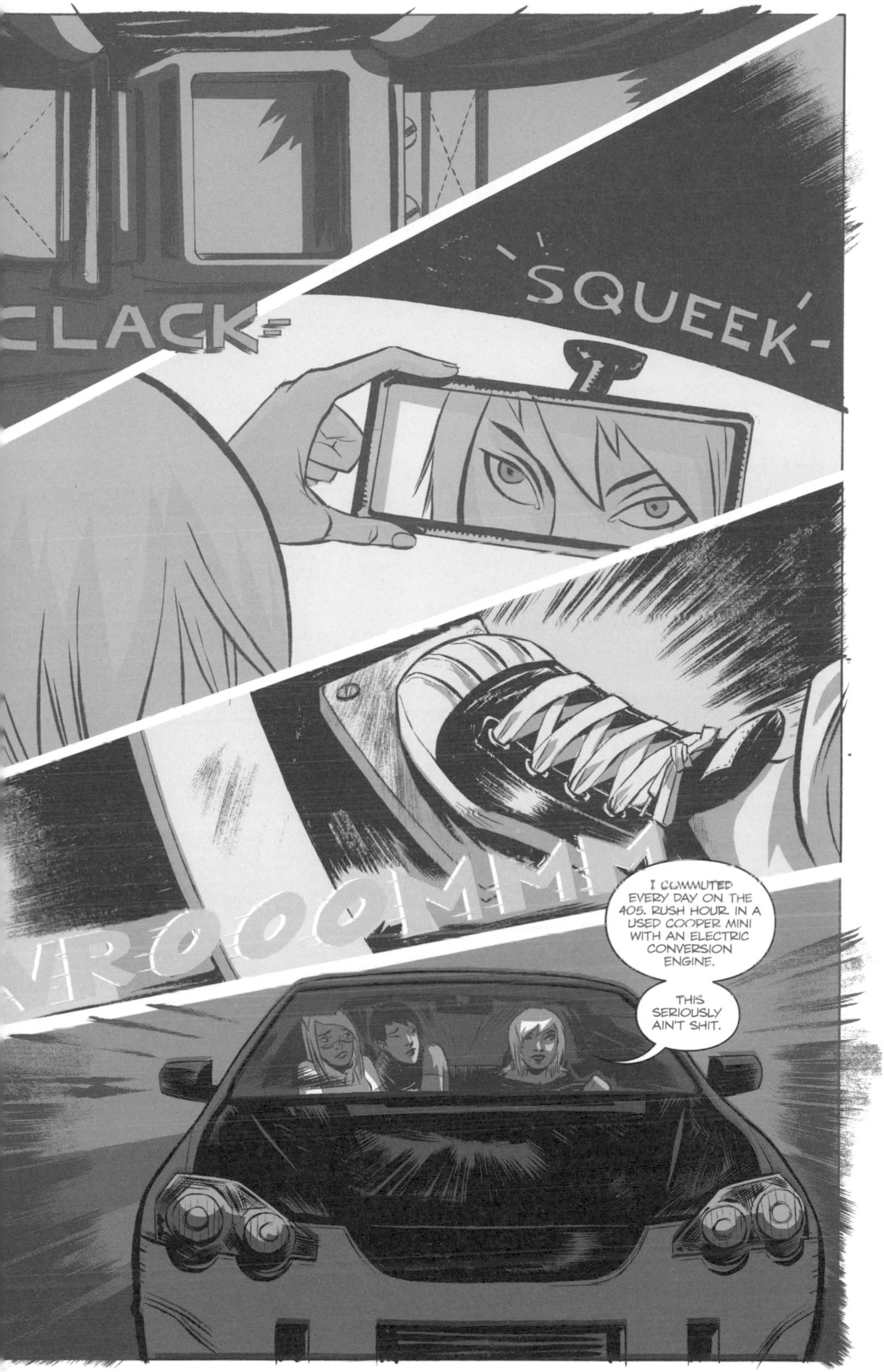
CLACK
SQUEEK
VROOOMMM
I COMMUTED EVERY DAY ON THE 405. RUSH HOUR IN A USED COOPER MINI WITH AN ELECTRIC CONVERSION ENGINE.
THIS SERIOUSLY AIN'T SHIT.

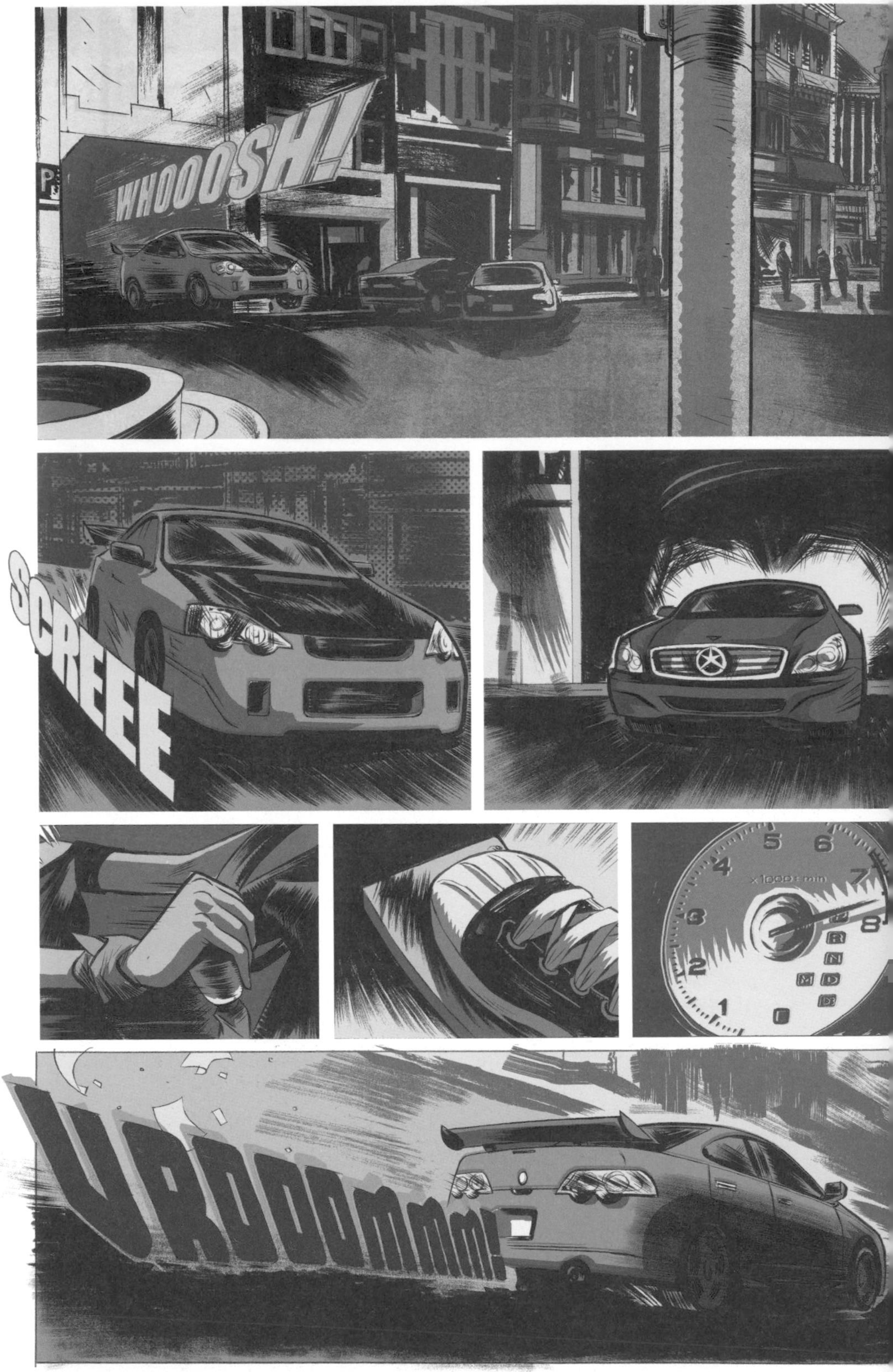
WHOOOSH!
SCREEE
VROOOMMM!

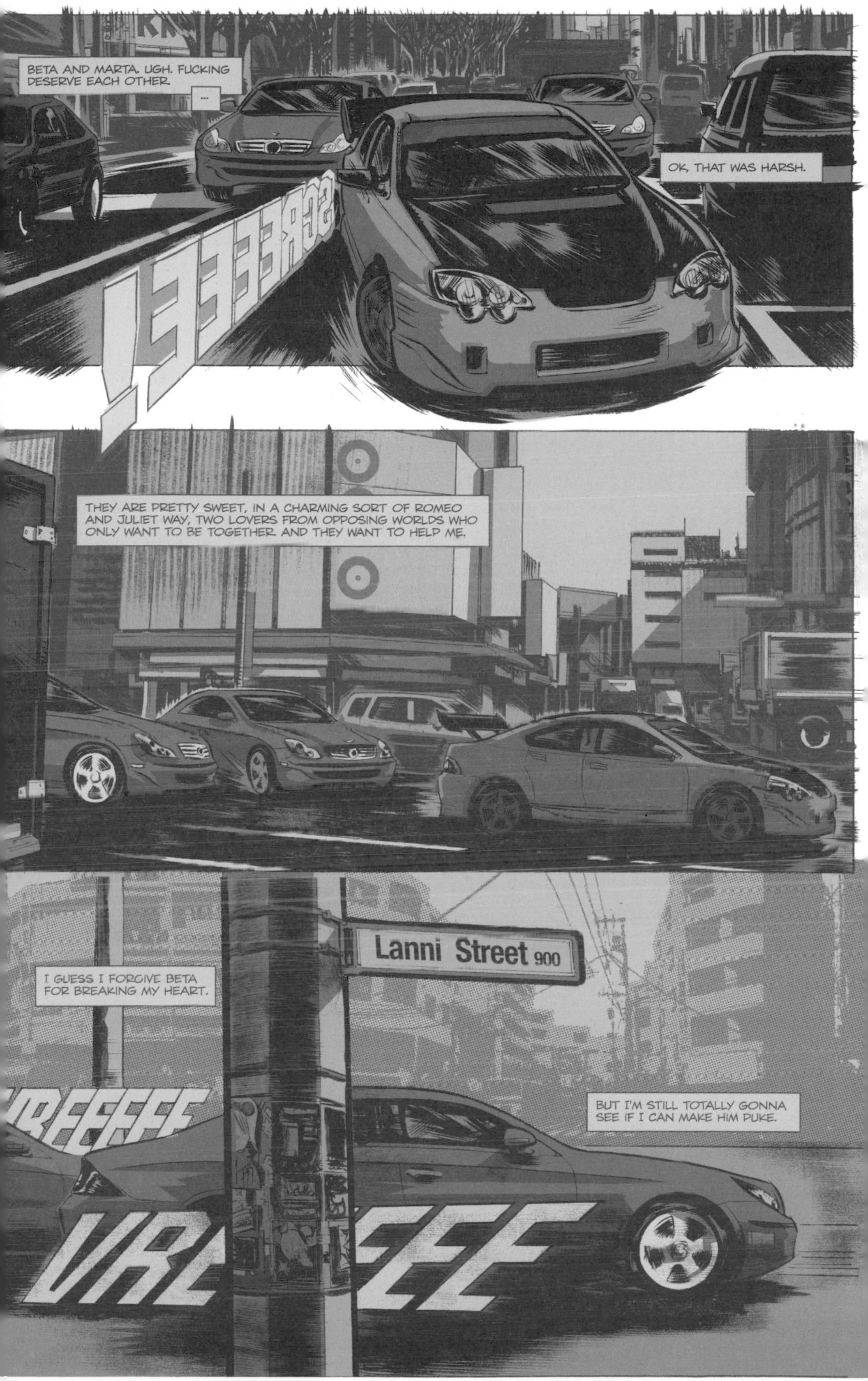
BETA AND MARTA. UGH. FUCKING DESERVE EACH OTHER.
...
SCREEEE!
OK, THAT WAS HARSH.
THEY ARE PRETTY SWEET, IN A CHARMING SORT OF ROMEO AND JULIET WAY, TWO LOVERS FROM OPPOSING WORLDS WHO ONLY WANT TO BE TOGETHER. AND THEY WANT TO HELP ME.
Lanni Street 900
I GUESS I FORGIVE BETA FOR BREAKING MY HEART.
BUT I'M STILL TOTALLY GONNA SEE IF I CAN MAKE HIM PUKE.

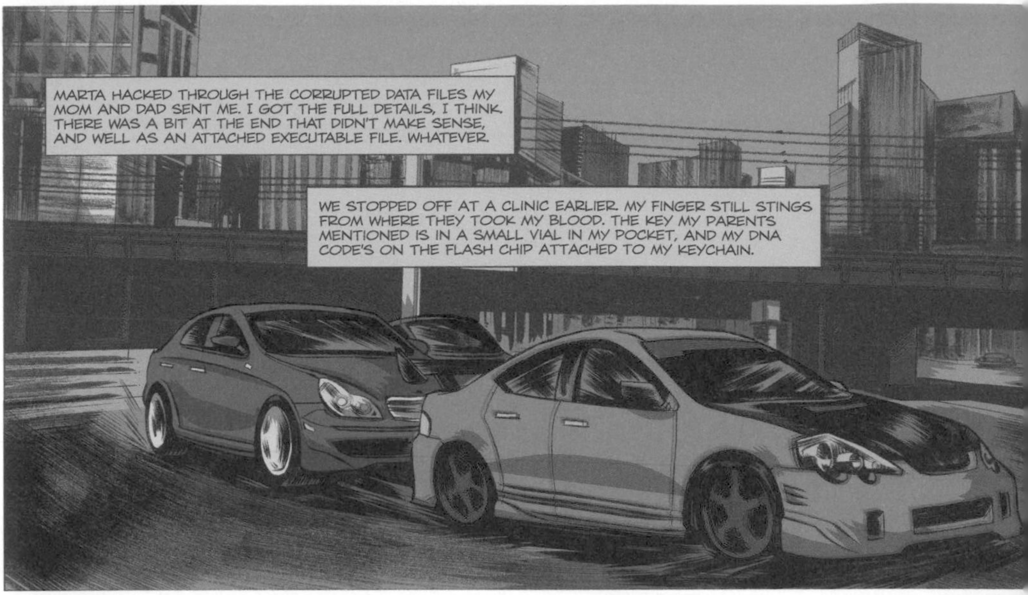
MARTA HACKED THROUGH THE CORRUPTED DATA FILES MY MOM AND DAD SENT ME. I GOT THE FULL DETAILS, I THINK. THERE WAS A BIT AT THE END THAT DIDN'T MAKE SENSE, AND WELL AS AN ATTACHED EXECUTABLE FILE. WHATEVER.
WE STOPPED OFF AT A CLINIC EARLIER. MY FINGER STILL STINGS FROM WHERE THEY TOOK MY BLOOD. THE KEY MY PARENTS MENTIONED IS IN A SMALL VIAL IN MY POCKET, AND MY DNA CODE'S ON THE FLASH CHIP ATTACHED TO MY KEYCHAIN.

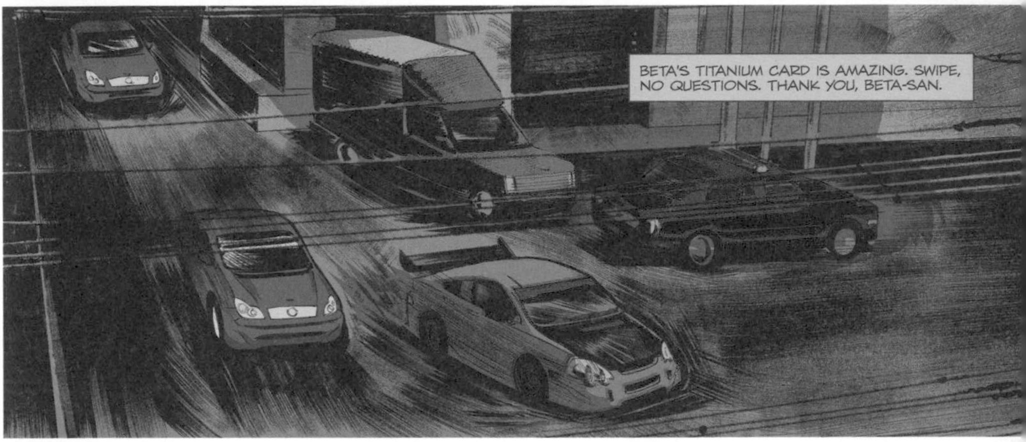
BETA'S TITANIUM CARD IS AMAZING. SWIPE, NO QUESTIONS. THANK YOU, BETA-SAN.

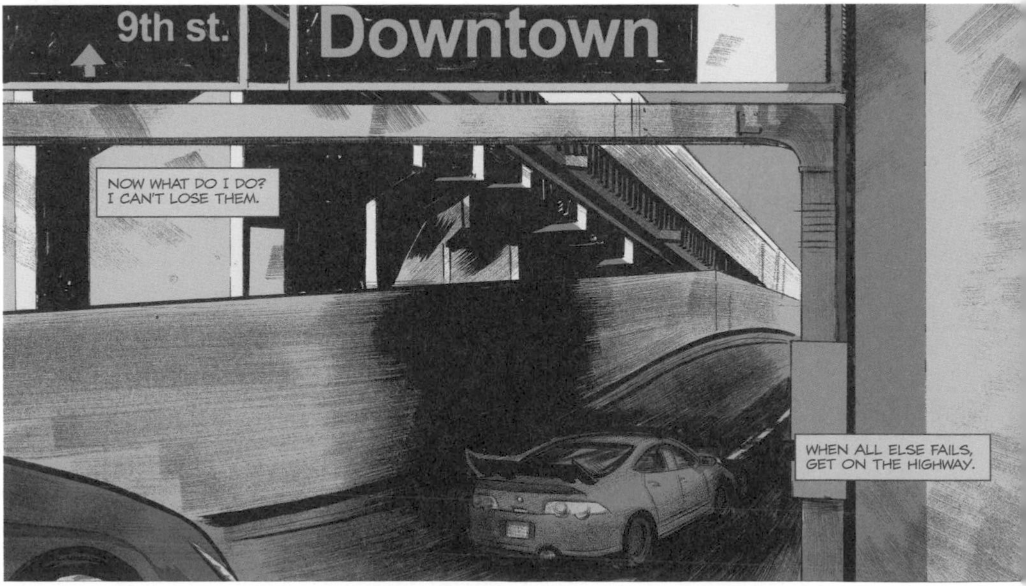
9th st.
Downtown
NOW WHAT DO I DO? I CAN'T LOSE THEM.
WHEN ALL ELSE FAILS, GET ON THE HIGHWAY.

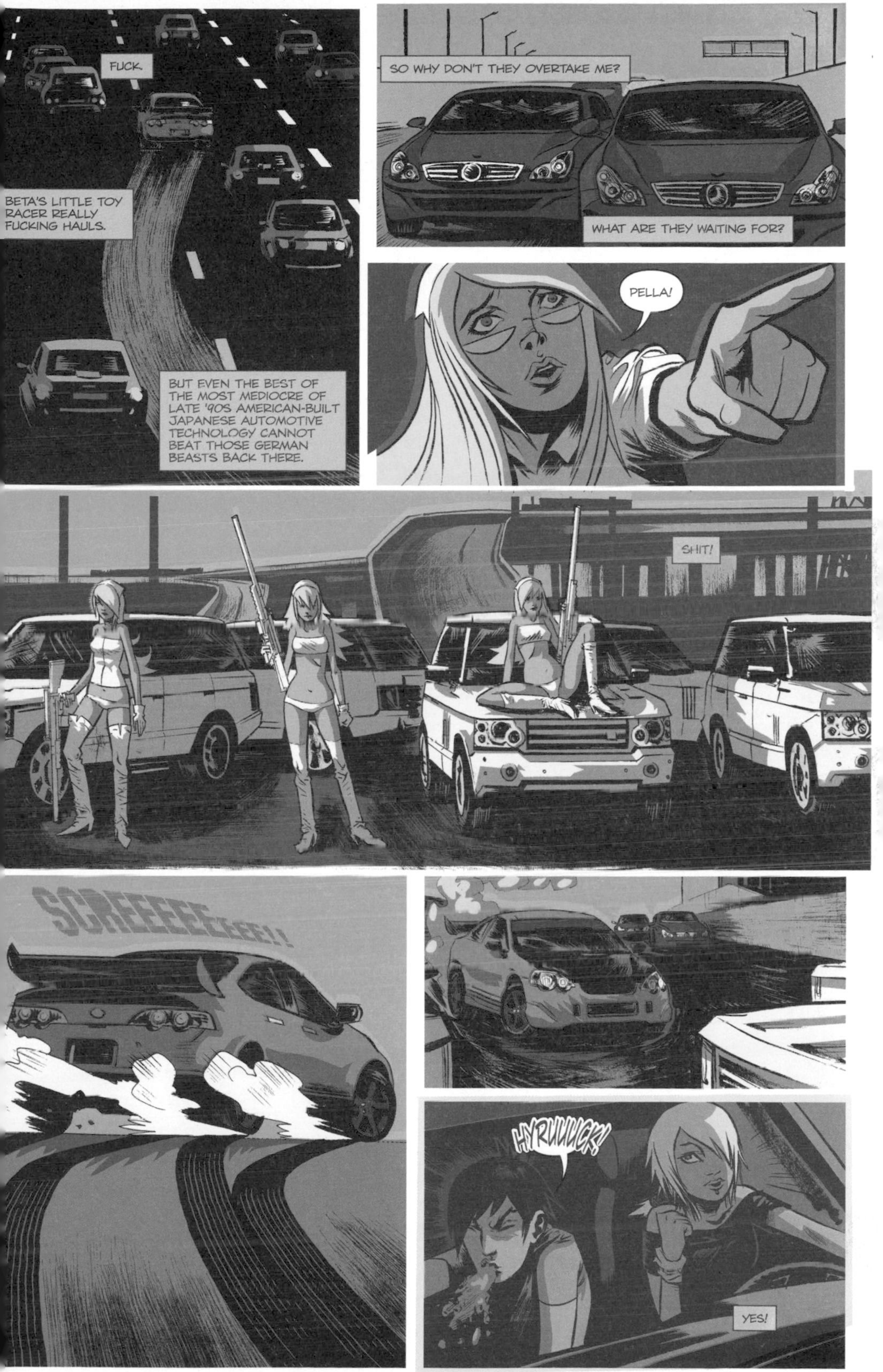
FUCK.
BETA'S LITTLE TOY RACER REALLY FUCKING HAULS.
BUT EVEN THE BEST OF THE MOST MEDIOCRE OF LATE '90S AMERICAN-BUILT JAPANESE AUTOMOTIVE TECHNOLOGY CANNOT BEAT THOSE GERMAN BEASTS BACK THERE.
SO WHY DON'T THEY OVERTAKE ME?
WHAT ARE THEY WAITING FOR?
PELLA!
SHIT!
SCREEEEEEEEE!!
HYRUUUCK!
YES!

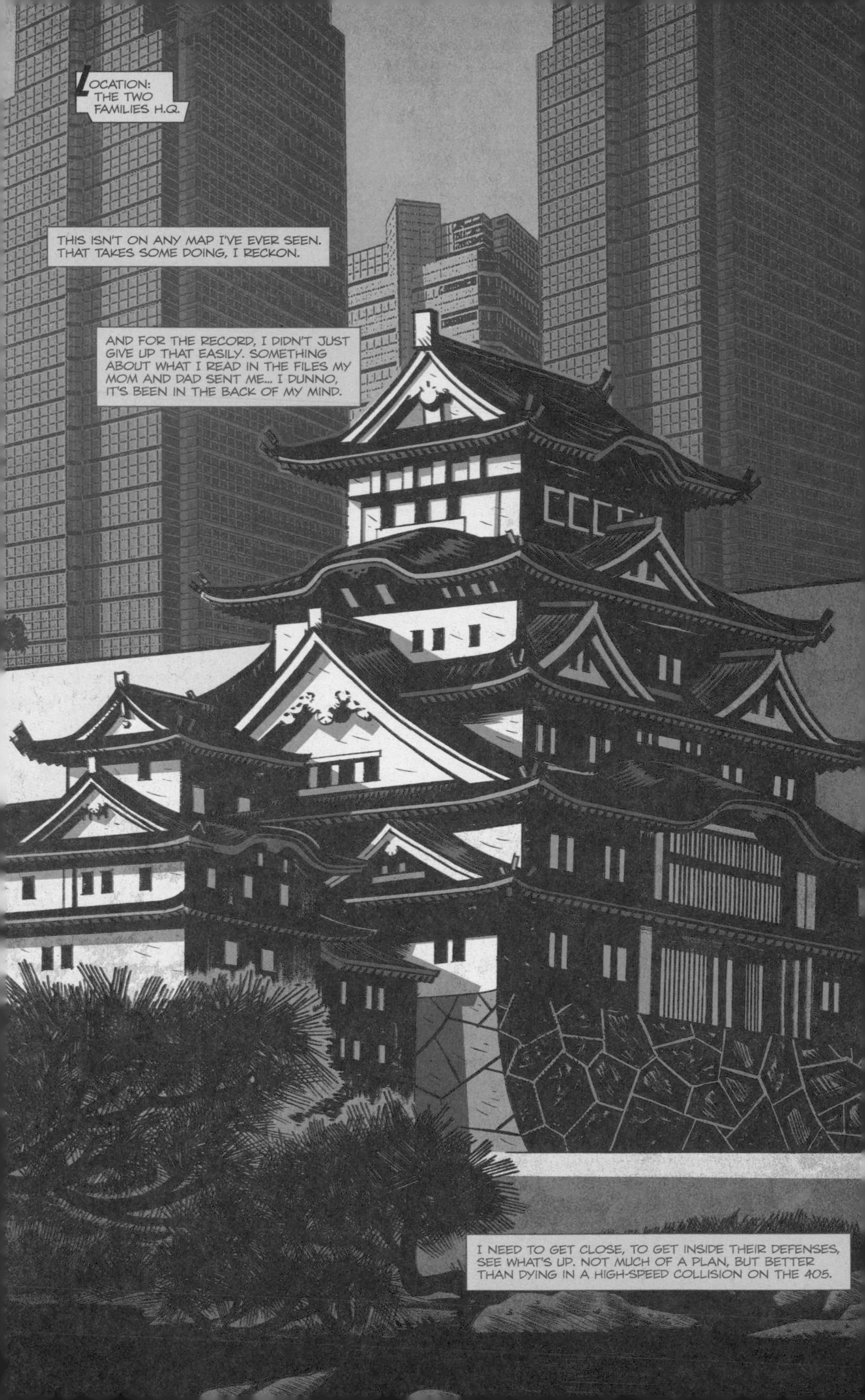
LOCATION: THE TWO FAMILIES H.Q.
THIS ISN'T ON ANY MAP I'VE EVER SEEN. THAT TAKES SOME DOING, I RECKON.
AND FOR THE RECORD, I DIDN'T JUST GIVE UP THAT EASILY. SOMETHING ABOUT WHAT I READ IN THE FILES MY MOM AND DAD SENT ME... I DUNNO, IT'S BEEN IN THE BACK OF MY MIND.
I NEED TO GET CLOSE, TO GET INSIDE THEIR DEFENSES, SEE WHAT'S UP. NOT MUCH OF A PLAN, BUT BETTER THAN DYING IN A HIGH-SPEED COLLISION ON THE 405.

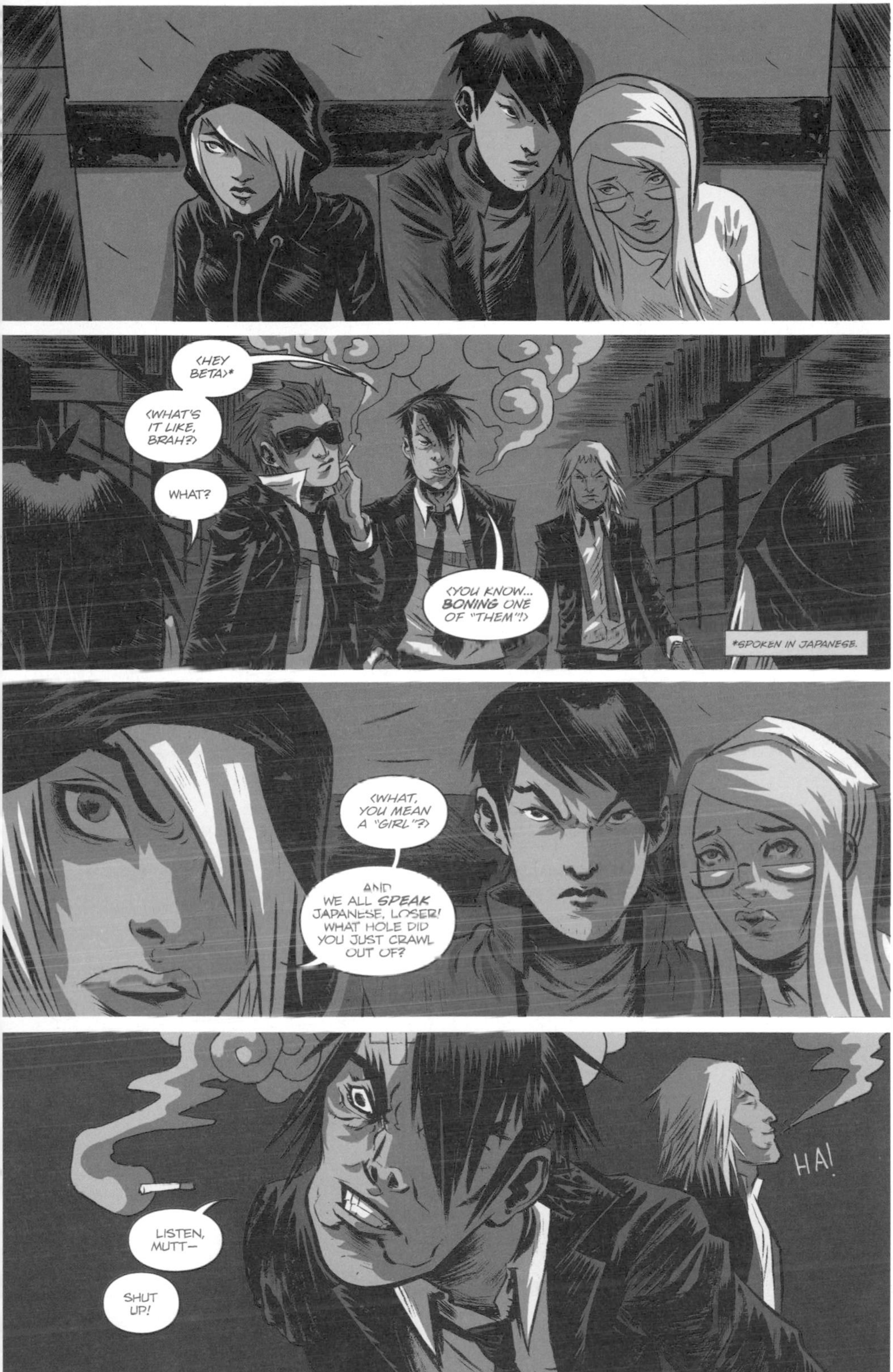
<HEY BETA>*
<WHAT'S IT LIKE, BRAH?>
WHAT?
<YOU KNOW... BONING ONE OF "THEM"!>
*SPOKEN IN JAPANESE.
<WHAT, YOU MEAN A "GIRL"?>
AND WE ALL SPEAK JAPANESE, LOSER! WHAT HOLE DID YOU JUST CRAWL OUT OF?
LISTEN, MUTT—
SHUT UP!
HA!

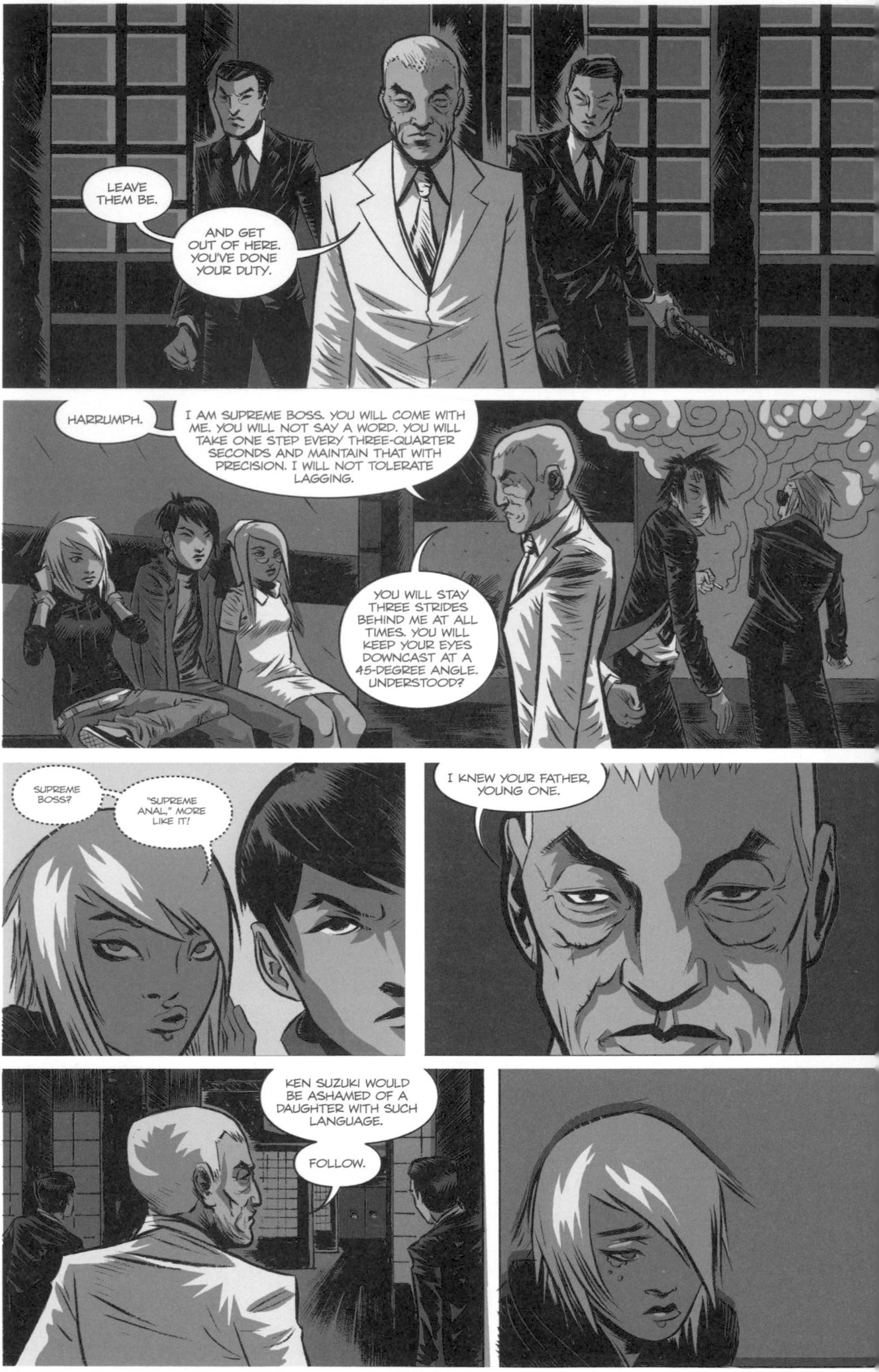
LEAVE THEM BE.
AND GET OUT OF HERE. YOU'VE DONE YOUR DUTY.
HARRUMPH.
I AM SUPREME BOSS. YOU WILL COME WITH ME. YOU WILL NOT SAY A WORD. YOU WILL TAKE ONE STEP EVERY THREE-QUARTER SECONDS AND MAINTAIN THAT WITH PRECISION. I WILL NOT TOLERATE LAGGING.
YOU WILL STAY THREE STRIDES BEHIND ME AT ALL TIMES. YOU WILL KEEP YOUR EYES DOWNCAST AT A 45-DEGREE ANGLE. UNDERSTOOD?
SUPREME BOSS?
"SUPREME ANAL," MORE LIKE IT!
I KNEW YOUR FATHER, YOUNG ONE.
KEN SUZUKI WOULD BE ASHAMED OF A DAUGHTER WITH SUCH LANGUAGE.
FOLLOW.

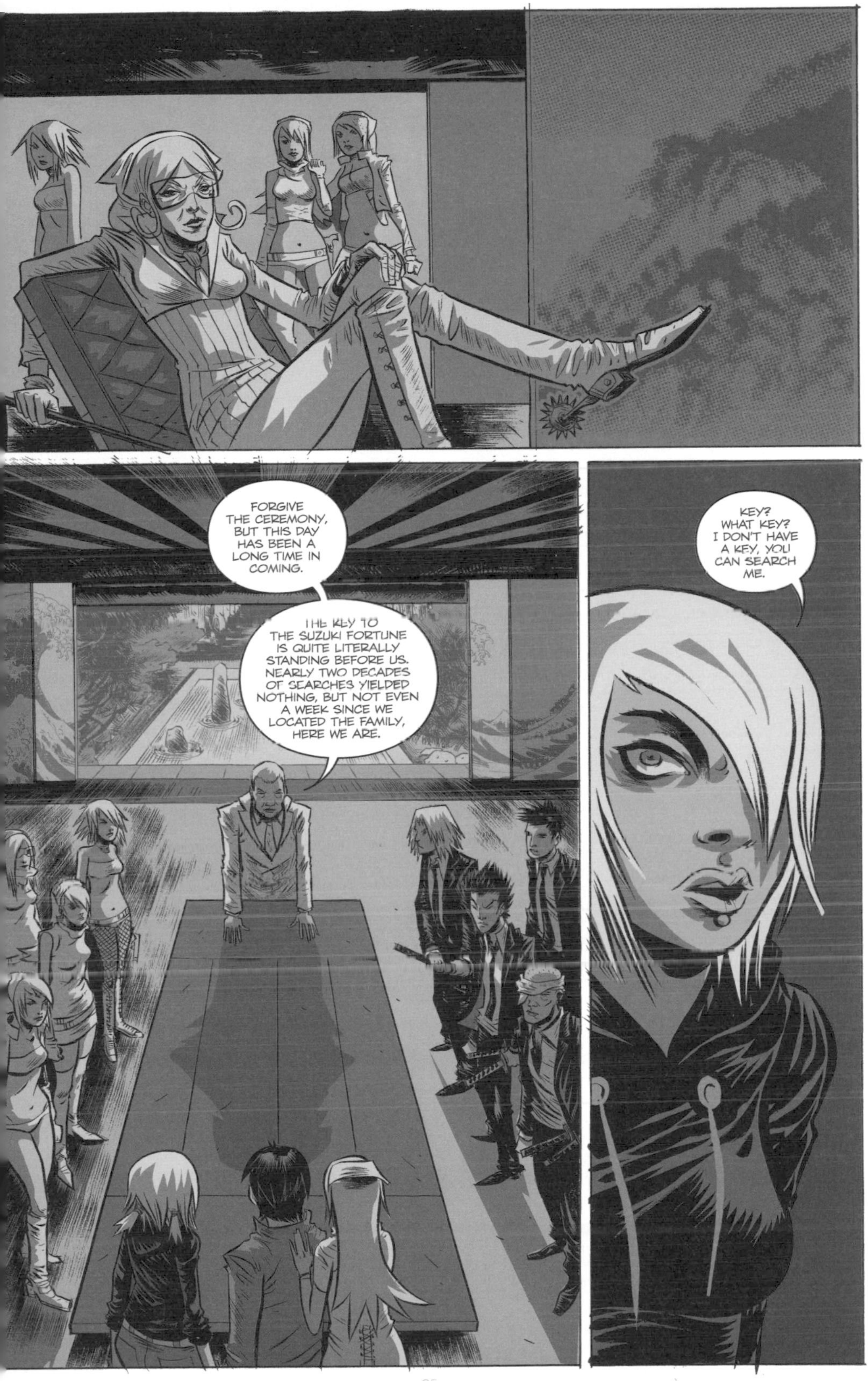
FORGIVE THE CEREMONY, BUT THIS DAY HAS BEEN A LONG TIME IN COMING.
THE KEY TO THE SUZUKI FORTUNE IS QUITE LITERALLY STANDING BEFORE US. NEARLY TWO DECADES OF SEARCHES YIELDED NOTHING, BUT NOT EVEN A WEEK SINCE WE LOCATED THE FAMILY, HERE WE ARE.
KEY? WHAT KEY? I DON'T HAVE A KEY, YOU CAN SEARCH ME.

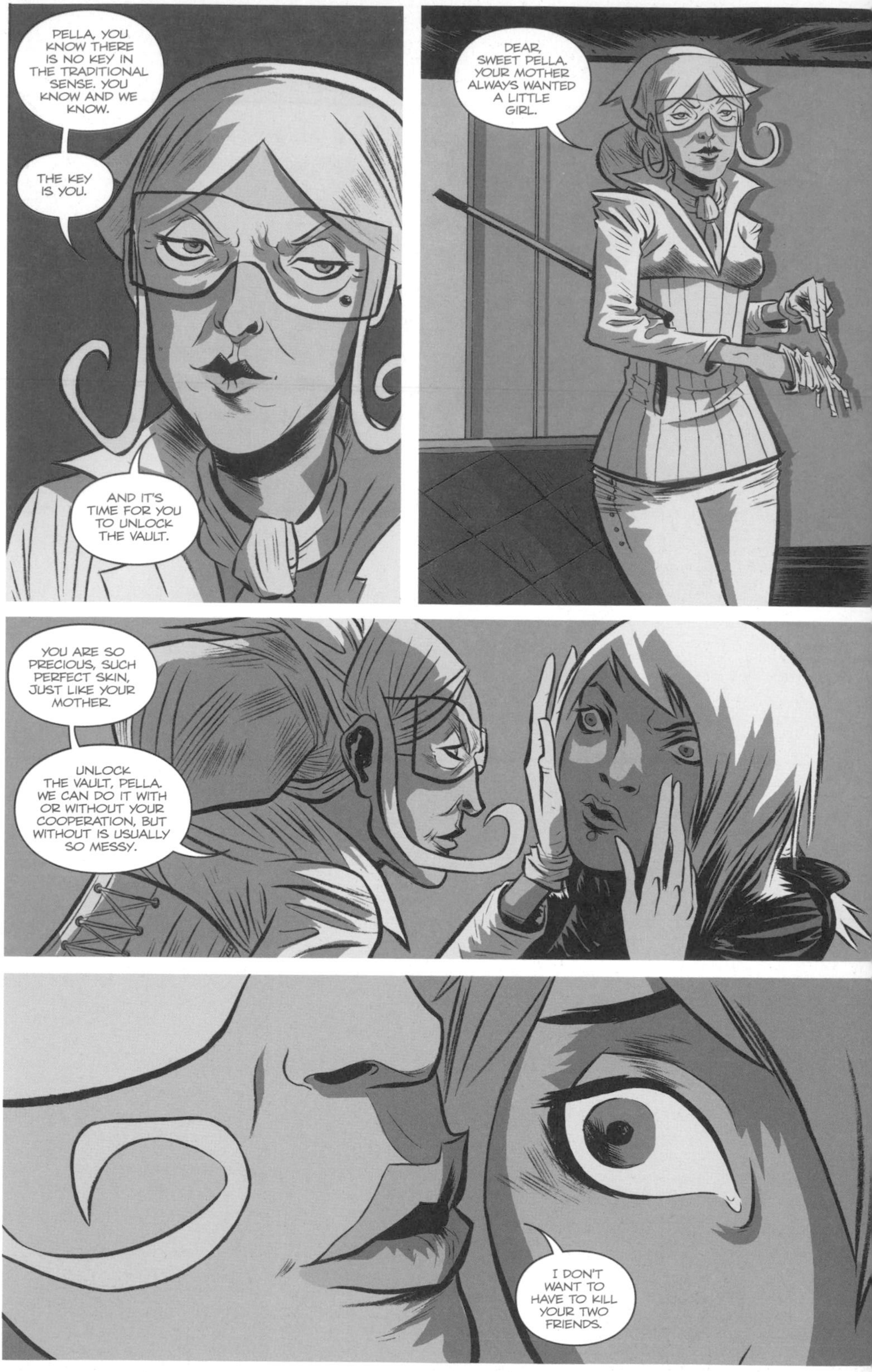

PELLA, YOU KNOW THERE IS NO KEY IN THE TRADITIONAL SENSE. YOU KNOW AND WE KNOW.
THE KEY IS YOU.
AND IT'S TIME FOR YOU TO UNLOCK THE VAULT.
DEAR, SWEET PELLA. YOUR MOTHER ALWAYS WANTED A LITTLE GIRL.
YOU ARE SO PRECIOUS, SUCH PERFECT SKIN, JUST LIKE YOUR MOTHER.
UNLOCK THE VAULT, PELLA. WE CAN DO IT WITH OR WITHOUT YOUR COOPERATION, BUT WITHOUT IS USUALLY SO MESSY.
I DON'T WANT TO HAVE TO KILL YOUR TWO FRIENDS.

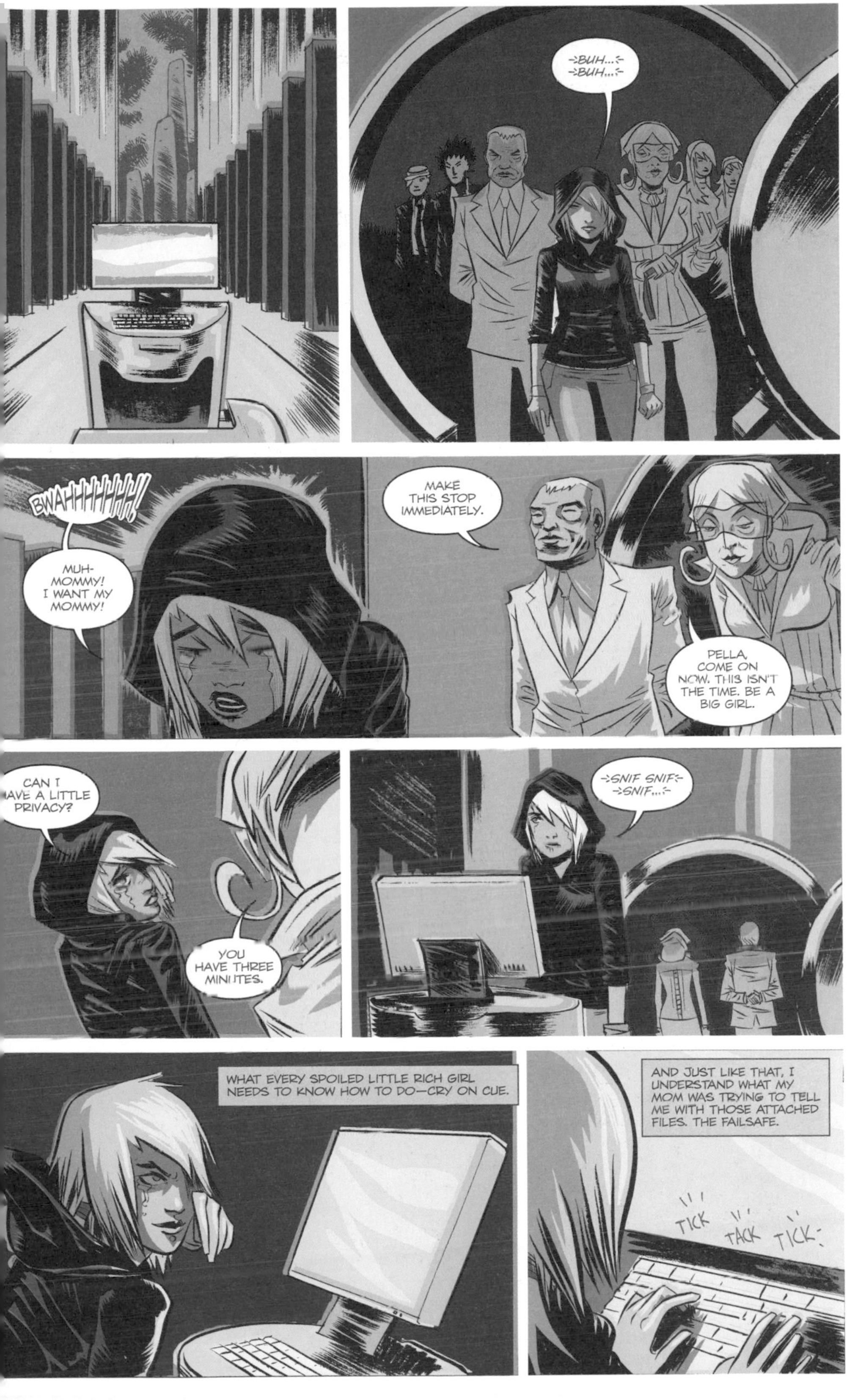

-BUH...-
-BUH...-
BWAHHHHHH!
MUH-MOMMY! I WANT MY MOMMY!
MAKE THIS STOP IMMEDIATELY.
PELLA, COME ON NOW. THIS ISN'T THE TIME. BE A BIG GIRL.
CAN I AVE A LITTLE PRIVACY?
YOU HAVE THREE MINUTES.
-SNIF SNIF-
-SNIF...-
WHAT EVERY SPOILED LITTLE RICH GIRL NEEDS TO KNOW HOW TO DO—CRY ON CUE.
AND JUST LIKE THAT, I UNDERSTAND WHAT MY MOM WAS TRYING TO TELL ME WITH THOSE ATTACHED FILES. THE FAILSAFE.
TICK
TACK
TICK

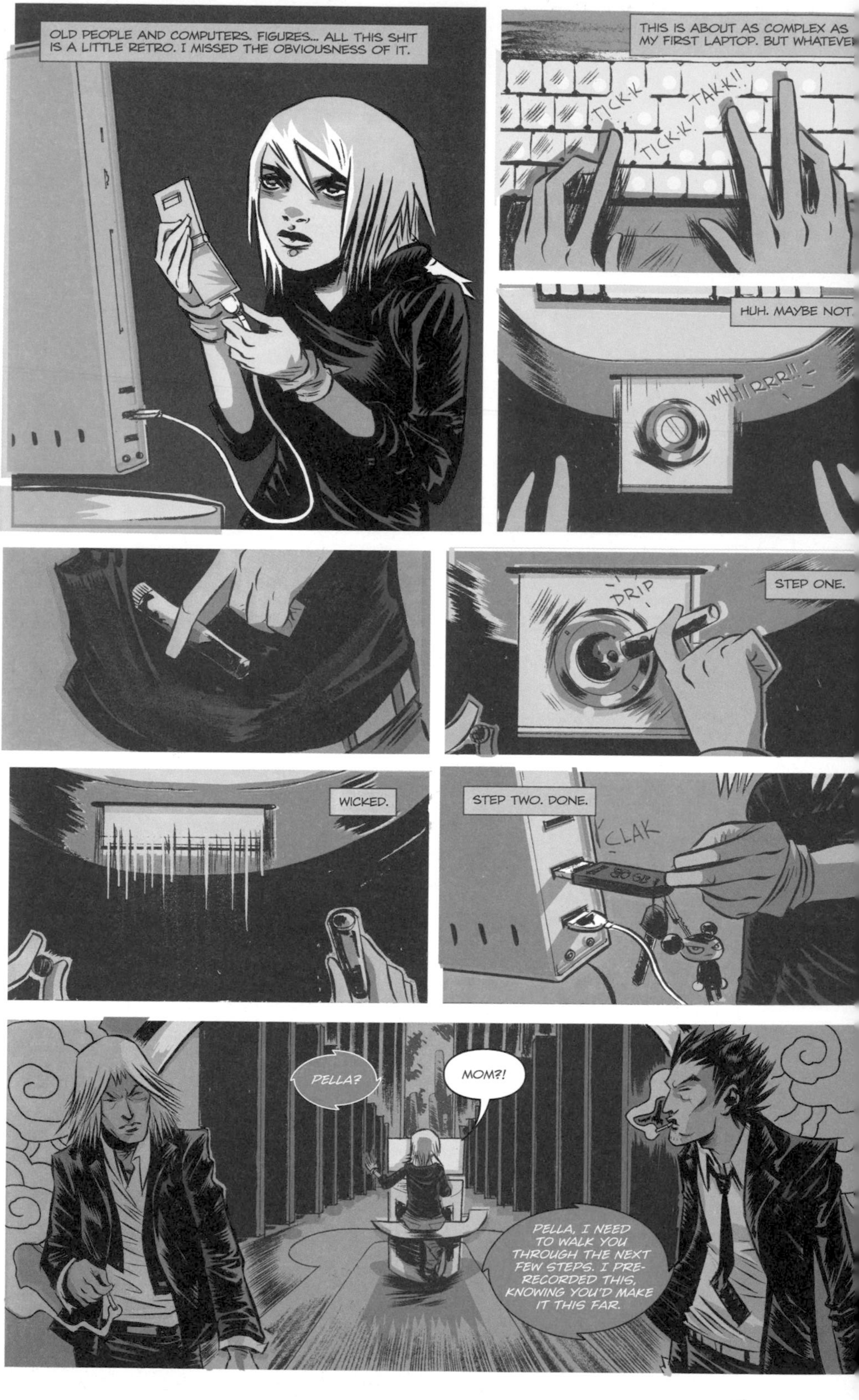

OLD PEOPLE AND COMPUTERS. FIGURES... ALL THIS SHIT IS A LITTLE RETRO. I MISSED THE OBVIOUSNESS OF IT.
THIS IS ABOUT AS COMPLEX AS MY FIRST LAPTOP. BUT WHATEVER
TICK-K
TICK-K!
TAKK!!
HUH. MAYBE NOT.
WHHIRRR!!
STEP ONE.
DRIP
WICKED.
STEP TWO. DONE.
CLAK
PELLA?
MOM?!
PELLA, I NEED TO WALK YOU THROUGH THE NEXT FEW STEPS. I PRE-RECORDED THIS, KNOWING YOU'D MAKE IT THIS FAR.

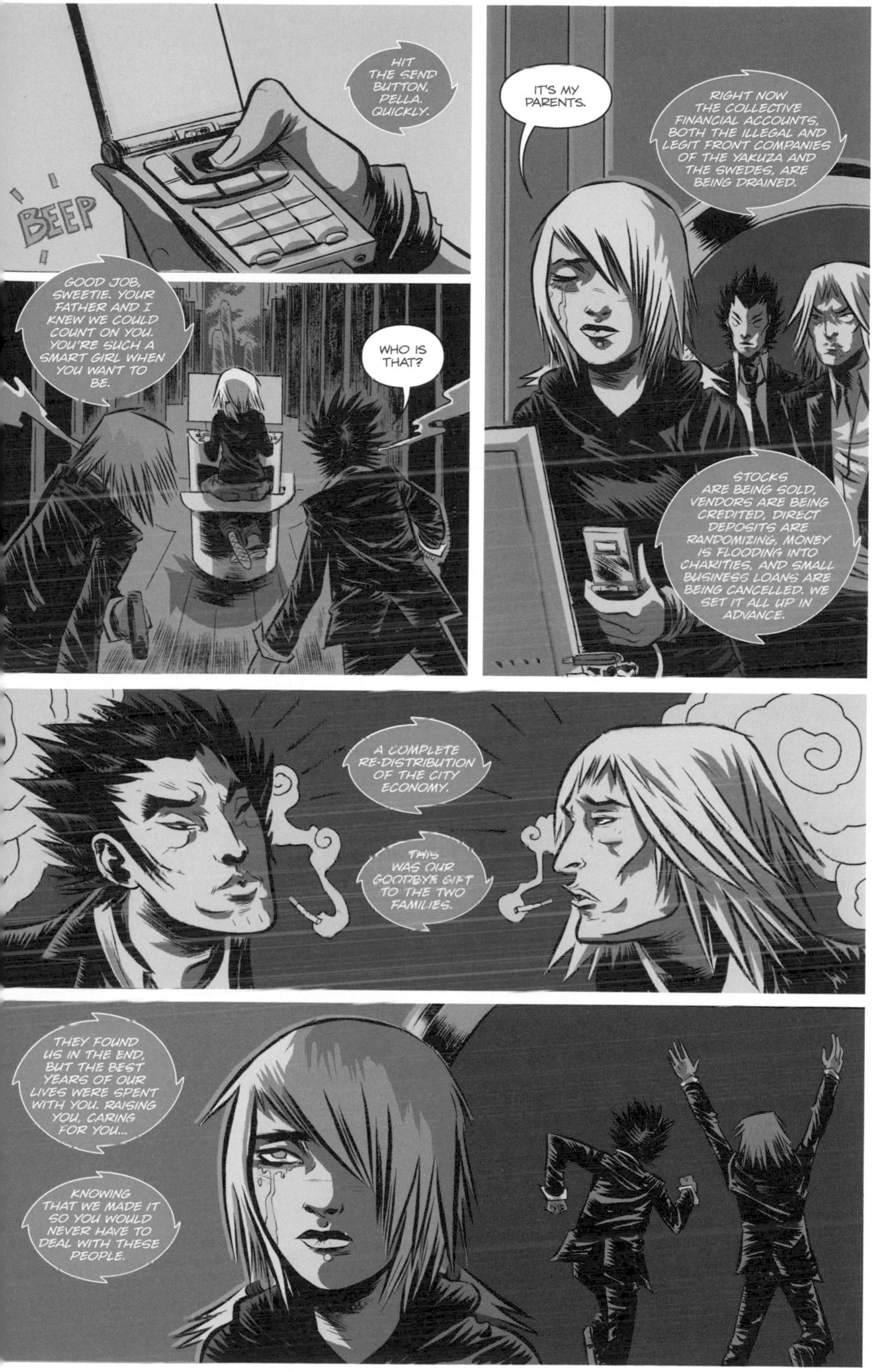
HIT THE SEND BUTTON, PELLA. QUICKLY.
BEEP
GOOD JOB, SWEETIE. YOUR FATHER AND I KNEW WE COULD COUNT ON YOU. YOU'RE SUCH A SMART GIRL WHEN YOU WANT TO BE.
WHO IS THAT?
IT'S MY PARENTS.
RIGHT NOW THE COLLECTIVE FINANCIAL ACCOUNTS, BOTH THE ILLEGAL AND LEGIT FRONT COMPANIES OF THE YAKUZA AND THE SWEDES, ARE BEING DRAINED.
STOCKS ARE BEING SOLD, VENDORS ARE BEING CREDITED, DIRECT DEPOSITS ARE RANDOMIZING, MONEY IS FLOODING INTO CHARITIES, AND SMALL BUSINESS LOANS ARE BEING CANCELLED. WE SET IT ALL UP IN ADVANCE.
A COMPLETE RE-DISTRIBUTION OF THE CITY ECONOMY.
THIS WAS OUR GOODBYE GIFT TO THE TWO FAMILIES.
THEY FOUND US IN THE END, BUT THE BEST YEARS OF OUR LIVES WERE SPENT WITH YOU. RAISING YOU, CARING FOR YOU...
KNOWING THAT WE MADE IT SO YOU WOULD NEVER HAVE TO DEAL WITH THESE PEOPLE.

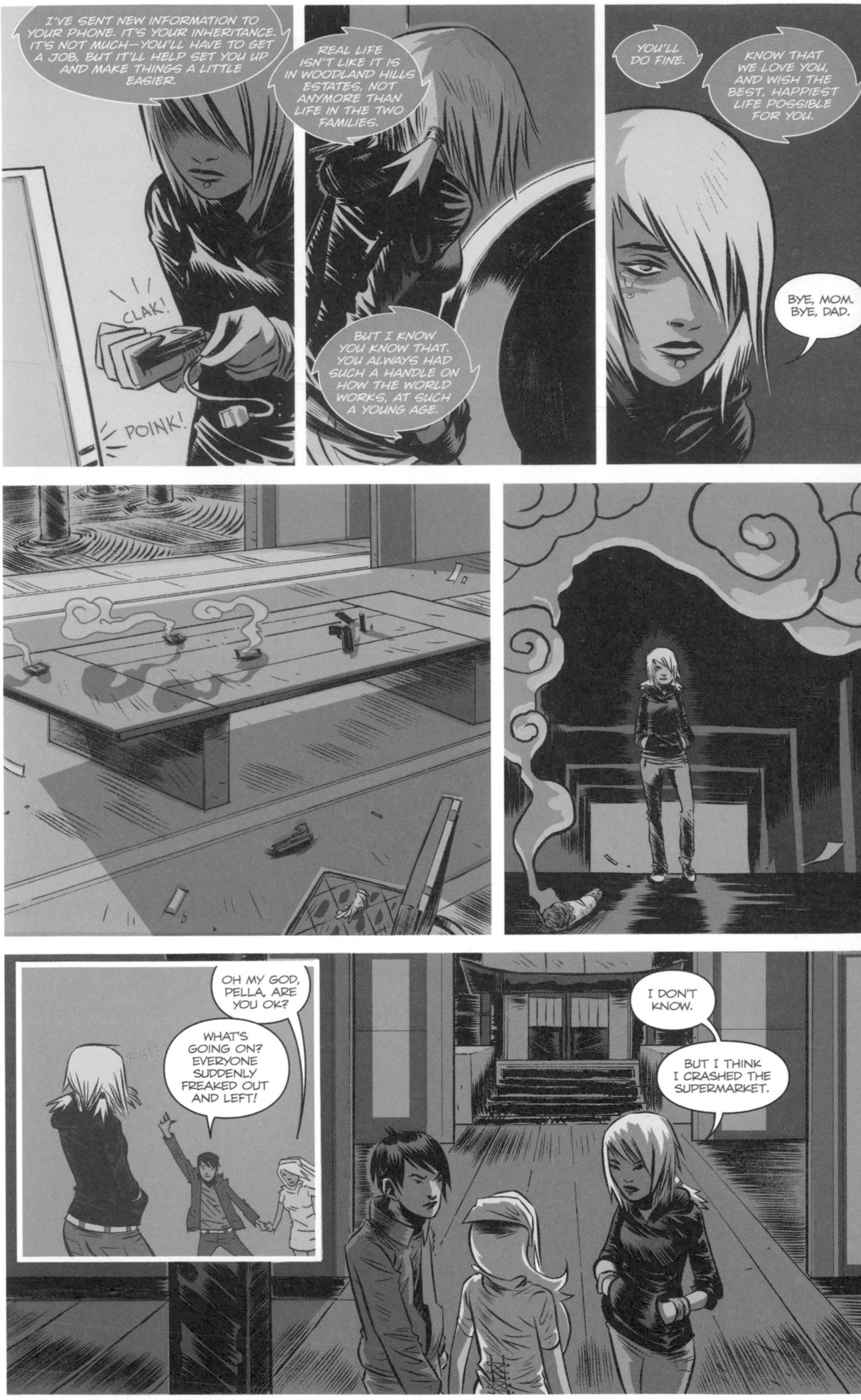
I'VE SENT NEW INFORMATION TO YOUR PHONE. IT'S YOUR INHERITANCE. IT'S NOT MUCH—YOU'LL HAVE TO GET A JOB, BUT IT'LL HELP SET YOU UP AND MAKE THINGS A LITTLE EASIER.
CLAK!
POINK!
REAL LIFE ISN'T LIKE IT IS IN WOODLAND HILLS ESTATES, NOT ANYMORE THAN LIFE IN THE TWO FAMILIES.
BUT I KNOW YOU KNOW THAT. YOU ALWAYS HAD SUCH A HANDLE ON HOW THE WORLD WORKS, AT SUCH A YOUNG AGE.
YOU'LL DO FINE.
KNOW THAT WE LOVE YOU, AND WISH THE BEST, HAPPIEST LIFE POSSIBLE FOR YOU.
BYE, MOM. BYE, DAD.
OH MY GOD, PELLA, ARE YOU OK?
WHAT'S GOING ON? EVERYONE SUDDENLY FREAKED OUT AND LEFT!
I DON'T KNOW.
BUT I THINK I CRASHED THE SUPERMARKET.

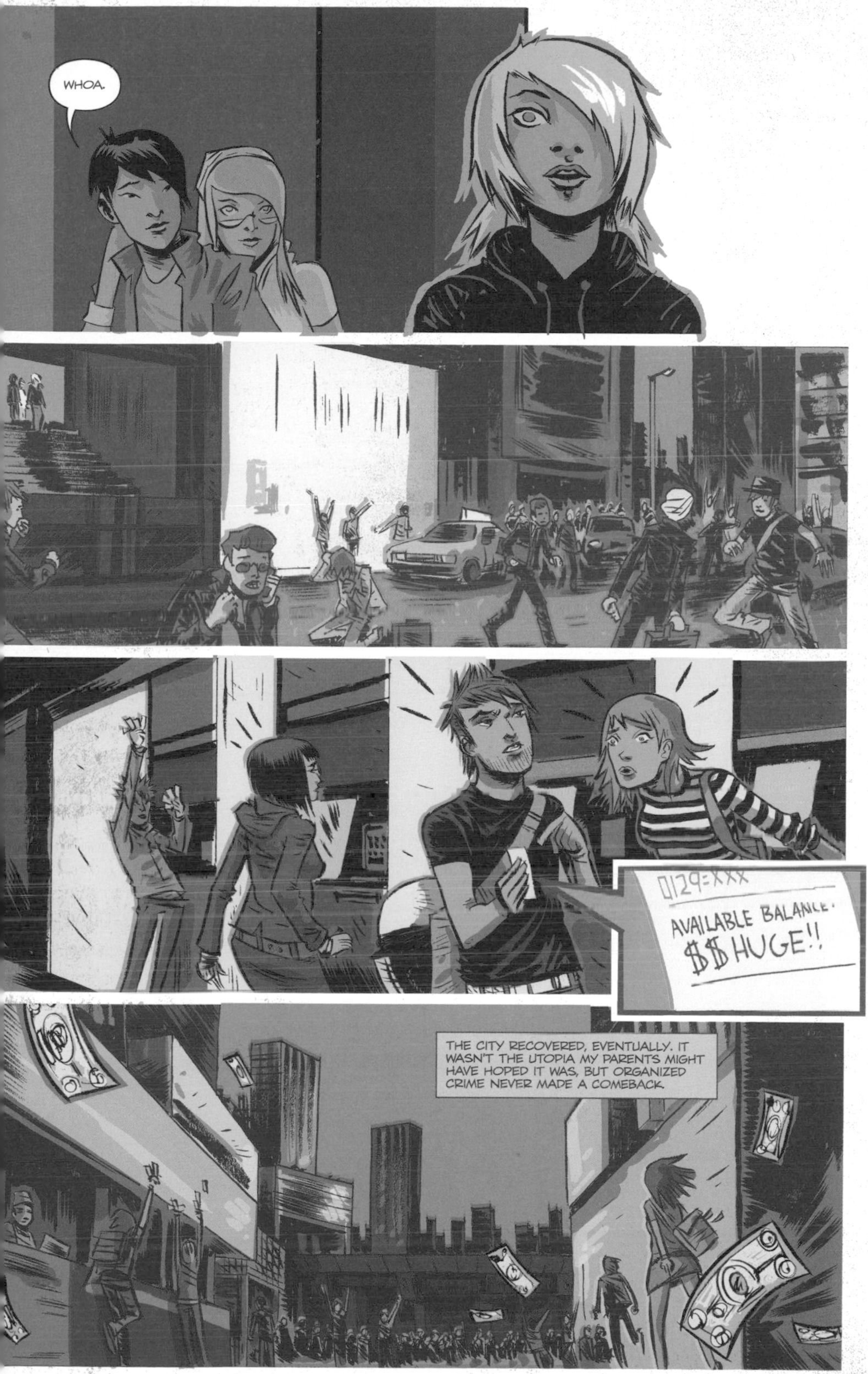
WHOA.
0129=XXX
AVAILABLE BALANCE:
$$ HUGE!!
THE CITY RECOVERED, EVENTUALLY. IT WASN'T THE UTOPIA MY PARENTS MIGHT HAVE HOPED IT WAS, BUT ORGANIZED CRIME NEVER MADE A COMEBACK.

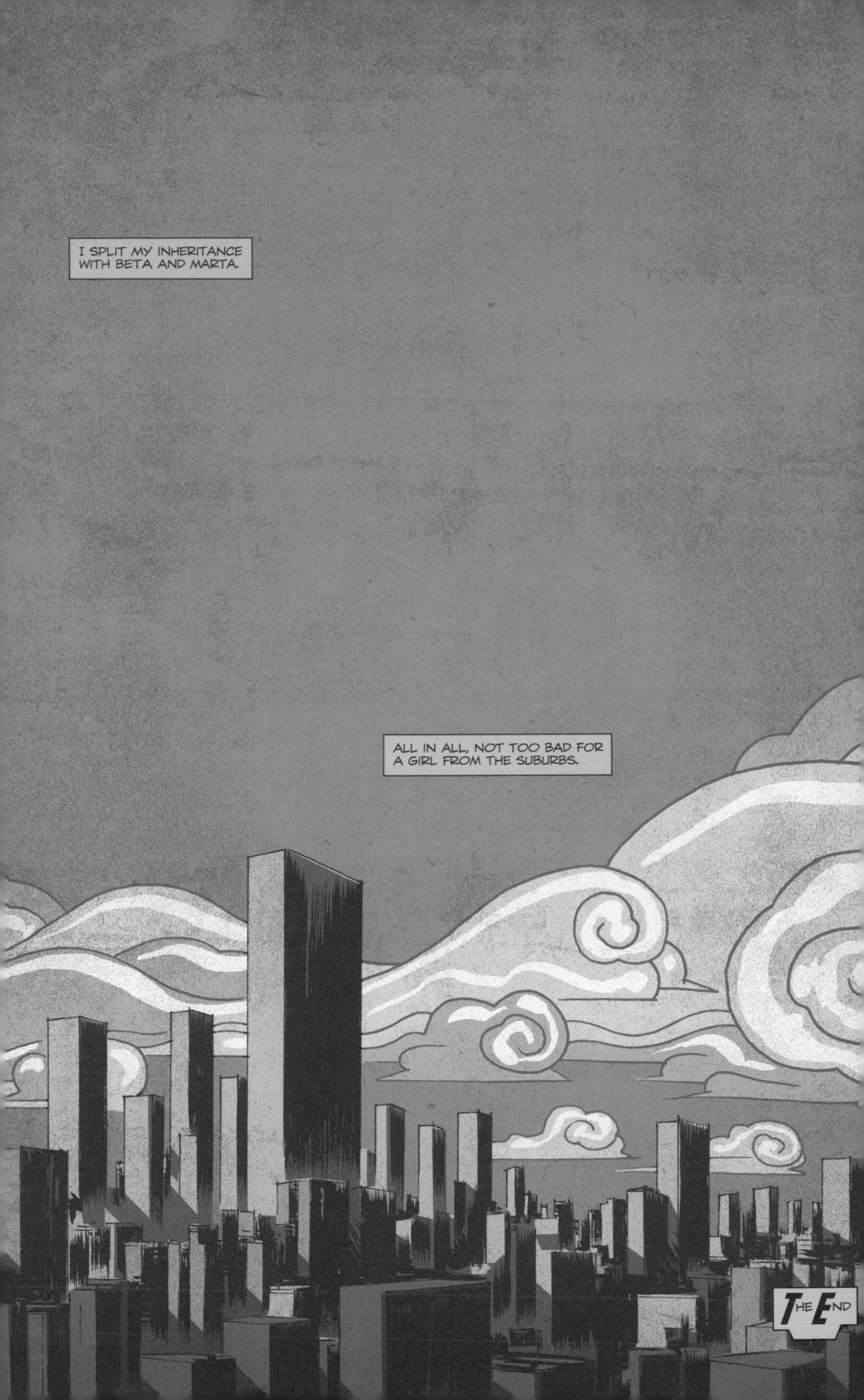
I SPLIT MY INHERITANCE WITH BETA AND MARTA.
ALL IN ALL, NOT TOO BAD FOR A GIRL FROM THE SUBURBS.
THE END

SUPERMARKET ART GALLERY

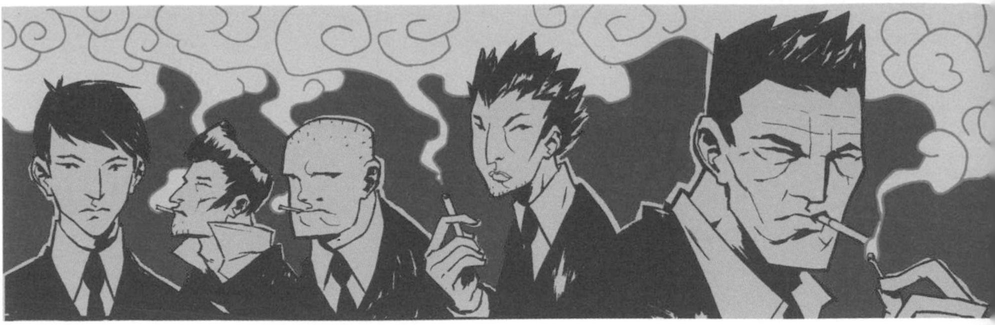

SUPERMARKET™

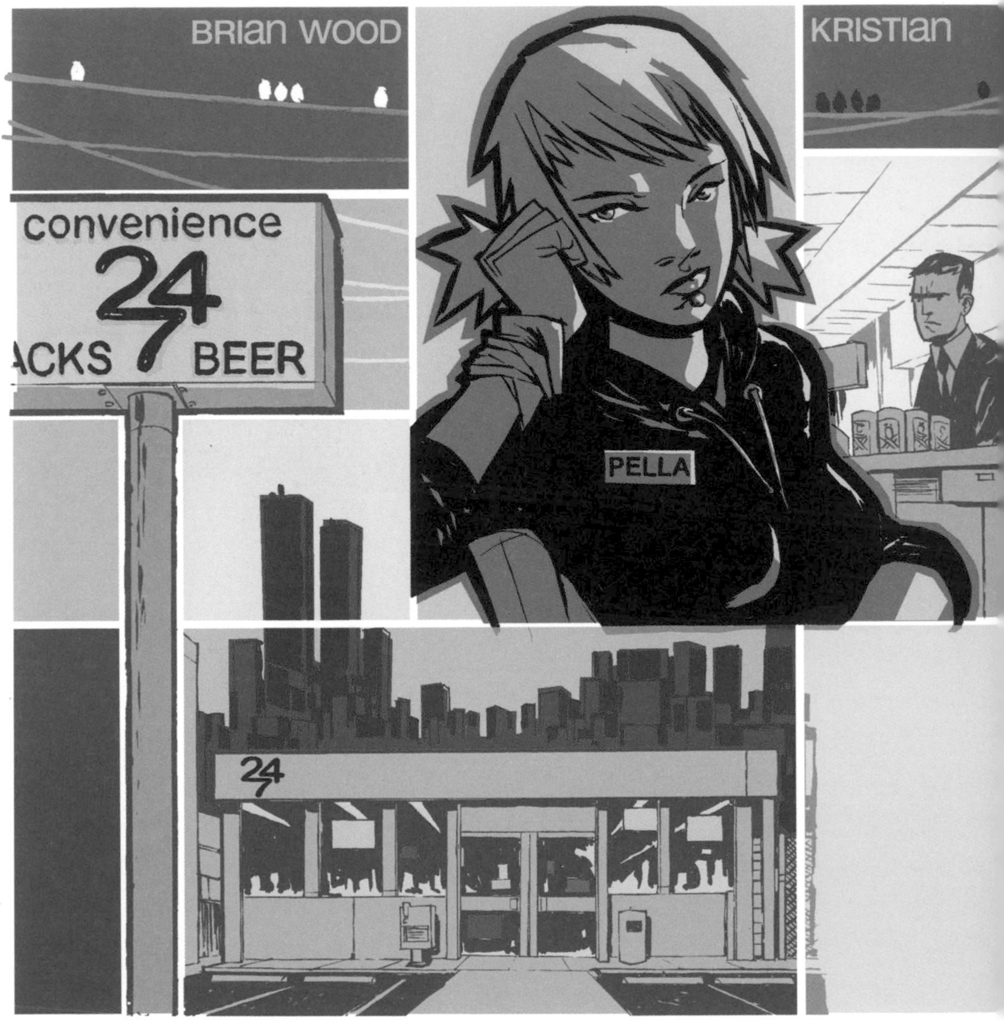

BRIAN WOOD
KRISTIAN
convenience
24
7
ACKS
BEER
PELLA
24
7

art by KRISTIAN DONALDSON

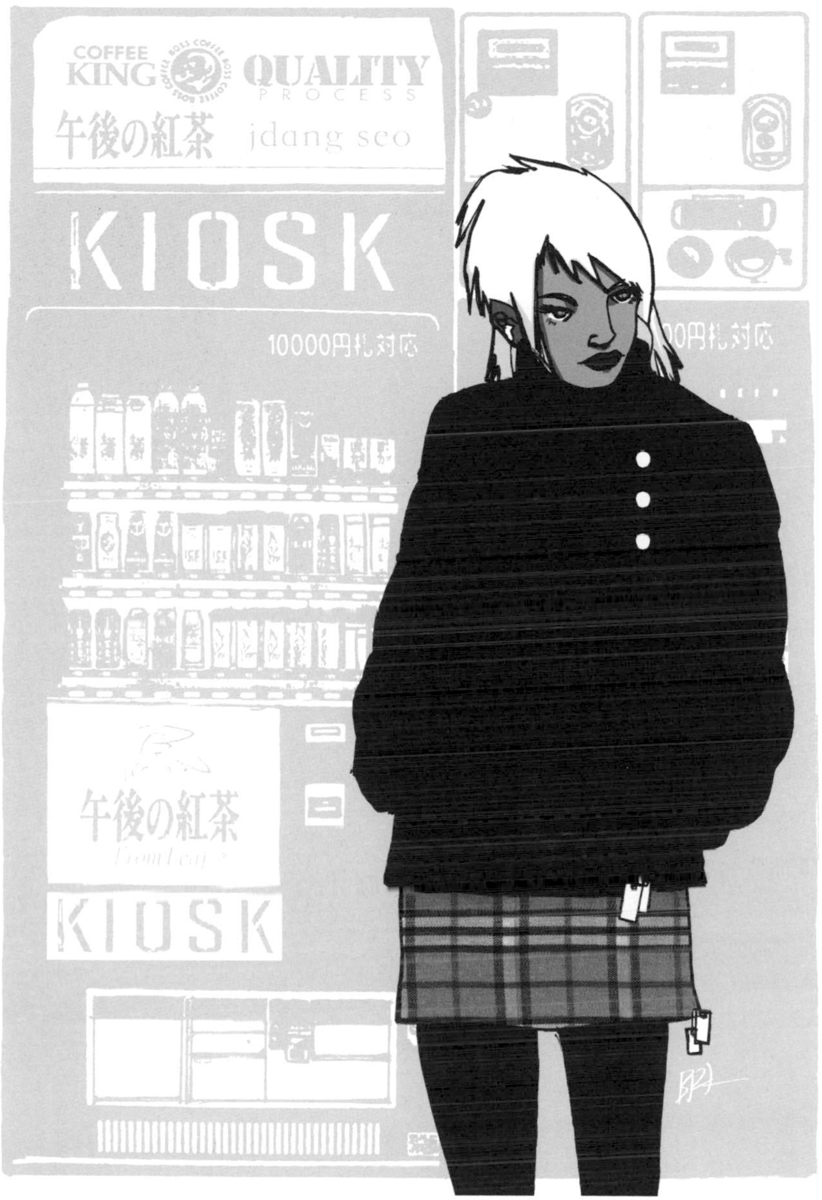
COFFEE KING
QUALITY PROCESS
午後の紅茶
jdang seo
KIOSK
10000円札対応
午後の紅茶
KIOSK

art by BRIAN WOOD

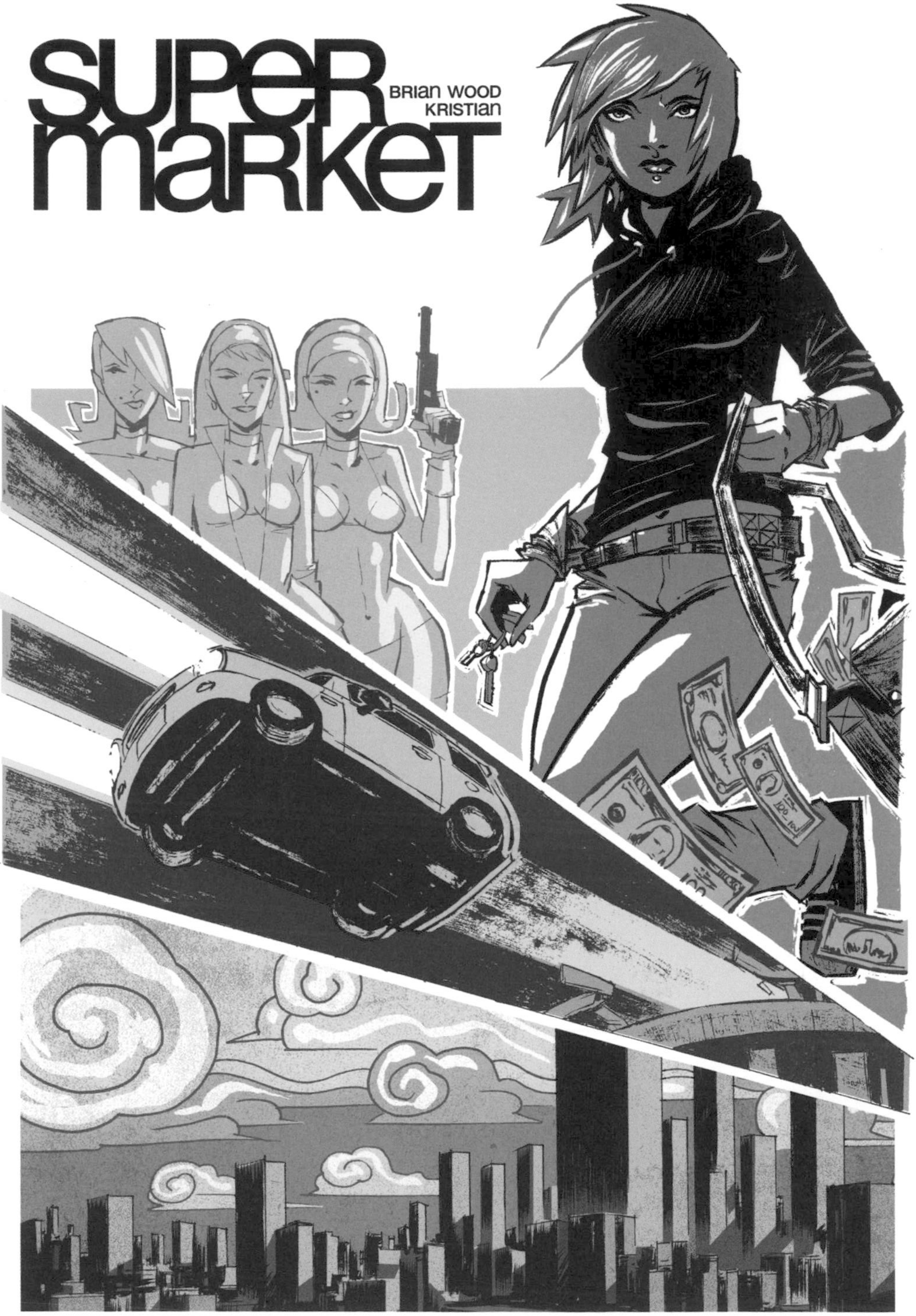
SUPER
market
BRIAN WOOD
KRISTIAN

art by KRISTIAN DONALDSON

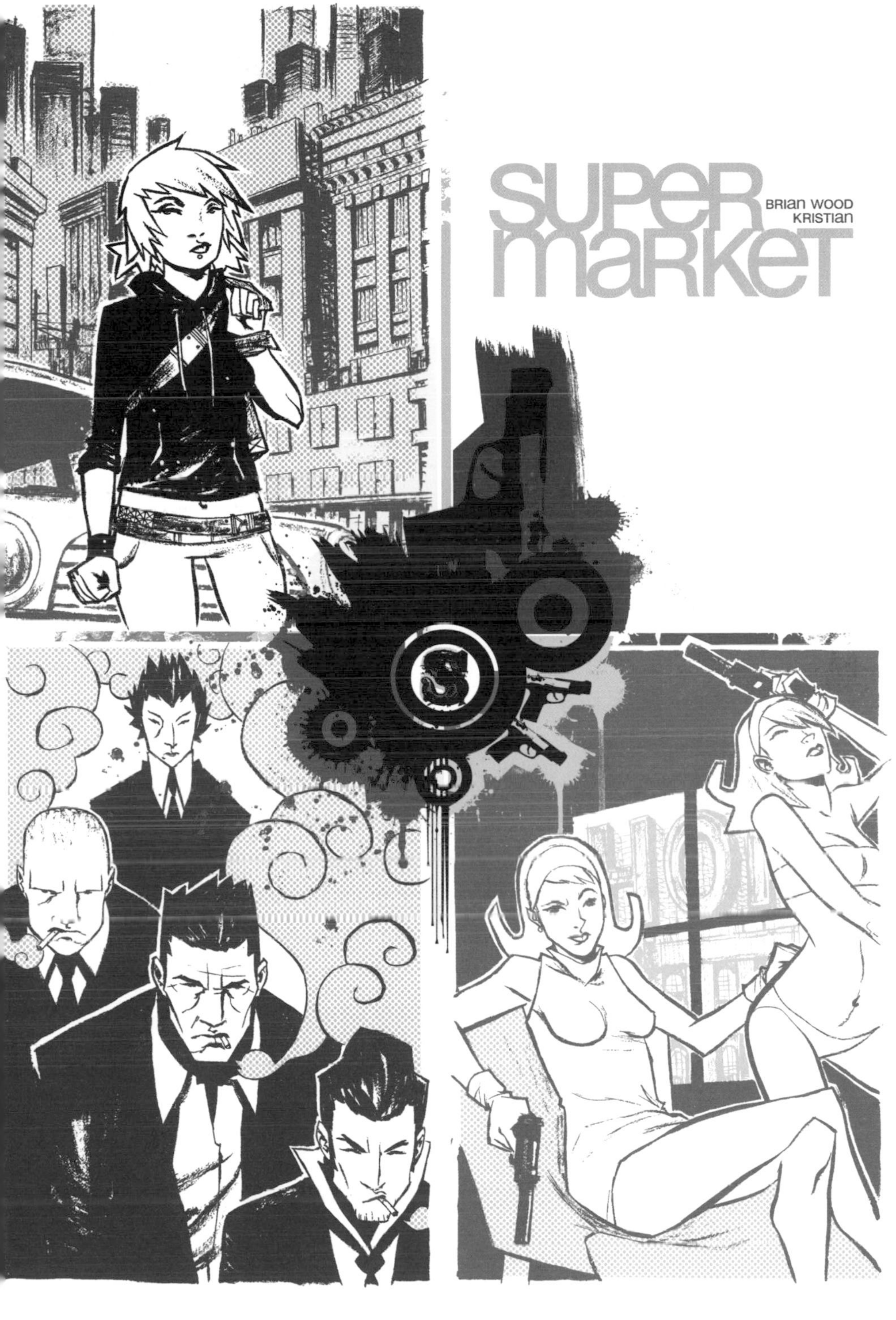
SUPER
MARKET
BRIAN WOOD
KRISTIAN

art by KRISTIAN DONALDSON

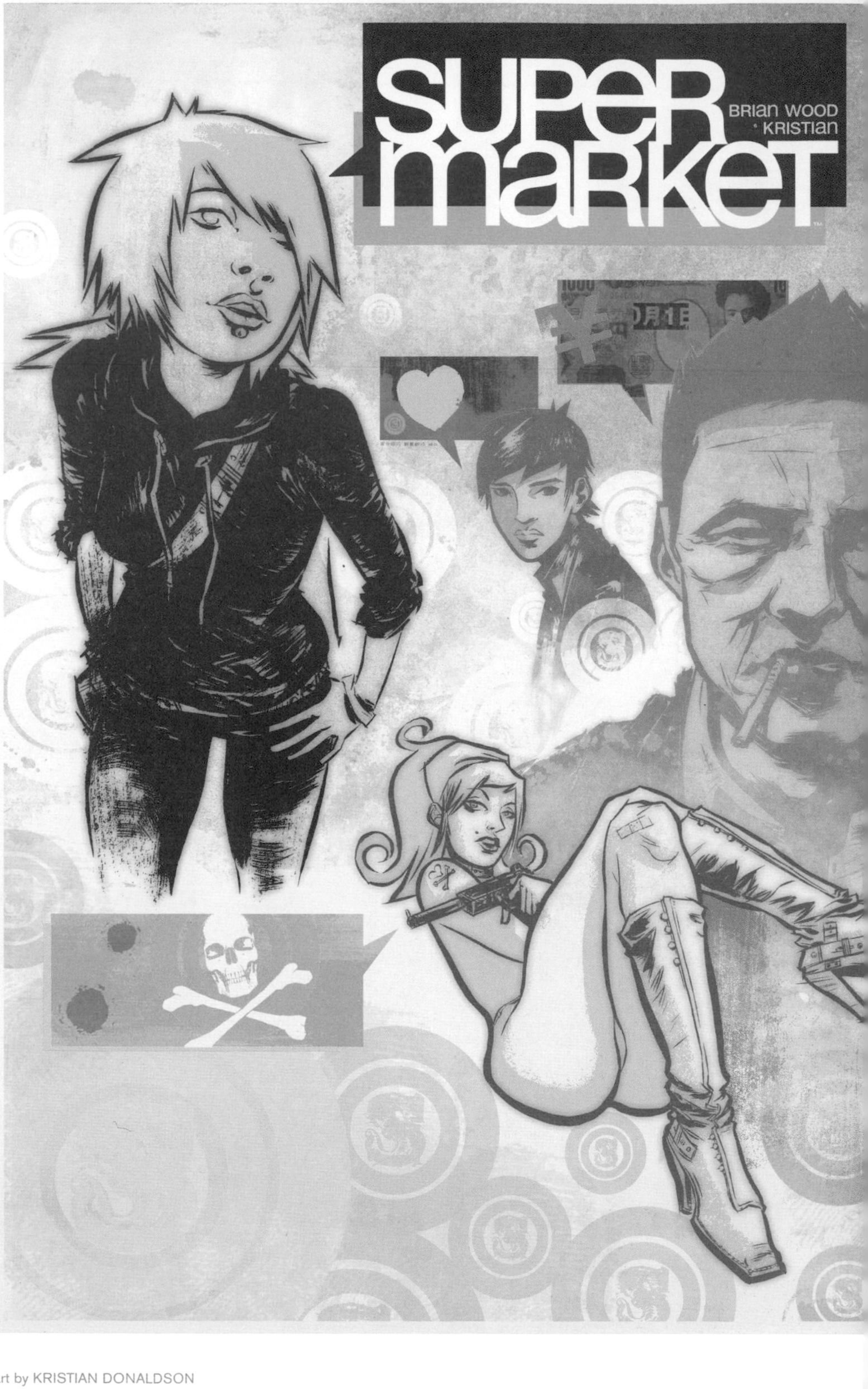
SUPER
market
BRIAN WOOD
KRISTIAN

art by KRISTIAN DONALDSON

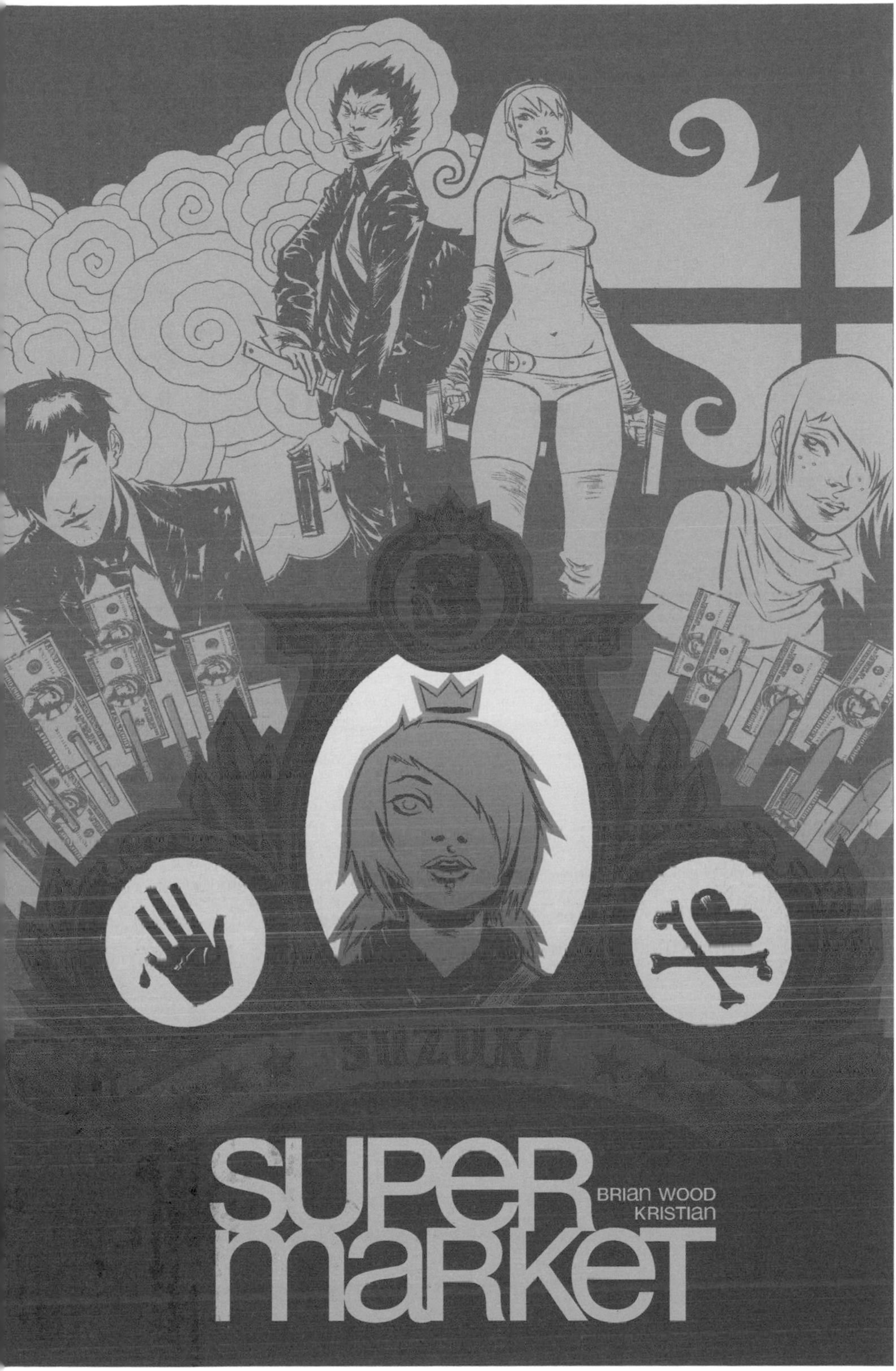
SUZUKI
SUPER
market
BRIAN WOOD
KRISTIAN

art by KRISTIAN DONALDSON

SUPERMARKET PIN-UP GALLERY

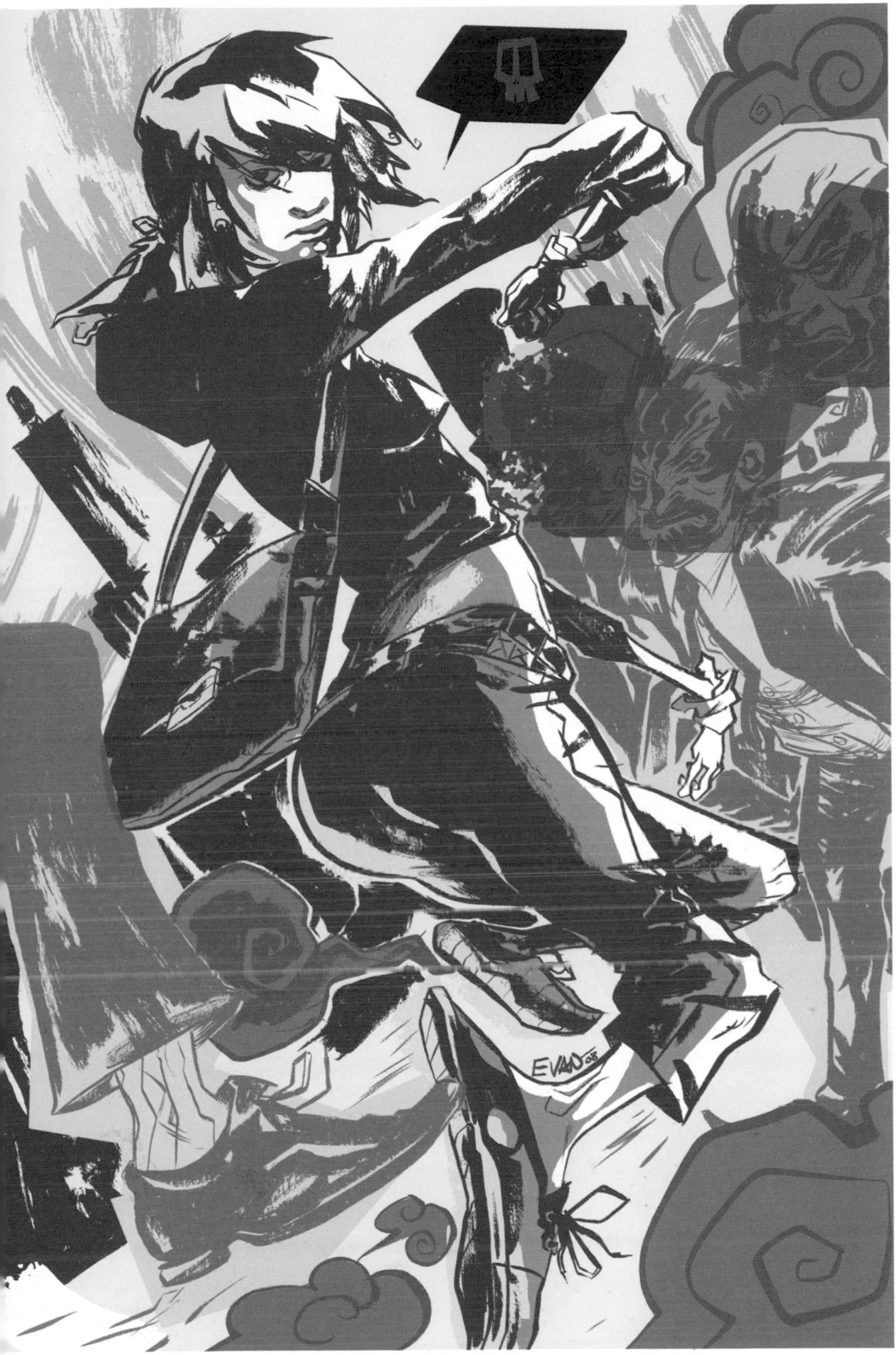

art by EVAN BRYCE

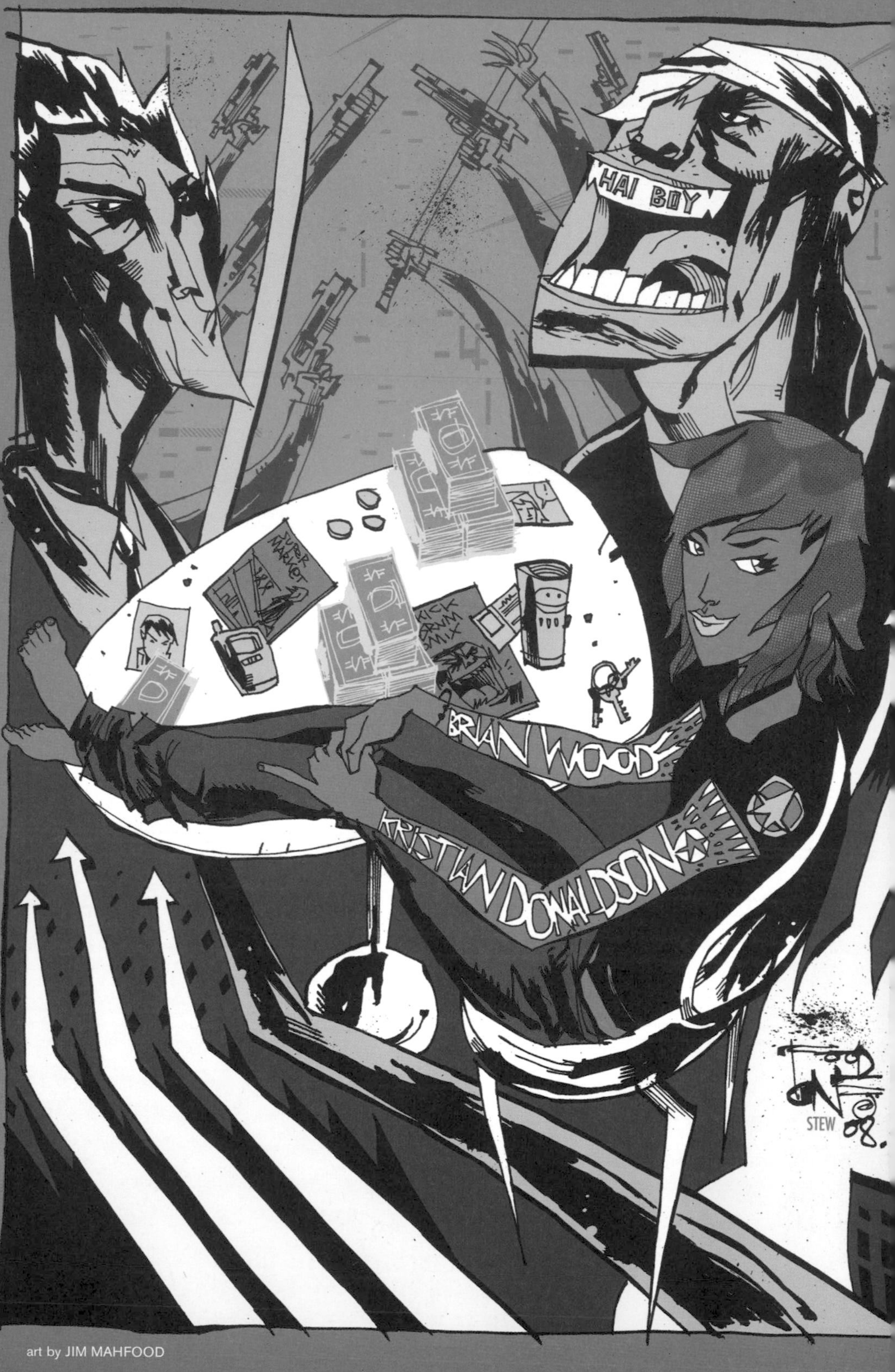
HAI BOY
SUPER MARKET
KICK
BRIAN WOOD
KRISTIAN DONALDSON
STEW
08

art by JIM MAHFOOD

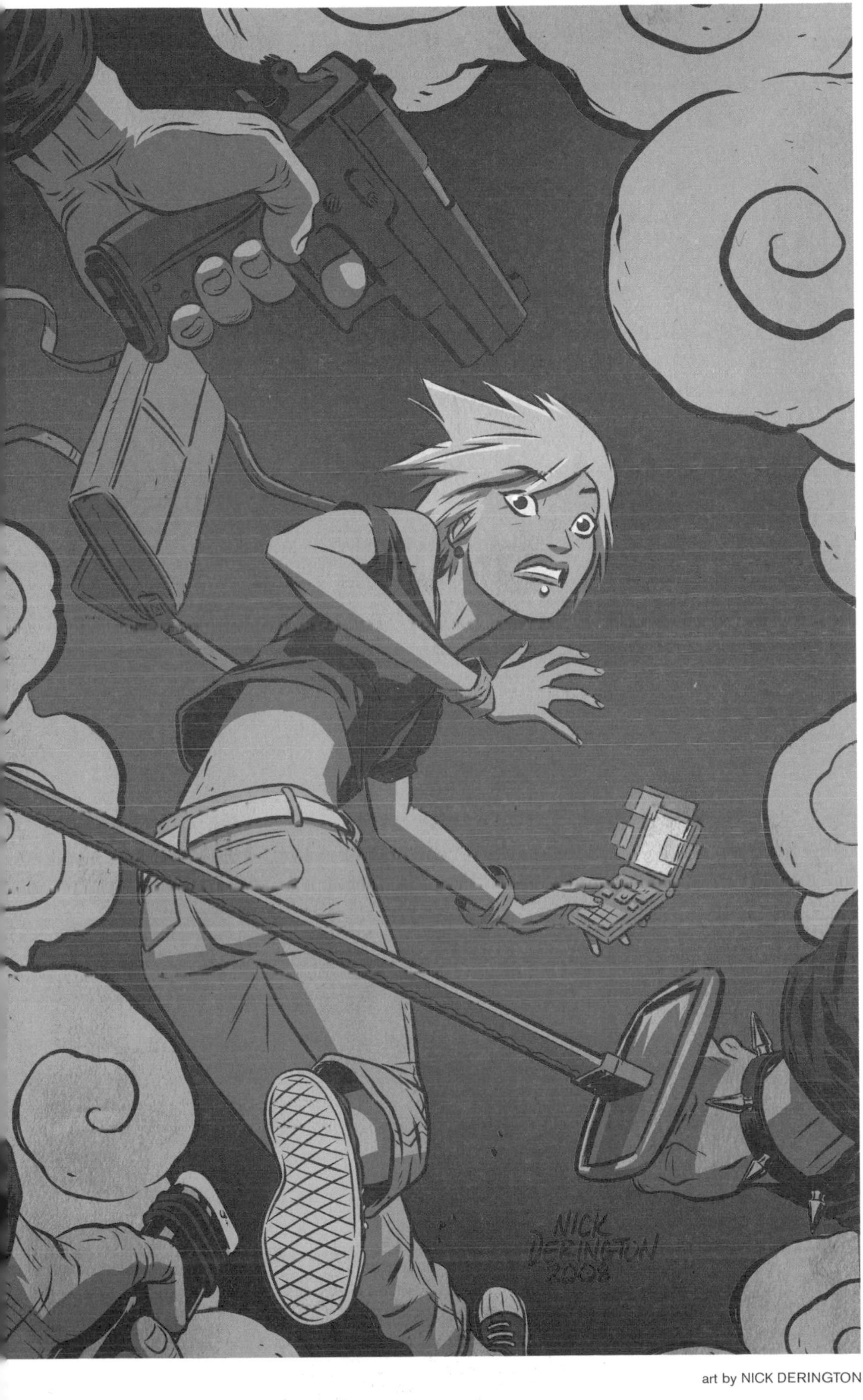
NICK DERINGTON 2008

art by NICK DERINGTON

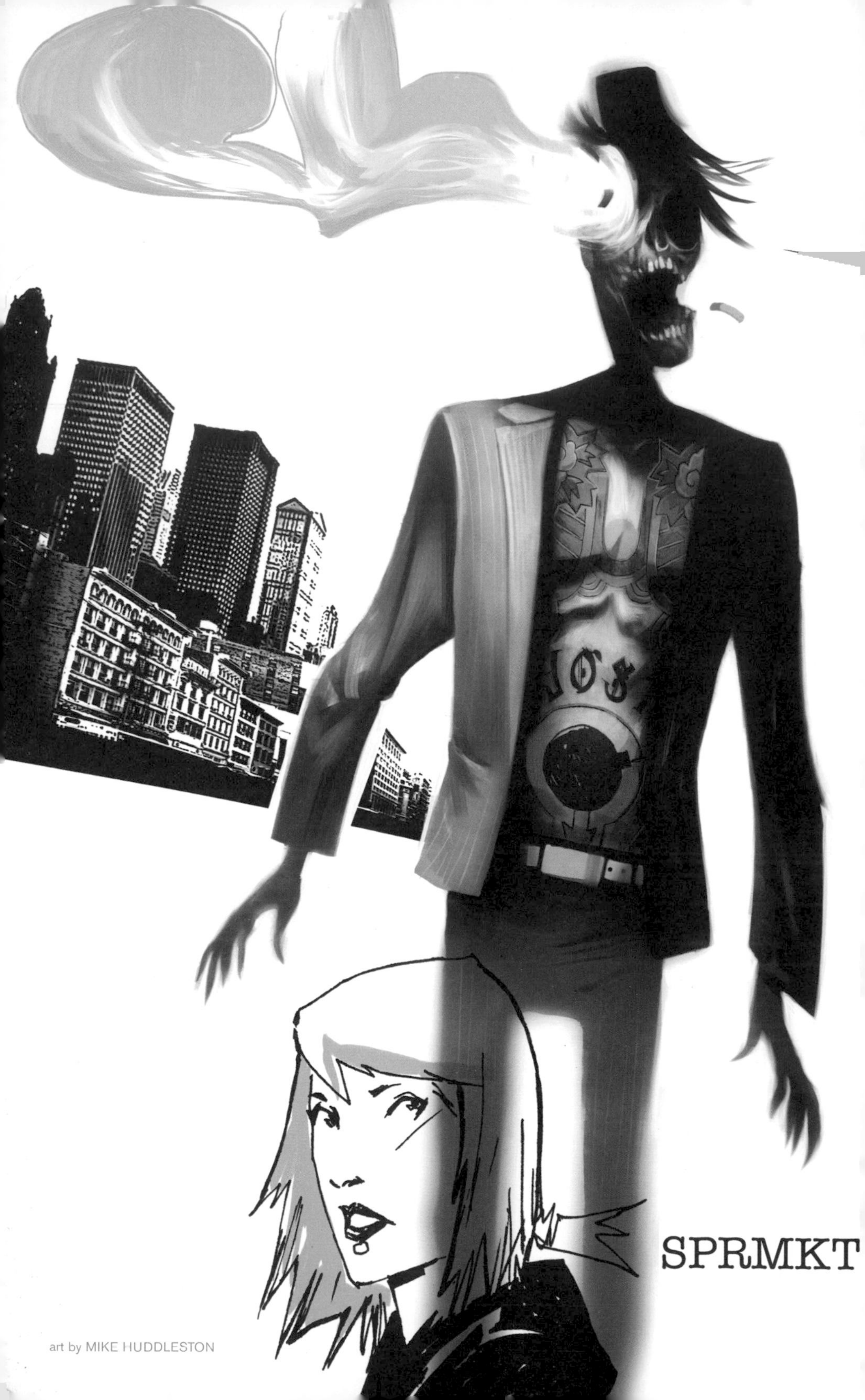
SPRMKT

art by MIKE HUDDLESTON